Increasing Returns and Path Dependence in the Economy

Economics, Cognition, and Society
This series provides a forum for theoretical and empirical investigations of social phenomena. It promotes works that focus on the interactions among cognitive processes, individual behavior, and social outcomes. It is especially open to interdisciplinary books that are genuinely integrative.

Editor: Timur Kuran

Editorial Board: Ronald Heiner
Sheila Ryan Johansson

Advisory Board: James M. Buchanan
Albert O. Hirschman
Mancur Olson

Increasing Returns and Path Dependence in the Economy

W. Brian Arthur

with a foreword by
Kenneth J. Arrow

Ann Arbor

THE UNIVERSITY OF MICHIGAN PRESS

Copyright © by the University of Michigan 1994
All rights reserved
Published in the United States of America by
The University of Michigan Press
Manufactured in the United States of America
⊗ Printed on acid-free paper

1997   1996   1995   1994   4   3   2   1

*A CIP catalogue record for this book is available from the British
Library.*

Library of Congress Cataloging-in-Publication Data

Arthur, W. Brian.
    Increasing returns and path dependence in the economy / W. Brian
Arthur.
        p.   cm. — (Economics, cognition, and society)
    Includes bibliographical references.
    ISBN 0-472-09496-3 (alk. paper). — ISBN 0-472-06496-7 (pbk. :
alk. paper)
    1. Economies of scale—Mathematical models.   2. Economic
development—Mathematical models.   3. Economics, Mathematical.
I. Title.   II. Series.
HD69.S5A77 1994
330'.01'51—dc20   94-9127
                                                                CIP

To my mother and father

Contents

Foreword

Kenneth J. Arrow

The concept of increasing returns has had a long but uneasy presence in economic analysis. The opening chapters of Adam Smith's *Wealth of Nations* put great emphasis on increasing returns to explain both specialization and economic growth. Yet the object of study moves quickly to a competitive system and a cost-of-production theory of value, which cannot be made rigorous except by assuming constant returns. The English school (David Ricardo, John Stuart Mill) followed the competitive assumptions and quietly dropped Smith's boldly-stated proposition that, "the division of labor is limited by the extent of the market," division of labor having been shown to lead to increased productivity.

Other analysts in different traditions, especially the French mathematician and economist, A. A. Cournot (1838), saw clearly enough the incompatibility of increasing returns and perfect competition and developed theories of monopoly and oligopoly to explain the economic system implied by increasing returns. But this tradition acts like an underground river, springing to the surface only every few decades. Alfred Marshall expanded broadly, if vaguely, on the implications of increasing returns, including those for economic growth, irreversible supply curves, and the like, as well as the novel and far-reaching concept of externalities, where some, at least, of the increasing returns are captured, not by the producer but by others.

The implications of increasing returns for imperfect competition were developed, though far from completely, by Edward Chamberlin and Joan Robinson in the 1930s. There was sporadic emphasis on the role of increasing returns in economic growth by Allyn Young (1928) (but only in very general terms) and then by Nicholas Kaldor in the 1950s. Many developmental theorists, particularly in the 1950s, advocated radical planning policies based on vague notions of increasing returns.

It is in this context that Brian Arthur's precise and fully-modeled papers caused us all to understand clearly and specifically what kinds of models have what kinds of implications. One outstanding characteristic of Arthur's viewpoint is its emphatically dynamic nature. Learning by using or doing plays an essential role, as opposed to static examples of returns to scale (e.g., those based on volume-area relations). The object of study is a history.

Another distinctive feature of most of the work is its stochastic character. This permits emphasis on the importance of random deviations for long-run tendencies. In particular, nonlinear Polya processes, studied by Arthur and his probabilistic colleagues, have very interesting properties. Among them are several essential implications of Arthur's viewpoint, in particular the multiplicity of possible long-run states, depending on initial conditions and on random fluctuations over time, and the specialization (in terms of process or geographical location) in an outcome achieved.

Increasing returns have more than one source. Arthur (in collaboration with David Lane) shows how the transmission of information based on experience may serve also as a reinforcement for early leading positions and so act in a manner parallel to more standard forms of increasing returns. A similar phenomenon occurs even in individual learning, where again successes reinforce some courses of action and inhibit others, thereby causing the first to be sampled more intensively, and so forth. There are in all of these models opposing tendencies, some toward achieving an optimum, some toward locking in on inefficient forms of behavior.

It is clear that Arthur's papers, collected in this volume, are an important part of the modern movement toward using positive feedback mechanisms to explain economic growth. Arthur's views are indeed more nuanced; they show how the same mechanisms can lead to inefficiency under suitable initial conditions or random fluctuations, and so they provide a necessary corrective to some overly optimistic current tendencies in thought.

Arthur's papers, while modeled according to the highest analytic standards, sometimes look different from standard economic analysis, and that is a compliment. Expectations are frequently myopic, based on limited information. Prices, though always present, are not always given the exaggerated importance of much current economic orthodoxy, though it must be added there is an excellent analysis of their strategic use in positive feedback situations. I must emphasize the importance of these variant approaches, particularly in areas where conventional tools simply fail.

It is a benefit to economists to have these papers from widely scattered sources brought together conveniently. The volume will be an important stimulus to new research in these areas.

Preface

When the University of Michigan Press approached me to bring out a book of collected papers on increasing returns in economics I was surprised. I had thought that only older researchers, venerable and near retirement, issued collected works. But Timur Kuran, my editor, and Colin Day, the Press's director, argued that although the papers collected here have been receiving much attention lately, several of them have appeared in obscure places and are not easy to track down. In book form they would be accessible. Moreover, if they were brought together, a wider picture might emerge from the mosaic they create than from the individual pieces. This sounded like sufficient rationalization to me, and I accepted their invitation with gusto.

Ideas that invoke some form of increasing returns are now acceptable in economics—indeed they have become highly fashionable. But this was not always so. As recently as the mid-1980s, many economists still regarded increasing returns with skepticism. In March 1987 I went to my old university, Berkeley, to have lunch with two of its most respected economists. What was I working on? Increasing returns. "Well, we know that increasing returns don't exist," said one. "Besides, if they do," said the other, "we couldn't allow them. Otherwise every two-bit industry in the country would be looking for a handout." I was surprised by these comments. Increasing returns *did* exist in the real economy, I believed. And while they might have unwelcome implications, that seemed no reason to ignore them.

Since then much has changed. The whole decade of the 1980s in fact saw an intense burst of activity in increasing returns economics. Nonconvexities and positive feedback mechanisms are now central to modern theorizing in international trade theory, growth theory, the economics of technology, industrial organization, macroeconomics, regional economics, economic development, and political economy.

Of course this turnabout did not happen in just a decade; it has been coming for a long time. In a sense, ideas that made use of increasing returns have *always* been part of the literature in economics. But in the past they were only partially articulated and were difficult to bring under mathematical control. And they tended to have disturbing implications. As a result many in our profession chose to disregard or dismiss them. This distaste reached its peak in the early 1970s with the broad acceptance in economics that all properly specified economic problems should show a unique equilibrium solution. I was a graduate student about this time, and all results in economics were served to us with the incantation that they were true, "providing there is sufficient convexity—that is, diminishing returns on the margin." I was curious about what might happen when there were *increasing* returns on the margin, but none of my professors seemed interested in the question or willing to answer it. Examples with increasing returns and nonconvexities were of course mentioned from time to time. But in the main they were treated like the pathological specimens in labeled jars that used to be paraded to medical students—anomalies, freaks, malformations that were rare, but that nevertheless could serve as object lessons against interference in the natural workings of the economy.

Part of the change, part of the very acceptance of the place of increasing returns, came out of the more formal part of economics itself. General-equilibrium and game theorists have known for many years that even under the most benign assumptions, multiple equilibria and indeterminate solutions occur naturally in the problems they deal with. Hence they found little difficulty accepting multiple equilibria when they arose from increasing returns. International trade theory, a less formal part of economics, needed to explain the peculiarity of intra-industry trade—France selling electronics to Germany and Germany selling electronics to France—and to deal more realistically with trade in manufactured goods. This forced it to include the possibility of increasing returns in production. Just as important as the broader acceptance of nonconvexities in trade theory and mathematical economics has been the development of new methods that deal analytically with the market imperfections and stochastic dynamics that arise in increasing returns problems. Economists can now explore into the terrain of increasing returns with much better equipment than they could ten or twenty years ago. As they do this they are rediscovering outposts from earlier expeditions: not just Adam Smith's familiar writings on specialization, Myrdal's notion of cumulative causation, Kaldor's work on mechanisms of regional disparity, Rosenstein-Rodan's Big Push; but Marshall's hopes for an organic economics, and the ideas of Frank Graham, Piero Sraffa, Allyn Young, Tord Palander, Magoroh Maruyama, and others more obscure.

All the essays brought together in this book were written between 1982 and 1992. In selecting papers to include I have dropped ones that were highly mathematical and ones that repeated arguments made in the papers here. Even so, there remains some overlap in the material included. Many of the papers have undergone several rewrites, each time becoming more compressed, more technical, and less discursive as they neared publication. In several cases I have deliberately selected an early version, in the hope of preserving some of the liveliness that later got edited out. And I have arranged the papers not by subject but more or less in the order in which they came to be written, with some exceptions to help the exposition along.

The papers in this collection largely deal with *allocation* problems under increasing returns or positive feedbacks. And they take a history-dependent, dynamic approach. There are of course other approaches to increasing returns, notably the imperfect-competition, static approach prominent in international trade theory, pioneered by Elhanan Helpman, Paul Krugman, and others, and the deterministic-dynamic approach of Paul Romer and others who have explored endogenous growth powered by increasing returns mechanisms. These other approaches are important; but they are not covered in the papers collected here.

The papers here reflect two convictions I have held since I started work in this area. The first is that increasing returns problems tend to show common properties and raise similar difficulties and issues wherever they occur in economics. The second is that the key obstacle to an increasing returns economics has been the "selection problem"—determining how an equilibrium comes to be selected over time when there are multiple equilibria to choose from. Thus the papers here explore these common properties—common themes—of increasing returns in depth. And several of them develop methods, mostly probabilistic, to solve the crucial problem of equilibrium selection.

As part of bringing together these essays in book form, I have been asked by the editors to give an account of how I came upon the ideas they contain. I will do this, hoping that the story that follows is not so detailed as to bore the reader.

My serious involvement with increasing returns did not begin until 1979. Before that, however, a couple of things had hinted in the right direction. I had studied electrical engineering as an undergraduate, so that the notion of positive feedback was familiar to me; though I remained vague about its consequences. And I had studied graduate-level economics at Berkeley, where I had become fascinated with the question of economic development; so that I was familiar with mechanisms that involved cumulative causation and self-reinforcement in Third World economies. As a result I remained curious about positive feedbacks and increasing returns in the economy; but I could not see how they might be incorporated into theory in a general and rigorous way.

This changed in 1979. I was working in the theory group of the International Institute for Applied Systems Analysis (IIASA) in Vienna and in April and May of that year got leave to spend eight weeks in Hawaii at the East-West Center. On my way through California, I picked up a copy of Horace

Freeland Judson's *The Eighth Day of Creation,* a beautifully written, seven-hundred page history of the discovery of the structure of DNA, the deciphering of the genetic code, and the discovery of the structure of the hemoglobin molecule. I became fascinated with Judson's book and in the next couple of weeks absorbed it in detail. This led to my reading in Hawaii whatever I could find in molecular biology and enzyme reactions. Among the books I got my hands on was Jacques Monod's *Chance and Necessity,* an insightful essay on the interplay between determinism and historical accident which was inspired by his discoveries of autocatalytic reactions that could go in more than one direction. Back in Vienna, in the fall of 1979, I followed some of these ideas from biochemistry and molecular biology into the domain of physics. A colleague, Mark Cantley, told me of the work the Brussels group had been doing on enzyme reactions, and lent me Ilya Prigogine's essay "Order through Fluctuation: Self-Organization and Social System." I began to learn thermodynamics so that I could study the work of Glansdorff, Nicolis, Prigogine, and others. At this time I also studied in detail the work of the German physicist Herman Haken.

That this body of theory represented a different point of view on science was clear to me at once. In this work outcomes were not predictable, problems might have more than one solution, and chance events might determine the future rather than be averaged away. The key to this work, I realized, lay not in the domain of the science it was dealing with, whether laser theory, or thermodynamics, or enzyme kinetics. It lay in the fact that these were processes driven by some form of self-reinforcement, or positive feedback, or cumulative causation—processes, in economics terms, that were driven by nonconvexities. Here was a framework that could handle increasing returns.

A great deal of my approach to increasing returns problems and to economics fell into place in a few weeks in October and November 1979. The problems in economics that interested me, I realized, involved competition among objects whose "market success" was cumulative or self-reinforcing. I discovered that wherever I found such problems, they tended to have similar properties. There was typically more than one long-run equilibrium outcome. The one arrived at was not predictable in advance; it tended to get locked in; it was not necessarily the most efficient; and its "selection" tended to be subject to historical events. If the problem was symmetrical in formulation, the outcome was typically asymmetrical.

In individual problems, some of these properties (especially the possibility of nonefficiency) had been noticed before. But there did not seem to be an awareness that they were generic to increasing returns problems and that they might form a framework for discussion and dissection of such problems. Further, it seemed that these properties had counterparts in condensed-matter physics. What I was calling multiple equilibria, nonpredictability, lock-in, inefficiency, historical dependence, and asymmetry, physicists were calling multiple metastable states, nonpredictability, phase or mode locking, high-energy ground states, nonergodicity, and symmetry breaking.

I became convinced that the key obstacle for economics in dealing with increasing returns was the indeterminacy introduced by the possibility of multiple equilibria. A statement that "several equilibria are possible" did not seem acceptable to economists. Missing was a means to determine how a particular solution might be arrived at. What was needed therefore was a method to handle the question of how one equilibrium, one solution, one structure, of the several possible came to be "selected" in an increasing returns problem. One possibility—popular at the time in game theory—would have been to add axioms that would settle the "selection problem." But this seemed artificial. Selection should not be predetermined I believed; in most problems it would happen naturally over time, often by historical accident. Thus the approach I sought needed to allow the possibility that random events, magnified by the inherent positive feedbacks or reinforcing mechanisms, might select the outcome probabilistically in increasing returns problems. Equilibrium selection, I believed, should be modeled by using nonlinear stochastic processes.

For a time master equations from probability theory seemed promising. But they were unnecessarily complicated and not very general—for example, they could not easily treat processes with growth. It became clear I needed to tailor my own methods.

In 1980 I experimented with various stochastic formulations of my economics problems with increasing returns, with mixed success. In the summer of 1981 I invited Joel Cohen, the mathematical biologist from Rockefeller University, to IIASA, and told him of my difficulties trying to find a suitable probabilistic framework to embed my problems in. Joel put me on to the Polya process, a path-dependent process in probability theory. He had in fact recently written a classic piece on the Polya process as a metaphor for how historical accidents could determine future structures. I was taken with the cleanness of the Polya framework, but realized that my problem did not exactly fit its specifications.

In fact, the Polya process turned out to be a very special case. It provided a growth process where units were added one at a time randomly into different categories with probabilities identical to their current proportions. What I needed to work with in my market-build-up problems was growth processes where probabilities of addition to the categories could be *an arbitrary function* of their current proportions (or market share). I believed that such "allocation processes" would converge to fixed points of this probability function, and convinced myself of the correctness of this conjecture using Fokker-Planck techniques. I asked a number of professional probability theorists for help in providing a rigorous proof. No one could oblige. I had mentioned the problem several times to my office mate at IIASA, the Soviet probability theorist Yuri Ermoliev. One day Yuri asked me to show him the formulation one more time; he thought he might have a possible idea that might point toward a proof. Ermoliev's idea was to reduce the dynamics of the process to a format that was well-understood in probability theory—that of the Robbins-Monroe stochastic approximation. It looked as if it would work. Ermoliev farmed the task of nailing the proof out to his protégé, Yuri Kaniovski, and a year later, in 1983, Ermoliev, Kaniovski, and I published a collection of theorems in the Soviet journal *Kibernetika*.

Not too long after the appearance of this article, a Soviet colleague passed us a copy of an article by three U.S. probability theorists, Bruce Hill, David Lane, and Bill Sudderth, in the 1980 *Annals of Probability,* formulating and solving much the same problem. We were naturally disappointed. But as it turned out the Hill, Lane, and Sudderth paper had solved a simpler, one-dimensional version of the problem; and we had solved the N-dimensional version. Moreover, our methods were different. We had used crude but powerful methods; they had used classic, but weaker methods. In the subsequent extensions of these theorems that we produced throughout the 1980s, we were able to borrow some of the Hill, Lane, and Sudderth techniques and use them in combination with our stochastic approximation methods. Much of this work was carried out by mail. Some took place in Vienna. Four times I visited the Soviet Union, staying for periods up to a month. To keep up with this collaboration I was forced to learn a great deal of professional-level probability theory. Working with Ermoliev and Kaniovski was a source of pure joy.

The result of all this concern with probability was a general procedure for settling the selection problem in increasing returns problems. It would work by redefining each problem as a corresponding stochastic process, usually involving allocations or transitions among categories. The process itself might have multiple asymptotic states (or random limits), and one of these would be "selected" in each realization, not necessarily the same one each time. Thus the fundamental indeterminacy would become a probabilistic indeterminacy; and selection could be studied by examining the workings of the transient dynamics of the process. Often the nonlinear Polya and stochastic approximation formats I had worked out with Ermoliev and Kaniovski could be applied; but sometimes other formats might be more appropriate. One paper here (chap. 2) uses a random-walk formulation; another (chap. 9) a master-equation format.

In casting around early on for examples of increasing returns at work within the economy, I had become fascinated in 1980 with the economics of technology. The standard technology problem in economics was that of figuring out the economic circumstances under which a new, superior technology might replace an old inferior one, and how long this process might take. But from my engineering studies as an undergraduate, I was aware that a new technology normally came along in several different versions or design format. Thus if a new technology were replacing an old one these alternatives might well be thought of as in competition for adopters. Further, it seemed that learning effects would provide advantage to any version that got ahead in cumulative adoptions; and so the adoption process could lock in, by historical chance, to whichever version of the technology got a better start. It was clear that this "competing-technologies problem" was *par excellence* one of increasing returns and it seemed just right for the approach I was trying to develop.

In 1980 and 1981 I tried various formulations of the competing technologies problem. I gave a plenary address on it at the International Conference on Systems in Caracas, Venezuela, in July 1981, and it was received with enthusiasm. It took another year or two to reduce the competing technologies problem to a form I was satisfied with. I wrote it up finally as a IIASA working paper in summer of 1983.

In the meantime, in 1982 I had moved to Stanford. I was heavily involved in economic and mathematical demography, and spent much of the next three years reorganizing Stanford's efforts in demography. At Stanford, I met the economic historian, Paul David. He was extremely sympathetic to my ideas, and indeed had been thinking along the same lines himself for quite some time before meeting me. The introduction to his 1975 book *Technical Choice, Innovation, and Economic Growth* contains several pages on the connection between nonconvexity and historical path dependence. Paul was intrigued at the prospect of an increasing-returns-path-dependence theory proper. Were there examples to go with this? I had been collecting papers on the history of the typewriter keyboard, and using the QWERTY keyboard as an example in papers and talks. Paul had thought of that, as had several others in the early 1980s. For argument he raised the standard objection that if there were a better alternative, people would be using it. I disagreed. We continued our discussions over the next two years, and in late 1984 Paul began to research the history of typewriters. The result, his 1985 "Clio and the Economics of QWERTY" paper in the *American Economic Association Papers and Proceedings* became an instant classic. For me this paper had two repercussions. One was that path dependence rapidly became a familiar part of the thinking of economists; it was legitimized by a well-known figure and finally had a place in the field. The other, less fortunate, was that because I had not yet been able to publish my own papers in the subject, many saw me as merely following up Paul's ideas.

My 1983 technologies working paper (chap. 2) had, in fact, received a great deal of attention, especially among economists interested in history and technology. But it did not do well at journals. In writing it up I had decided to keep the exposition as simple as I could so that the ideas would be accessible to the widest readership possible, even undergraduates. Many of my previous papers were highly technical, and several were in professional mathematical journals; and I saw no reason to dress the paper up in mathematical formalisms merely to impress the reader. I admired the lucidity and simplicity of George Akerlof's classic "The Market for 'Lemons'" and tried to write the paper at that level. This turned out to be a crucial mistake. The straightforward random-walk mathematics I used could not pass as an exercise in technique; yet the paper could not be categorized as a solution to any standard, accepted economic problem. The paper began an editorial and refereeing career that was to last six years. I submitted it in turn to the *American Economic Review,* the *Quarterly Journal of Economics,* the *American Economic Review* again (which had changed editors), and the *Economic Journal.* In 1989 after a second appeal it was finally published in the *Economic Journal.*

In early 1984 I began work on increasing returns and the industry location problem. I had been reading Jane Jacobs's *Cities and the Wealth of Nations* and had been greatly taken by her haunting accounts of places and regions that had got "passed by" historically in favor of other places and regions that had got ahead merely, it seemed, because they had got ahead. To prepare for working out a stochastic dynamics that would model industry clusters forming by historical chance under agglomeration economies I read a good deal of the German literature on spatial location. It appeared there were two points of view. Most authors, the better known ones mainly, favored an equilibrium approach in which industry located in a unique predetermined way. But others, usually obscure and untranslated, emphasized the role of chance in history and the evolutionary, path-dependent character of industry location over time. In the 1930s the path dependence ideas, it seemed, had been largely abandoned by theorists. There had been no means by which to settle how one location pattern among the many possible might be selected and theory did not at the time accept indeterminacy. This problem was thus a natural for a probabilistic dynamic approach that could deal with the selection problem; and my resulting 1986 paper "Industry Location and the Importance of History" (chap. 4) received attention at Stanford. But in the editorial process it met a fate similar to the competing technologies piece. After turndowns from two mainstream journals, partially on lack of understanding that this was a legitimate problem for economic theory ("the paper would be better suited to a regional economics journal"), I finally managed to place it in *Mathematical Social Sciences* in 1990.

In looking back on the difficulties in publishing these papers, I realize that I was naive in expecting they would be welcomed immediately in the journals.

The field of economics is notoriously slow to open itself to ideas that are different.

The problem, I believe, is not that journal editors are hostile to new ideas. The lack of openness stems instead from a belief embedded deep within our profession that economics consists of rigorous deductions based on a fixed set of foundational assumptions about human behavior and economic institutions. If the assumptions that mirror reality are indeed etched in marble somewhere, and apply uniformly to all economic problems, and we know what they are, there is of course no need to explore the consequences of others. But this is not the case. The assumptions economists need to use vary with the context of the problem and can not be reduced to a standard set. Yet, at any time in the profession, a standard set seems to dominate. These are often originally adopted for analytical convenience but then become used and accepted by economists mainly because they are used and accepted by other economists. Deductions based on different assumptions then look strange and can easily be dismissed as "not economics." I am sure this state of affairs is unhealthy. It deters many economists, especially younger ones, from attempting approaches or problems that are different. It encourages use of the standard assumptions in applications where they are not appropriate. And it leaves us open to the charge that economics is rigorous deduction based upon faulty assumptions. At this stage of its development economics does not need orthodoxy and narrowness; it needs openness and courage.

My fortunes changed rapidly in 1987. The Guggenheim Foundation awarded me a Fellowship to study increasing returns in early 1987, and in April of that year, Kenneth Arrow invited me to come to a small institute in Santa Fe for a ten-day meeting in September that would take the form of a series of discussions between physicists and economists. I went; and from this much else flowed. The physicists there, particularly Phil Anderson, Richard Palmer, and David Pines, immediately recognized the similarities between my outlook in economics and condensed-matter physics, and their endorsement did much to legitimize my work. The overall meeting succeeded enormously, and led to the idea of an Economics Research Program at Santa Fe. I was asked to be its first director and accepted. The two years I spent at Santa Fe in 1988 and 1989 were the most exciting of my professional life.

At Santa Fe in September 1987 I had shared a house with John Holland, and had become intrigued—entranced—with his ideas on adaptation. These ideas seemed a long way from increasing returns; and indeed I did not particularly push research in increasing returns at Santa Fe in the first two years. Learning and adaptation, I believed were more important. But as I read into the literature I realized that where learning took place, beliefs could become self-reinforcing, whether at the Hebbian neural-synapse level, or in Holland's classifier-system learning, or in learning in macro-economic problems. Thus I began to see a strong connection between learning problems and increasing returns, and as if to confirm this, much of the stochastic mathematics that applied to increasing returns turned out to apply also to learning problems. Although my recent work on learning is outside the scope of this volume, I have included a paper here that at least hints at the increasing-returns connection with learning.

As of writing this, increasing returns are currently the subject of intense research in economics. Paul Romer's theories of endogenous growth have taken off, and are now being connected with the international trade literature. Paul Krugman has taken up the industry-location-under-increasing-returns problem to great effect, and has done much to popularize it. Andrei Shleifer, Robert Vischny, and Kevin Murphy's modern revival of the Rosenstein-Rodin "Big Push" argument has launched a renewed interest in increasing returns among development economists. Paul David and Douglass North have gone deeper into path dependency and its meaning for economics in general, and economic history in particular. Timur Kuran is applying increasing returns to problems of social choice and political upheaval. Paul Milgrom and John Roberts have worked out a theory of complementarity. And Steven Durlauf and Kiminori Matsuyama are pursuing the stochastic, equilibrium-selection point of view. Several other first-rate economists are involved; and the subject, I am happy to say, is flourishing.

From time to time an economist will ask me where I am heading with my own viewpoint on economics. I used to believe I had no intended direction—that I was just following where the ideas led. But in reading through these essays I realize that from the first I have had a very definite direction and vision. The actual economic world is one of constant transformation and change. It is a messy, organic, complicated world. If I have had a constant purpose it is to show that transformation, change, and messiness are natural in the economy. These are not at odds with theory; they can be upheld by theory. The increasing-returns world in economics is a world where dynamics, not statics, are natural; a world of evolution rather than equilibrium; a world of probability and chance events. Above all, it is a world of process and pattern change. It is not an anomalous world, nor a miniscule one—a set of measure zero in the landscape of economics. It is a vast and exciting territory of its own. I hope the reader journies in this world with as much excitement and fascination as I have.

W. Brian Arthur
Stanford, May 1993

Acknowledgments

Among the people whose ideas have influenced the work collected here are Herman Haken, John Holland, and Ilya Prigogine; and of course my coauthors, Yuri Ermoliev, David Lane, Yuri Kaniovski, and Andrzej Ruszczynski. Over the years Martin Shubik has greatly supported and heartened me. Kenneth Boulding and Tjalling Koopmans helped bolster my courage in the early days to go ahead with work on increasing returns. And I am particularly grateful to Kenneth Arrow who has not only encouraged my own work, but done an enormous amount to encourage in general nonstandard approaches in economics in the last few years, and the Santa Fe program in particular.

At Santa Fe I thank Philip Anderson, George Cowan, Murray Gell-Mann, Stuart Kauffman, Richard Palmer, Ginger Richardson, and Mike Simmons for their constant backing, suggestions, and support. Over the last twelve years or so, I have had conversations, discussions, and arguments with a great many people on the material of this book. Always I learned much. Besides the people already mentioned, in particular I thank Peter Allen, Michel Balinski, Joel Cohen, Robin Cowan, Paul David, Giovanni Dosi, Marc Feldman, Frank Hahn, Ward Hanson, Richard Herrnstein, Ernesto Illy, Martin Krieger, Paul Krugman, Mordecai Kurz, Asoka Mody, Richard Nelson, Evgeny Nurminski, Nathan Rosenberg, Jonathan Roughgarden, David Rumelhart, Tom Sargent, Mitchell Waldrop, Gavin Wright, and Peyton Young. Several institutions and individuals provided financial support: Stanford's Center for Economic Policy Research, the Guggenheim Foundation, the Russell Sage Foundation, the International Schumpeter Society, the International Institute for Applied Systems Analysis, Dean and Virginia Morrison, the Illy family, and John Reed and Henry Lichstein of Citicorp.

In producing the book, the University of Michigan Press has done an excellent job, and I thank Colin Day, its director. I also thank Timur Kuran, the Series's editor, for his very useful help and suggestions.

Finally I thank my wife, Susan P. Arthur, for her unwavering support during the time of trying to bring these ideas into acceptance in the economics profession.

CHAPTER 1

Positive Feedbacks in the Economy

This paper, written for a wide audience at a popular level, will serve as an introduction to many of the themes that follow in this book.

It appeared in *Scientific American* (February 1990): 92–99. A few of the diagrams in the original have been omitted.

Conventional economic theory is built on the assumption of diminishing returns. Economic actions engender a negative feedback that leads to a predictable equilibrium for prices and market shares. Such feedback tends to stabilize the economy because any major changes will be offset by the very reactions they generate. The high oil prices of the 1970s encouraged energy conservation and increased oil exploration, precipitating a predictable drop in prices by the early 1980s. According to conventional theory, the equilibrium marks the "best" outcome possible under the circumstances: the most efficient use and allocation of resources.

Such an agreeable picture often does violence to reality. In many parts of the economy, stabilizing forces appear not to operate. Instead positive feedback magnifies the effects of small economic shifts; the economic models that describe such effects differ vastly from the conventional ones. Diminishing returns imply a single equilibrium point for the economy, but positive feedback—increasing returns—makes for many possible equilibrium points. There is no guarantee that the particular economic outcome selected from among the many alternatives will be the "best" one. Furthermore, once random economic events select a particular path, the choice may become locked-in regardless of the advantages of the alternatives. If one product or nation in a competitive marketplace gets ahead by "chance," it tends to stay ahead and even increase its lead. Predictable, shared markets are no longer guaranteed.

During the past few years I and other economic theorists at Stanford University, the Santa Fe Institute in New Mexico and elsewhere have been developing a view of the economy based on positive feedback. Increasing-returns economics has roots that go back 70 years or more, but its application to the economy as a whole is largely new. The theory has strong parallels with modern nonlinear physics (instead of the pre-twentieth-century physical models that underlie conventional economics), it requires new and challenging mathematical techniques and it appears to be the appropriate theory for understanding modern high-technology economies.

The history of the videocassette recorder furnishes a simple example of positive feedback. The VCR market started out with two competing formats selling at about the same price: VHS and Beta. Each format could realize increasing returns as its market share increased: large numbers of VHS recorders would encourage video outlets to stock more prerecorded tapes in VHS format, thereby enhancing the value of owning a VHS recorder and leading more people to buy one. (The same would, of course, be true for Beta-format players.) In this way, a small gain in market share would improve the competitive position of one system and help it further increase its lead.

Such a market is initially unstable. Both systems were introduced at about the same time and so began with roughly equal market shares; those shares fluctuated early on because of external circumstance, "luck," and corporate maneuvering. Increasing returns on early gains eventually tilted the competition toward VHS: it accumulated enough of an advantage to take virtually the entire VCR market. Yet it would have been impossible at the outset of the competition to say which system would win, which of the two possible equilibria would be selected. Furthermore, if the claim that Beta was technically superior is true, then the market's choice did not represent the best economic outcome (fig. 1).

Conventional economic theory offers a different view of competition between two technologies or products performing the same function. An example is the competition between water and coal to generate electricity. As hydroelectric plants take more of the market, engineers must exploit more costly dam sites, thereby increasing the chance that a coal-fired plant will be cheaper. As coal plants take more of the market, they bid up the price of coal (or trigger the imposition of costly pollution controls) and so tip the balance toward hydropower. The two technologies end up sharing the market in a predictable proportion that best exploits the potentials of each, in contrast to what happened to the two video-recorder systems.

The evolution of the VCR market would not have surprised the great Victorian economist Alfred Marshall, one of the founders of today's conventional economics. In his 1890 *Principles of Economics,* he noted that if firms' production costs fall as their market shares increase, a firm that simply by good fortune gained a high proportion of the market early on would be able to best its rivals; "whatever firm first gets a good start" would corner the market. Marshall did not follow up this observation, however, and theoretical economics has until recently largely ignored it.

Marshall did not believe that increasing returns applied everywhere; agriculture and mining—the mainstays of the economies of his time—were

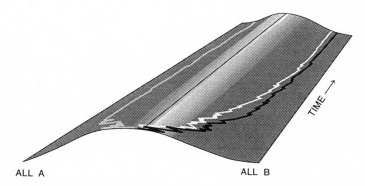

ALL A   ALL B

Fig. 1. Random walk on a convex surface illustrates increasing-returns competition between two technologies. Chance determines early patterns of adoption and so influences how fast each competitor improves. As one technology gains more adherents (corresponding to motion downhill toward either edge of the surface), further adoption is increasingly likely.

subject to diminishing returns caused by limited amounts of fertile land or high-quality ore deposits. Manufacturing, on the other hand, enjoyed increasing returns because large plants allowed improved organization. Modern economists do not see economies of scale as a reliable source of increasing returns. Sometimes large plants have proved more economical; often they have not.

I would update Marshall's insight by observing that the parts of the economy that are resource-based (agriculture, bulk-goods production, mining) are still for the most part subject to diminishing returns. Here conventional economics rightly holds sway. The parts of the economy that are knowledge-based, on the other hand, are largely subject to increasing returns. Products such as computers, pharmaceuticals, missiles, aircraft, automobiles, software, telecommunications equipment, or fiber optics are complicated to design and to manufacture. They require large initial investments in research, development, and tooling, but once sales begin, incremental production is relatively cheap. A new airframe or aircraft engine, for example, typically costs between $2 and $3 billion to design, develop, certify, and put into production. Each copy thereafter costs perhaps $50 to $100 million. As more units are built, unit costs continue to fall and profits increase.

Increased production brings additional benefits: producing more units means gaining more experience in the manufacturing process and achieving greater understanding of how to produce additional units even more cheaply. Moreover, experience gained with one product or technology can make it easier to produce new products incorporating similar or related technologies.

Japan, for example, leveraged an initial investment in building precision instruments into a capacity for building consumer electronics products and then the integrated circuits that went into them.

Not only do the costs of producing high-technology products fall as a company makes more of them, but the benefits of using them increase. Many items such as computers or telecommunications equipment work in networks that require compatibility; when one brand gains a significant market share, people have a strong incentive to buy more of the same product so as to be able to exchange information with those using it already.

If increasing returns are important, why were they largely ignored until recently? Some would say that complicated products—high technology—for which increasing returns are so important, are themselves a recent phenomenon. This is true but is only part of the answer. After all, in the 1940s and 1950s, economists such as Gunnar K. Myrdal and Nicholas Kaldor identified positive-feedback mechanisms that did not involve technology. Orthodox economists avoided increasing returns for deeper reasons.

Some economists found the existence of more than one solution to the same problem distasteful—unscientific. "Multiple equilibria," wrote Joseph A. Schumpeter in 1954, "are not necessarily useless, but from the standpoint of *any* exact science the existence of a uniquely determined equilibrium is, of course, of the utmost importance, even if proof has to be purchased at the price of very restrictive assumptions; without any possibility of proving the existence of [a] uniquely determined equilibrium—or at all events, of a small number of possible equilibria—at however high a level of abstraction, a field of phenomena is really a chaos that is not under analytical control."

Other economists could see that theories incorporating increasing returns would destroy their familiar world of unique, predictable equilibria and the notion that the market's choice was always best. Moreover, if one or a few firms came to dominate a market, the assumption that no firm is large enough to affect market prices on its own (which makes economic problems easy to analyze) would also collapse. When John R. Hicks surveyed these possibilities in 1939 he drew back in alarm. "The threatened wreckage," he wrote, "is that of the greater part of economic theory." Economists restricted themselves to diminishing returns, which presented no anomalies and could be analyzed completely.

Still others were perplexed by the question of how a market could select one among several possible solutions. In Marshall's example, the firm that is the largest at the outset has the lowest production costs and must inevitably win in the market. In that case, why would smaller firms compete at all? On the other hand, if by some chance a market started with several identical firms, their market shares would remain poised in an unstable equilibrium forever.

Fig. 2. Florence cathedral clock has hands that move "counterclock-
wise" around its twenty-four-hour dial. When Paolo Uccello designed
the clock in 1443, a convention for clockfaces had not emerged. Competing designs were subject to increasing returns: the more clockfaces of
one kind were built, the more people became used to reading them.
Hence, it was more likely that future clockfaces would be of the same
kind. After 1550, "clockwise" designs displaying only twelve hours had
crowded out other designs. The author argues that chance events
coupled with positive feedback, rather than technological superiority,
will often determine economic developments.

Studying such problems in 1979, I believed I could see a way out of many of
these difficulties. In the real world, if several similar-size firms entered a
market at the same time, small fortuitous events—unexpected orders, chance
meetings with buyers, managerial whims—would help determine which ones
achieved early sales and, over time, which firm dominated. Economic activity
is quantized by individual transactions that are too small to observe, and these
small "random" events can accumulate and become magnified by positive
feedbacks so as to determine the eventual outcome. These facts suggested that
situations dominated by increasing returns should be modeled not as static,
deterministic problems but as dynamic processes based on random events and
natural positive feedbacks, or nonlinearities.

   With this strategy an increasing-returns market could be re-created in a theoretical model and watched as its corresponding process unfolded again and again. Sometimes one solution would emerge, sometimes (under identical conditions) another. It would be impossible to know in advance which of the many solutions would emerge in any given run. Still, it would be possible to record the particular set of random events leading to each solution and to study the probability that a particular solution would emerge under a certain set of initial conditions. The idea was simple, and it may well have occurred to economists in the past. But making it work called for nonlinear random-process theory that did not exist in their day.

Every increasing-returns problem need not be studied in isolation; many turn out to fit a general nonlinear probability schema. It can be pictured by imagining a table to which balls are added one at a time; they can be of several possible colors—white, red, green, or blue. The color of the ball to be added next is unknown, but the probability of a given color depends on the current proportions of colors on the table. If an increasing proportion of balls of a given color increases the probability of adding another ball of the same color, the system can demonstrate positive feedback. The question is, Given the function that maps current proportions to probabilities, what will be the proportions of each color on the table after many balls have been added?

In 1931 the mathematician George Polya solved a very particular version of this problem in which the probability of adding a color always equaled its current proportion. Three U.S. probability theorists, Bruce M. Hill of the University of Michigan at Ann Arbor and David A. Lane and William D. Sudderth of the University of Minnesota at Minneapolis, solved a more general, nonlinear version in 1980. In 1983 two Soviet probability theorists, Yuri M. Ermoliev and Yuri M. Kaniovski, both of the Glushkov Institute of Cybernetics in Kiev, and I found the solution to a very general version. As balls continue to be added, we proved, the proportions of each color must settle down to a "fixed point" of the probability function—a set of values where the probability of adding each color is equal to the proportion of that color on the table. Increasing returns allow several such sets of fixed points (fig. 3).

This means that we can determine the possible patterns or solutions of an increasing-returns problem by solving the much easier challenge of finding the sets of fixed points of its probability function. With such tools economists can now define increasing-returns problems precisely, identify their possible solutions and study the process by which a solution is reached. Increasing returns are no longer "a chaos that is not under analytical control."

In the real world, the balls might be represented by companies and their colors by the regions where they decide to settle. Suppose that firms enter an industry one by one and choose their locations so as to maximize profit. The

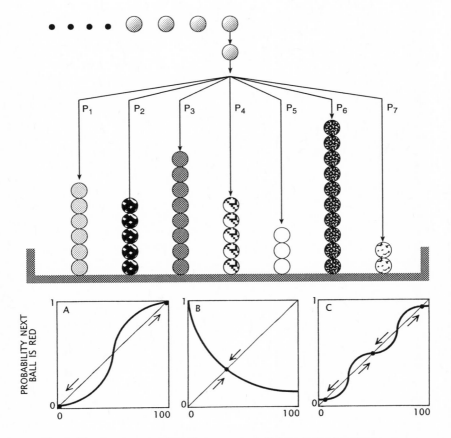

Fig. 3. Nonlinear probability theory can predict the behavior of systems subject to increasing returns. In this model, balls of different shades are added to a table; the probability that the next ball will have a specific shade depends on the current proportions of shades (*top*). Increasing returns occur in *A* (the graph shows the two-shade case; arrows indicate likely directions of motion): a grey ball is more likely to be added when there is already a high proportion of grey balls. This case has two equilibrium points: one at which almost all balls are grey; the other at which very few are grey. Diminishing returns occur in *B*; a higher proportion of grey balls lowers the probability of adding another. There is a single equilibrium point. A combination of increasing and diminishing returns (*C*) yields many equilibrium points.

geographic preference of each firm (the intrinsic benefits it gains from being in a particular region) varies; chance determines the preference of the next firm to enter the industry. Also suppose, however, that firms' profits increase if they are near other firms (their suppliers or customers). The first firm to enter the industry picks a location based purely on geographic preference. The second firm decides based on preference modified by the benefits gained by locating near the first firm. The third firm is influenced by the positions of the first two firms, and so on. If some location by good fortune attracts more firms than the others in the early stages of this evolution, the probability that it will attract more firms increases. Industrial concentration becomes self-reinforcing.

The random historical sequence of firms entering the industry determines which pattern of regional settlement results, but the theory shows that not all patterns are possible. If the attractiveness exerted by the presence of other firms always rises as more firms are added, some region will always dominate and shut out all others. If the attractiveness levels off, other solutions, in which regions share the industry, become possible. Our new tools tell us which types of solutions can occur under which conditions.

Do some regions in fact amass a large proportion of an industry because of historical chance rather than geographic superiority? Santa Clara County in California (Silicon Valley) is a likely example. In the 1940s and early 1950s certain key people in the U.S. electronics industry—the Varian brothers, William Hewlett and David Packard, William Shockley—set up shop near Stanford University; the local availability of engineers, supplies and components that these early firms helped to create made Santa Clara County extremely attractive to the 900 or so firms that followed. If these early entrepreneurs had preferred other places, the densest concentration of electronics in the country might well be somewhere else (fig. 4).

On a grander scale, if small events in history had been different, would the location of cities themselves be different? I believe the answer is yes. To the degree that certain locations are natural harbors or junction points on rivers or lakes, the pattern of cities today reflects not chance but geography. To the degree that industry and people are attracted to places where such resources are already gathered, small, early chance concentrations may have been the seeds of today's configuration of urban centers. "Chance and necessity," to use Jacques Monod's phrase, interact. Both have played crucial roles in the development of urban centers in the United States and elsewhere.

Self-reinforcing mechanisms other than these regional ones work in international high-tech manufacturing and trade. Countries that gain high volume and experience in a high-technology industry can reap advantages of lower cost and higher quality that may make it possible for them to shut out other

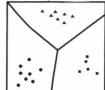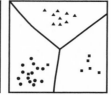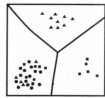

Fig. 4. Industry grows in a region with three locations, as firms of three different types choose locations to maximize profit. Location is determined by intrinsic geographic preference and by the presence of other companies. In this computer-generated example, early companies settle in their geographically preferred regions. But the southwest by chance pulls ahead, and so all new companies eventually settle there. Such clustering might appear to imply that the southwest is somehow superior. In other runs of the program, however, the north and southeast regions dominate instead.

countries. For example, in the early 1970s, Japanese automobile makers began to sell significant numbers of small cars in the United States. As Japan gained market volume without much opposition from Detroit, its engineers and production workers gained experience, its costs fell and its products improved. These factors, together with improved sales networks, allowed Japan to increase its share of the U.S. market; as a result, workers gained still more experience, costs fell further and quality improved again. Before Detroit responded seriously, this positive-feedback loop had helped Japanese companies to make serious inroads into the U.S. market for small cars. Similar sequences of events have taken place in the markets for television sets, integrated circuits and other products.

How should countries respond to a world economy where such rules apply? Conventional recommendations for trade policy based on constant or diminishing returns tend toward low-profile approaches. They rely on the open market, discourage monopolies, and leave issues such as R&D spending to companies. Their underlying assumption is that there is a fixed world price at which producers load goods onto the market, and so interference with local costs and prices by means of subsidies or tariffs is unproductive. These policies are appropriate for the diminishing-returns parts of the economy, not for the technology-based parts where increasing returns dominate.

Policies that are appropriate to success in high-tech production and international trade would encourage industries to be aggressive in seeking out product and process improvements. They would strengthen the national research base on which high-tech advantages are built. They would encourage firms in a single industry to pool their resources in joint ventures that share upfront costs, marketing networks, technical knowledge, and standards. They might even foster strategic alliances, enabling companies in several countries to enter a complex industry that none could tackle alone. Increasing-returns theory also points to the importance of timing when undertaking research initiatives in new industries. There is little sense in entering a market that is already close to being locked-in or that otherwise offers little chance of success. Such policies are slowly being advocated and adopted in the United States.

The value of other policies, such as subsidizing and protecting new industries—bioengineering, for example—to capture foreign markets, is debatable. Dubious feedback benefits have sometimes been cited to justify government-sponsored white elephants. Furthermore, as Paul R. Krugman of the Massachusetts Institute of Technology and several other economists have pointed out, if one country pursues such policies, others will retaliate by subsidizing their own high-technology industries. Nobody gains. The question of optimal industrial and trade policy based on increasing returns is currently being studied intensely. The policies countries choose will determine not only the shape of the global economy in the 1990s but also its winners and its losers.

Increasing-returns mechanisms do not merely tilt competitive balances among nations; they can also cause economies—even such successful ones as those of the United States and Japan—to become locked into inferior paths of development. A technology that improves slowly at first but has enormous long-term potential could easily be shut out, locking an economy into a path that is both inferior and difficult to escape.

Technologies typically improve as more people adopt them and firms gain experience that guides further development. This link is a positive-feedback loop: the more people adopt a technology, the more it improves and the more attractive it is for further adoption. When two or more technologies (like two or more products) compete, positive feedbacks make the market for them unstable. If one pulls ahead in the market, perhaps by chance, its development may accelerate enough for it to corner the market. A technology that improves more rapidly as more people adopt it stands a better chance of surviving—it has a "selectional advantage." Early superiority, however, is no guarantee of long-term fitness.

In 1956, for example, when the United States embarked on its nuclear-power program, a number of designs were proposed: reactors cooled by gas, light water, heavy water, even liquid sodium. Robin Cowan of New York University has shown that a series of trivial circumstances locked virtually the entire U.S. nuclear industry into light water. Light-water reactors were originally adapted from highly compact units designed to propel nuclear submarines. The role of the U.S. Navy in early reactor-construction contracts, efforts by the National Security Council to get a reactor—any reactor—working on land in the wake of the 1957 *Sputnik* launch as well as the predilections of some key officials all acted to favor the early development of light-water reactors. Construction experience led to improved light-water designs and, by the mid-1960s, fixed the industry's path. Whether other designs would, in fact, have been superior in the long run is open to question, but much of the engineering literature suggests that high-temperature, gas-cooled reactors would have been better.

Technological conventions or standards, as well as particular technologies, tend to become locked-in by positive feedback, as my colleague Paul A. David of Stanford has documented in several historical instances. Although a standard itself may not improve with time, widespread adoption makes it advantageous for newcomers to a field—who must exchange information or products with those already working there—to fall in with the standard, be it the English language, a high-definition television system, a screw thread or a typewriter keyboard. Standards that are established early (such as the 1950s-vintage computer language FORTRAN) can be hard for later ones to dislodge, no matter how superior would-be successors may be.

Until recently conventional economics texts have tended to portray the economy as something akin to a large Newtonian system, with a unique equilibrium solution preordained by patterns of mineral resources, geography, population, consumer tastes, and technological possibilities. In this view, perturbations or temporary shifts—such as the oil shock of 1973 or the stock-market crash of 1987—are quickly negated by the opposing forces they elicit. Given future technological possibilities, one should in theory be able to forecast accurately the path of the economy as a smoothly shifting solution to the analytical equations governing prices and quantities of goods. History, in this view, is not terribly important; it merely delivers the economy to its inevitable equilibrium.

Positive-feedback economics, on the other hand, finds its parallels in modern nonlinear physics. Ferromagnetic materials, spin glasses, solid-state lasers and other physical systems that consist of mutually reinforcing elements show the same properties as the economic examples I have given. They "phase lock" into one of many possible configurations; small perturbations at critical times influence which outcome is selected, and the chosen outcome may have higher energy (that is, be less favorable) than other possible end states.

This kind of economics also finds parallels in the evolutionary theory of punctuated equilibrium. Small events (the mutations of history) are often averaged away, but once in a while they become all-important in tilting parts of the economy into new structures and patterns that are then preserved and built on in a fresh layer of development.

In this new view, initially identical economies with significant increasing-returns sectors do not necessarily select the same paths. Instead they eventually diverge. To the extent that small events determining the overall path always remain beneath the resolution of the economist's lens, accurate forecasting of an economy's future may be theoretically, not just practically, impossible. Steering an economy with positive feedbacks into the best of its many possible equilibrium states requires good fortune and good timing—a feel for the moments when beneficial change from one pattern to another is most possible. Theory can help identify these states and times, and it can guide policymakers in applying the right amount of effort (not too little but not too much) to dislodge locked-in structures.

The English philosopher of science Jacob Bronowski once remarked that economics has long suffered from a fatally simple structure imposed on it in the eighteenth century. I find it exciting that this is now changing. With the acceptance of positive feedbacks, economists' theories are beginning to portray the economy not as simple but as complex, not as deterministic, predictable and mechanistic but as process-dependent, organic, and always evolving.

BIBLIOGRAPHY

Arthur, W. Brian. 1988. "Self-Reinforcing Mechanisms in Economics." In *The Economy as an Evolving Complex System,* ed. Philip W. Anderson, Kenneth J. Arrow, and David Pines. Reading, Mass.: Addison-Wesley Publishing Co.
———. 1989. "Competing Technologies, Increasing Returns, and Lock-in by Historical Events." *The Economic Journal* 99 (394 March):116–31.
Arthur, W. Brian, Y. M. Ermoliev, and Y. M. Kaniovski. 1987. "Path-Dependent Processes and the Emergence of Macro-Structure." *European Journal of Operational Research* 30:294–303.
David, Paul. 1988. "Path-Dependence: Putting the Past into the Future of Economics." I.M.S.S. Tech Report No. 533, November. Stanford University.
Helpman, Elhanan, and Paul Krugman. 1985. *Market Structure and Foreign Trade.* Cambridge: MIT Press.

CHAPTER 2

Competing Technologies, Increasing Returns, and Lock-In by Historical Small Events

This paper uses the notion of technologies competing for adoption to explore the properties of allocation under increasing returns. It was already well-known that allocation problems under increasing returns could show multiple equilibria and possible inefficiency. To these properties the paper adds the possibility of *lock-in* (or inflexibility) and *nonergodicity* (or path dependence).

The paper is also concerned with the "selection problem"—how one allocation outcome comes to be "selected" over time by small, chance events when there are several possible long-run outcomes.

The paper first appeared in September 1983 as Working Paper WP-83-90 at the International Institute for Applied Systems Analysis under the title "On Competing Technologies and Historical Small Events: The Dynamics of Choice under Increasing Returns." The version reproduced here is an update that appeared as Center for Economic Policy Research Publication No. 43, Stanford, 1985. The paper was published, in somewhat abbreviated form, in the *Economic Journal* 99 (March 1989): 116–31.

The statics of markets where commodities show increasing returns or decreasing supply costs are by now becoming familiar.[1] It is well known that in such markets nonconvexities appear, so that multiple equilibria are called into being. These equilibria are typically "corner solutions" with one commodity or one firm monopolizing the market. But while information on preferences, endowments, and transformation possibilities allows us to locate and describe these various possible equilibria, it is usually insufficient to tell us which one will be "selected." There is an indeterminacy of outcome.

The author would like to thank the International Institute for Applied Systems Analysis, Laxenburg, Austria for financial support in summer 1983; and Paul David, Ward Hanson, Richard Nelson, Nathan Rosenberg, Martin Shubik, Gavin Wright, and the members of the Technological Innovation Project Workshop at Stanford for useful suggestions, comments and criticisms.

1. Increasing-return studies address a much wider variety of issues than are treated here. See among others: Arrow and Hahn (chap. 7, 1971), Beato (1982), Brown and Heal (1976, 1979), Farrell and Saloner (1985), Flaherty (1980), Guesneries (1975), Katz and Shapiro (1983, 1985), Kehoe (1985), Krugman (1980), Scarf (1981), Schelling (1978), Spence (1981), and Weitzman (1982). The Schelling and Spence treatments are closest in spirit to the one here.

Marshall (1891, p. 485) noticed this indeterminacy a century or so ago in the case of firms with long-run decreasing cost curves competing for a market. Ultimately one firm achieves a monopoly of the industry, but *which* firm dominates can not be deduced in advance. To proceed farther we need to examine the possible paths by which an outcome comes to be selected. We need, in other words, to examine the dynamics of allocation under increasing returns.

To set ideas and a possible strategy for analysis, consider a simple example. Suppose in a certain island cars are introduced, all at more or less the same time. Drivers may choose between the right- and left-hand sides of the road. Each side possesses increasing returns: as a higher proportion of drivers chooses one side, the payoff to choosing that side rapidly rises. Casual thought tells us that we would observe a good deal of randomness to the proportions initially driving on each side, but that, if one side by chance got sufficiently ahead, other drivers would "fall in" on this side, so that eventually all cars would drive on (would allocate themselves to) the same side of the road. Of course the side that "wins"—that comes to "dominate the market"—cannot be deduced in advance. The outcome is indeterminate.

In such a situation the actual outcome would likely be decided by a host of "small events" outside our knowledge—drivers' reactions, dogs running into the road, the timing or positioning of traffic lights. One way then to bring allocation under increasing returns within the bounds of analysis would be to make explicit these "small events," add them to the model, and examine in detailed "slow-motion" the dynamic process by which they cumulate into an aggregate outcome. This would be difficult in our imaginary example. But as a strategy it may be possible in better-defined cases.

Notice that our hypothetical example displays the familiar increasing-returns properties of *potential inefficiency* and *nonpredictability:* even though individual choices are rational, there is no guarantee that the side "selected" is, from any long-term collective viewpoint, the better of the two; and *ex-ante* knowledge of drivers' preferences and possibilities does not suffice to predict the "market outcome." But notice also two new properties inherent in the dynamics. As time passes inducements to individual drivers to change sides, if offered, would gradually become ineffective; the allocation of cars to sides of the road becomes progressively more rigid and "locked-in." We will call this lock-in property *inflexibility.* And "historical small events" are not averaged away and "forgotten" by the dynamics. History may decide the outcome. This property is *nonergodicity.*

In this paper we explore the dynamics of allocation with increasing returns present. To keep matters concrete we do this in the context of a simple model of an adoption market for technologies which improve with adoption. We pay particular attention to circumstances where "historical small events" can cumulate step-by-step to lock the market in to the monopoly of a possibly inferior technology. We examine the mechanisms by which increasing returns dynamically generate inefficiency, inflexibility, nonpredictability, and non-ergodicity. And we illustrate circumstances under which increasing returns lead not to monopoly but rather to market sharing.

We begin by introducing the notion of competing technologies, then go on to set up the simple model of allocation.

Competing Technologies

Preliminaries

Usually there are several ways to carry through any given economic purpose. We shall call these "ways" (or methods) *technologies* and we will be interested in technologies that can potentially fulfill the same purpose, that is, technologies that *compete,* albeit unconsciously, for shares of a "market" of potential adopters. Technologies, in this study, may exist as pure method or pure information; or they may be embodied in physical plant or machinery. We shall also distinguish between what we call *sponsored* technologies, those like the Sony Betamax system, that are marketed and priced as products, and *unsponsored* technologies, generic ones like jet propulsion, that are openly available to all and incapable of being priced. In most of this paper, we will treat technologies as unsponsored and embodied in physical machinery.

In this paper competition assumes a stronger form than in the standard diffusion case where a new and superior technology competes with an old and inferior one. Here two or more superior technologies compete with *each other* to replace an outmoded horse-and-buggy technology. For example, in the 1890s, the steam engine, the electric motor, and the gasoline engine competed as power sources for the new automobile. In the 1800s and on into this century, spinning mules competed with ring-frames in cotton manufacturing (Saxonhouse and Wright 1984). More recently the nuclear technology competes with hydroelectric, coal, and other technologies, for part capture of the electricity generation market. And gallium arsenide competes with doped silicon in the manufacture of fast semiconductors.

It need not be the case that the number of technologies competing for a given purpose is few. If we consider the arrangement of the 40 or so keys on a typewriter as a technology, then in principle 40-factorial or 10^{48} possible keyboards compete with the standard QWERTY keyboard.

We introduce increasing returns to adoption by invoking Rosenberg's concept of Learning by Using (Rosenberg 1982; see also Lieberman 1985). A technology that is not a mere standard or convention tends to be fluid: it mutates, changing in design and sometimes in purpose, typically existing in several or many *variants*. As adoption cumulates, the usage and experience that cumulate with it become incorporated into more reliable and effective variants. Rosenberg documents several cases: jet aircraft—like the Boeing 727 or the DC-8, for example—are constantly modified in design and they improve significantly in structural soundness, reliability, wing design, payload capacity, and engine efficiency as they accumulate actual airline use. Obviously time may be a factor here. But we will abstract from learning-by-using a pure increasing-returns case, where returns rise only with the numbers who have chosen a technology.

Not all technologies generate increasing returns with adoption. The very popularity of a factor-intensive technology may bid its inputs up in price, so that diminishing returns accompany adoption. Hydroelectric power, for example, becomes more costly as suitable dam sites become scarcer and hydrodynamically less efficient. And of course some technologies are unaffected by adoption—their returns are constant.

In the model that follows we contrast competition between technologies with increasing, decreasing, and constant returns to adoption.

An Adoption Market with Heterogeneous Adopters

Assume that two unsponsored technologies, A and B, compete for adoption by a large number of economic agents who are currently using an outmoded technology of the one-horse-shay type. (For simplicity we can treat the pool of agents as infinite in size.) It pays agent i to retain his obsolete equipment until its demise at time t_i; but he cannot afford to be without working machinery, so that at this point he adopts the latest variant of either technology A or technology B and holds it thereafter. The variant each agent chooses is fixed or frozen in design at his time of choice, so that his payoff is not affected by future changes in or future adoption of either technology. (Later we allow payoffs to be affected by future adoptions.) Agents fall into two types, R and S, with equal numbers in each, the two types independent of the times of choice but differing in their preferences, or in their economic environment.

The monetary returns-in-use or payoff to adoption to a particular agent are simply the (discounted) value of the output of his variant less its factor cost over an appropriate time horizon. For simplicity we shall suppose that variants of A or B available for choice change with the numbers n_A and n_B of previous adoptions so that the n_Ath adopter of A adopts variant n_A of A (similarly for B), with payoff-utility fixed for this variant at the level given in table 1.[2]

---

2. More realistically, where the technologies have uncertain monetary returns we can assume von Neumann-Morgenstern agents, with table 1 interpreted as the resulting determinate expected-utility payoffs.

TABLE 1. Returns to Choosing *A* or *B* Given Previous Adoptions

	Technology A	Technology B
R-Agent	$a_R + rn_A$	$b_R + rn_B$
S-Agent	$a_S + sn_A$	$b_S + sn_B$

We can contrast the dynamics of the adoption process under increasing, diminishing, or constant returns regimes by allowing r and s to be simultaneously positive, negative, or zero. We assume $a_R > b_R$ and $a_S < b_S$ so that *R*-agents have a natural preference for *A,* and *S*-agents have a natural preference for *B*.

To complete this market model, it remains to define a set of "historical small events." Recall that in the earlier side-of-the-road example, our lack of knowledge of certain events—drivers' reactions, weather conditions, traffic-light timings—caused the outcome to be indeterminate. Were we to have infinitely detailed knowledge of such events and conditions, the outcome—the side of the road that would be selected—would presumably be determinable in advance.[3] We can conclude that our limited discerning power, or more precisely the limited discerning power of an implicit *observer,* causes the indeterminacy. We may therefore define "historical small events" to be those events or conditions that are outside the knowledge of the observer—beyond the resolving power of his "model" or abstraction of the situation.

To return to *our* model, we assume an observer who has full knowledge of all the conditions and returns functions, *except* the set of times of choice $\{t_i\}$. The observer thus "sees" the choice order as a binary sequence of *R* and *S* types with the property that an *R* or an *S* stands in the *n*th position in the line with equal likelihood, that is, with probability one half.

We now have a simple neoclassical allocation model where two types of agents choose between *A* and *B,* each agent choosing his preferred option when his times comes. The supply cost (or returns) functions are known, as is the demand (each agent demands one unit inelastically). Only one small element is left open, and that is the set of events that determine the sequence in which the agents make their choice. Of interest is whether the fluctuations in the order of choices that these small events introduce make a difference to the market-share outcome in the different cases of constant, diminishing, and increasing returns.

We will need some properties. Describe the process by the sequence $\{x_n\}$ where x_n is the market share of *A* at stage *n*, when *n* choices in total have been

---

3. This is not to deny that "God plays dice"; it is merely to take the Laplacian position that, given complete knowledge of the world, the dice become determinate. Randomness follows then from lack of knowledge, and the notion of "pure chance" need not be invoked.

made. With the small degree of uncertainty we have built in, we cannot expect precise determination of market shares at the outset. We will say that the process is *predictable* if initial fluctuations average away so that the observer has enough information to accurately predetermine market shares in the long-run; that is, if the observer can, *ex ante,* construct a forecasting sequence $\{\hat{x}_n\}$ with the property that $|\hat{x}_n - x_n| \to 0$, with probability one, as $n \to \infty$. We will say that the process is *flexible* if the amount of tax or subsidy on one of the technologies' returns needed to influence future market choices always remains small, less than some constant g say. We will say that it is *ergodic* if different sequences of historical events in all likelihood lead to the same market outcome; more precisely, if, given two samples from the observer's set of possible historical events, $\{t_i\}$ and $\{t_i'\}$, with corresponding time paths $\{x_n\}$ and $\{x_n'\}$, then $|x_n' - x_n| \to 0$, with probability one, as $n \to \infty$. Efficiency requires some special comment. In this allocation problem choices define a "path" or sequence of A- and B-variants that become "developed," with externalities present because previous choices affect present-variant payoffs. Thus a "good" path might require some "investment" sacrifices by early adopters to arrive at better variants. By analogy with other dynamic problems we might choose total or aggregate payoff (after n choices) as the criterion. But here we have two agent types with different preferences operating under the "greedy algorithm" of each agent taking the best choice for himself at hand and it is easy to show that under any returns regime, maximization of total payoffs is never guaranteed.[4] However, our interest lies more in whether the market causes the potentially "right" technology to emerge. Accordingly we will adopt a "no-regret" criterion and say that the process is *path-efficient* if at all times equal development (equal adoption) of the technology that is behind in adoption would not have paid off better. More precisely, suppose at any time n, an agent chooses the more-adopted technology α, which stands at variant m, with payoff to him of $\Pi_\alpha(m)$. (The less adopted technology β stands at variant $k < m$.) We will say that the process is *path-efficient* if

$$\Pi_\alpha(m) \geq \text{Max}_j\{\Pi_\beta(j)\} \text{ for } k \leq j \leq m$$

that is, if variants of the lagging technology would not have delivered more, if they had been developed and available for adoption.

---

4. Aggregate payoff is maximal, under constant and diminishing returns, providing agents are all of one type; but when agent types differ, post-adoption trading of choices between types may occasionally raise aggregate payoff. Increasing returns, of course, may deliver choices that are far from maximal in aggregate.

Allocation in the Three Regimes

Homogeneous Agents—A Digression

Before looking at the outcome of choices in our R and S agent model, it is instructive to take a glance at how the dynamics would run if all agents were of one type only. Here choice order does not matter; agents are homogeneous and indistinguishable; and there are no unknown events so that ergodicity is not an issue. We bypass the trivial constant returns case where agents always choose the higher payoff technology.

Where both technologies show diminishing returns—the standard text-book case—market-sharing in general takes place. As demand increases, adoption follows the composite supply curve obtained from lateral addition of the separate returns curves for each technology. The outcome is predictable—our observer can determine in advance market shares after n choices exactly in this situation—and it is easy to show it is path-efficient. It is also flexible: adjustment of either returns curve can always shift the composite supply curve and hence market share.

Where both technologies show increasing returns, the result is more interesting. The first agent chooses the more favorable technology, A say. This enhances the returns to adopting A. The next agent *a-fortiori* chooses A too. This continues, with A chosen each time, and B incapable of "getting started." The end result is that A "corners the market" and B is excluded. This outcome is trivially predictable, and path-efficient if returns rise at the same rate. Notice though that if returns increase at different rates, the adoption process may easily become path-inefficient, as table 2 shows. In this case after thirty choices in the adoption process—all of which are A—equivalent adoption of B would have delivered higher returns. But this situation cannot at any time be remedied by the given tax or subsidy g. If the process has gone far enough, g can no longer close the gap between the returns to A and the returns to B at the starting point. Flexibility is not present here; and the market becomes increasingly "locked-in" to an inferior choice.

TABLE 2. Increasing-Return Adoption Payoffs (Homogeneous Agents)

Adoptions	0	10	20	30	40	50	60	70	80	90	100
Technology A	10	11	12	13	14	15	16	17	18	19	20
Technology B	4	7	10	13	16	19	22	25	28	31	34

The R and S Agent Model

Now let us return to the case of interest, where the unknown choice sequence of two types of agents allows us to include some notion of historical "small-events." Begin with the constant-returns situation, and let $n_A(n)$ and $n_B(n)$ be the number of choices of A and B respectively, when n choices in total have been made. We will write the difference in adoption, $n_A(n) - n_B(n)$ as d_n. The market share of A is then expressible as

$$x_n = 0.5 + d_n/2n. \qquad (1)$$

Note that through the variables d_n and n—the difference and total—we can fully describe the dynamics of adoption of A versus B. In this constant returns situation R-agents always choose A and S-agents always choose B, regardless of the number of adopters of either technology. Thus the way in which adoption of A and B cumulates is determined simply by the sequence in which R- and S-agents "line up" to make their choice, $n_A(n)$ increasing by one unit if the next agent in line is an R, $n_B(n)$ increasing by one unit if the next agent in line is an S, with the difference in adoption, d_n, moving upward by one unit or downward one unit accordingly.

To our observer, the choice-order is random, with agent types equally likely. Hence to him, the "state" d_n appears to perform a simple coin-toss gambler's random walk with each "move" having equal probability 0.5.

In the diminishing-returns situation, these simple dynamics are modified. Figure 1 illustrates the returns functions of each agent type. Observe that, although at the outset R-agents will choose the higher-returns (to them) technology A, adoption bids its returns downward, so that future R-agents will switch their preference to B if the numbers using A become sufficiently greater than the numbers using B. That is, R-agents will "switch" their preferred choice in our model if

$$d_n = n_A(n) - n_B(n) > \Delta_R \qquad (2)$$

$$= \frac{(a_R - b_R)}{-r}.$$

Similarly S-agents will switch preference to A if numbers adopting B become sufficiently ahead of the numbers adopting A, that is, if

$$d_n = n_A(n) - n_B(n) < \Delta_S \qquad (3)$$

$$= \frac{(a_S - b_S)}{s}.$$

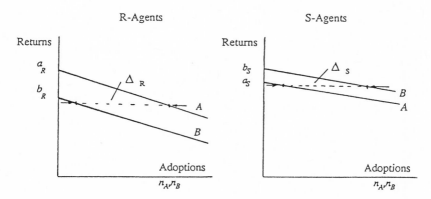

Fig. 1. Returns to adoption of *A* and *B*: diminishing returns case

We see now (in fig. 2) that there are three distinct regions in the d_n, n plane where the directions of choice (indicated by arrows) differ. In region I, where adoption of both technologies shows little difference *R*-types choose *A* and *S*-types choose *B*. But in regions II and III both agent types choose the same technology—the one that is "behind." Thus d_n may wander at will in region I but cannot enter regions II or III. The allocation process with diminishing returns appears to our observer as a random walk with reflecting barriers.

We obtain slightly different dynamics in the increasing returns situation. Now *R*-agents, who start with a natural preference for *A*, will switch allegiance if adoption pushes *B* far enough *ahead* of *A* in numbers and in payoff. Similarly, *S*-agents, with a natural preference for *B*, will switch their choices to *A* if adoption pushes *A* far enough ahead of *B*. Regions of choice again appear in the d_n, n plane (see fig. 3), defined by inequalities similar to (2) and (3). Once region II or III is entered, both agent types choose the same technology, but in this case the difference is that they will choose the technology that is "ahead," with the result that this technology further increases its lead. The choice process is "locked into" either region II or region III from then on. In the d_n, n plane the boundaries of these regions become barriers which "absorb" the process. Once either is reached by random movement of d_n, the process ceases to involve both technologies—it is "locked-in" to one technology only. We are now in a good position. We need only use the elementary theory of random walks to derive the properties of this choice process under the different linear returns regimes. For convenient reference we summarize the results in table 3.

Proofs of these results are not difficult. Before outlining them it is useful to look at market shares. In the increasing-linear-returns situation, we know from random-walk theory that d_n becomes absorbed with probability one.

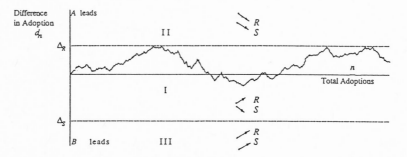

Fig. 2. Diminishing returns: random walk with reflecting barriers

Therefore, the market share of *A* *must* eventually become zero or one. The two technologies cannot coexist indefinitely and one *must* exclude the other. In the diminishing returns situation, by contrast, the market is shared. The difference-in-adoption, d_n, is trapped between finite constants; hence $d_n/2n$ in equation (1) tends to zero as n goes to infinity, and x_n must approach 0.5. (Here the 50-50 market split results from the equal proportions of agent types.) Under constant returns, again the market is shared. In this case the random walk ranges free, but we know from random-walk theory that the standard deviation of d_n increases with $\sqrt{n}$. It follows that the $d_n/2n$ term disappears and that x_n tends to 0.5, with probability one, so that again the market is split fifty-fifty.

Now look at the observer's problem in predicting the market outcome. Under increasing returns, to come close, he must predict *A*'s eventual share either as 0.0 or 1.0. But whichever he chooses he will be wrong with probability one-half. The process is nonpredictable. Notice though that the observer *can* predict that one technology will take the market; if he knows some random-walk theory he can also predict that it will be *A* with probability $s(a_R - b_R)/\{s(a_R - b_R) + r(b_S - a_S)\}$; but he cannot predict the actual market-share outcome with any accuracy—in spite of his knowledge of supply and demand conditions. This state of affairs is quite different where returns are constant, or diminishing. In both cases a forecast that the market will settle to fifty-fifty will be correct, with probability one. Predictability is guaranteed.

Policy adjustments to the returns can affect choices at all times in the constant-returns situation but only if they are large enough to bridge the gap in preferences between technologies. Flexibility here is at best partial. In the two other regimes adjustments correspond to a shift of one or both of the barriers. Once the increasing-returns process is absorbed into *A* or *B*, however, the amount of subsidy or tax necessary to shift the barriers enough to influence choices (a precise index of the degree to which the system is "locked-in") increases without bound. Flexibility is lost. In the diminishing-returns situation, a given subsidy or tax *g* can always affect future choices (in absolute

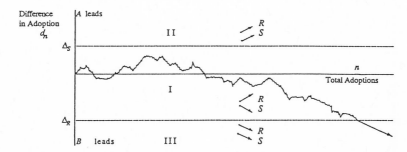

Fig. 3. Increasing returns: random walk with absorbing barriers

numbers, if not in market shares), because reflecting barriers continue to influence the process (with probability one) at times in the future. Diminishing returns are flexible.

Ergodicity can be shown easily in the constant and diminishing returns cases. Any sequence of historical events—any line-up of the agents—drives the market to fifty-fifty in the diminishing returns case; and only truly extraordinary happenstance events (for example, twice as many R-agents as S-agents joining the line indefinitely) with associated probability zero can cause deviation from fifty-fifty in the constant returns case. The line-up caused by the historical timing of agent choices therefore has no effect on eventual market shares, and the process is ergodic—it forgets its small-event history. In the increasing returns case the situation is quite different. A nonzero proportion of the choice sequences causes the market outcome to "tip" toward A, the remaining proportion causes it to "tip" toward B. (The extraordinary line-ups— say S followed by R followed by S followed by R and so on indefinitely—that could cause market sharing, have proportion or measure zero.) Thus, the historical sequence of the choices (which depends on the small events $\{t_i\}$) *decides* the path of market shares, and the process is non-ergodic—it remembers its small-event history.

Path efficiency is easy to prove in the constant- and diminishing-returns cases. Under constant returns, adoption, by definition, does not affect payoff. Each agent type chooses its preferred technology and there is no gain foregone

TABLE 3. Properties of the Three Regimes

	Predictable	Flexible	Ergodic	Necessarily Path-Efficient
Constant returns	Yes	No	Yes	Yes
Diminishing returns	Yes	Yes	Yes	Yes
Increasing returns	No	No	No	No

by the failure of the lagging technology to receive further development (further adoption). Under diminishing returns, suppose at any stage an agent chooses variant m of the leading technology over the currently available variant k of the less used technology. Since returns are diminishing he must also prefer variant m of the leading technology to the still-lower payoffs of variant $k + 1$ through m of the less used technology. Thus the agents' self-interested rule of adopting the highest-return choice at hand is again not causing the "wrong" technology mix to be developed. Under increasing returns, however, path efficiency is not guaranteed. Suppose without loss of generality that the market locks in to technology A. R-agents do not lose; but S-agents would each gain $(b_S - a_S)$ if their favored technology B had been equally developed and available for choice. Things are worse still if the technologies improve at different rates. Now an early run of agent-types who initially prefer the slow-to-improve option can lock the market in to this inferior option; equal development of the excluded technology in the long run would have paid off better to both types.

Robustness

Would these results have been materially different if we had made weaker assumptions in our model? The answer is a qualified no.

We can show that the same qualitative results hold for M technologies in competition, and for agent types in unequal proportions (here the random walk "drifts"). Where returns to one technology depend also on the numbers adopting the *other* technology, switching barriers again appear, again causing lock-in or reflection. And if the technologies arrive in the market at different times, once again the dynamics go through as before, with the process now starting with initial n_A or n_B not at zero. Thus in practice an early-start technology may already be locked in, so that a new arrival, although potentially superior, cannot gain a footing.

We assumed earlier for convenience that the market is ever expanding. More realistically where agent numbers are finite, absorption or reflection and the properties that depend on them still assert themselves providing agent numbers are large relative to the numerical width of the gap between switching barriers.

Discussion

Some Examples

In our simple theoretical model, the economy, under increasing returns, can dynamically lock itself in by small historical events to a technological path that is neither guaranteed to be efficient, nor easily altered, nor entirely predictable in advance. This model might apply best to competition between unsponsored generic technologies embodied in machinery, like steam versus gasoline for automobile propulsion or light-water versus gas-cooled for nuclear reactors. The most common case is that of technologies chosen for sound engineering reasons at the time but now locked-in by user externalities, denying later, more appropriate technologies a footing. Examples are the narrow gauge of British railroads; the U.S. color television system; the 1950s programming language FORTRAN; and the QWERTY typewriter keyboard.[5] If our path-efficiency criterion is more than a theoretical construct, the past should contain a "fossil record" of technologies that, given equal adoption, might have been better than those that eventually predominated. It is indeed claimed that Algol, if adopted, would have been superior to FORTRAN; that high-temperature gas-cooled reactors would have been superior to the predominant light-water reactor; and that the Dvorak 1932 typewriter keyboard, if equally prevalent, would have been superior to QWERTY.[6]

We should not conclude that every case of competing technologies shows tendencies toward dynamic lock-in. Conventional power-generation technologies, for example, are factor-intensive and show eventual diminishing returns. We would expect these to share the market in a more-or-less predictable and efficient way.

When Does Lock-In Occur?

It is often supposed that increasing returns *must* cause market exclusion or monopoly outcomes, as in the Marshall citation earlier. But in fact, with consumer heterogeneity present, increasing returns do not necessarily imply monopoly outcomes. Suppose our problem now has nonlinear learning-by-using increasing returns of the form $\Pi_A^R = a_R(1 - e^{-rn_A})$, $\Pi_B^R = b_R(1 - e^{-rn_B})$ for R-agents (with similar form for S-agents). Then we might suspect that if agent-types early on are fairly equally distributed in the queue, learning effects might be more or less simultaneously exhausted, so that both technologies may be bid up to their upper bounds without one of them ever getting sufficiently ahead to cause lock-in. Heterogeneity of preferences

---

5. See Paul David (1985) for a fascinating study of how QWERTY became locked-in. Also Kindleberger (1983) on railroad gauges and other standards; and Hartwick (1985).

6. The HTGR reactor has high thermal mass which has considerable safety advantages; but the LWR reactor dominated because it was lighter, and hence better suited to early nuclear submarines. (Personal communication from Alan Manne and Harvey Brooks.) A pure example of an equally good but excluded technology is the anticlockwise turning convention of the hands on some early clocks (the Uccello clock of 1433 in Florence cathedral for example) which disappeared by 1550 (see also Cipolla 1967, 65).

would not be overcome by increased returns and the market would ultimately be equally shared. Theory confirms that this can happen. With general returns functions, the crossover point at which the difference in adoption d_n causes switching may vary as total choices n increase. The barriers may then widen or narrow with total adoptions n, and if they widen fast enough no switching may occur at all. The precise condition we need is that switching—market exclusion in the increasing-returns case—occurs with probability one if the nonconstant barriers lie within the iterated-logarithm-law limits, from some finite stage onward. Market-sharing is still guaranteed in the diminishing-returns case. But in the general increasing-returns case, possible outcomes may indeed include interior solutions besides monopoly ones.

Often technologies are *sponsored* by firms, like personal computers or videorecorders which gain peripheral-product support as their market-share increases, or like technological networks that offer transportation, communication, or distribution services whose costs decrease with traffic carried. Would the possibility of strategic pricing alter the phenomena described earlier? A complete answer is not yet known. In a stochastic duopoly analysis based on the linear-increasing returns model above, Hanson (1985) shows that again market exclusion goes through: firms engage in penetration pricing, taking losses early on in exchange for potential monopoly profits later—all but one firm exit with probability one. Under discounting and weaker increasing returns, however, market sharing reappears. (See also Mookherjee and Ray 1985.)

In the case of *competing standards,* early adopters are affected by the choices of *later* adopters, who may or may not fall in with one's choice and follow suit. Now agents will choose partly on the basis of their expectations. Katz and Shapiro (1983, 1985) have shown that in this case expectations of what is likely to prevail, even if founded on very little, can become self-fulfilling.[7] We can confirm their two-period analysis in our dynamic case. In the Appendix we show that with rational expectations and increasing returns once again market exclusion goes through. But now, if a technology gets ahead by chance, expectations that it will eventually lock in narrow the absorption barriers—the fundamental market instability is exacerbated.

Proving market-exclusion or market-sharing in general increasing returns problems is equivalent to investigating the limit properties of random processes with increments (consumer choices) that are path-dependent. Powerful techniques now exist for this in the probability theory literature.[8]

---

7. In an important related case, Farrell and Saloner (1985) investigate whether expectations about other firms' behavior cause firms to be locked-in to an inferior standard when all would be better off with an alternative one.

8. Such as the path-dependent strong-law theorems of Arthur, Ermoliev, and Kaniovski (1983, 1985a, 1985b) or Hill, Lane, and Sudderth (1980). See Arthur (1985).

On Historical Explanation and on Policy

The argument of this paper suggests that the interpretation of economic history should be different in the three regimes. Under constant and diminishing returns, the evolution of the market is *ergodic*—ultimate market shares are built in *a priori* to the endowments, preferences, and transformation possibilities that describe the economy and small events cannot sway the outcome. Here the dynamics of the market reveal the superior choice. But while this is comforting, it reduces history to the status of mere carrier—the deliverer of the inevitable. Under increasing returns, by contrast, the process becomes path-dependent. It is *nonergodic*—many outcomes are possible, and heterogeneities, small indivisibilities, or chance meetings become magnified by positive feedbacks to "tip" the system into the actual outcome "selected." History becomes all-important.[9]

Where we observe the predominance of one technology or one economic institution over its competitors we should then be cautious of the standard exercise that seeks the means by which the winner's innate "superiority" came to be translated into adoption. Gasoline's superiority over steam as the propulsion device for automobiles, for example, we take for granted. But among engineers it is still in dispute, just as it was in 1900.[10]

Policy deserves a brief comment. Where diminishing-returns technologies compete it is usually best to let the superior aggregate choice, or the superior mix of choices, reveal itself in the outcome that eventually dominates. But in the increasing-returns case, laissez-faire gives no guarantee that the "fittest" technology (in the long-run sense) will be the one that survives. More effective policy in the (unsponsored) increasing-returns case would be

---

9. Modern historiography as in Conrad and Meyer (1964) takes a comfortable compromise position on this ancient inevitability-versus-"Cleopatra's-nose" debate arguing that causality is part deterministic, part "random." Interestingly, we find no such compromise. Causality resides either deterministically within the given economic structure, or "randomly" in the small events and circumstances outside the given structure. (Strictly speaking, "random events" are not invoked or defined in this paper—only circumstances that lie outside the main description of the dynamic structure.) For earlier recognition of the significance of both nonconvexity and ergodicity for economic history see David (1975).

10. Amusingly, Fletcher writes in 1904: ". . . unless the objectionable features of the petrol carriage can be removed, it is bound to be driven from the road by its less objectionable rival, the steam-driven vehicle of the day." Seventy-two years later, Burton (1976) concludes that certain realizable advances (uniflow expanders with impulse valves and lower powerplant weight) "make the vehicular steam engine competitive with the Otto cycle [gasoline] engine in terms of fuel mileage, and greatly superior in terms of pollutant emissions." (See also Strack 1970). Of course, if this claim is true, Detroit may still be rational in continuing to pursue gasoline, given the auto engine's technological interrelatedness with a distributional, maintenance, and refinery infrastructure specialized to gasoline. See also McLaughlin (1954) and Arthur (1984) on the steam versus gasoline question.

predicated on the nature of the market breakdown: in our model early adopters impose externalities on later ones by rationally choosing variants best for themselves alone; missing is an inter-agent market to induce them to explore promising but costly infant technologies that might pay off handsomely to later adopters.[11] The standard remedy of assigning to early developers rights of compensation by later users would be effective here only to the degree that early developers can appropriate later payoffs. Moreover, restricting such "patents" to tightly defined variants allows easy bypass by latecomers; widening them to generic technologies (nuclear power, for example) is impracticable and would restrict exploration by others. As a second possibility, the central authority, acting as a super-agent, could underwrite adoption and exploration along promising but less popular technological paths. But where eventual returns to a technology are hard to ascertain—as in solar energy for example—the super-agent then faces a classic multi-arm bandit problem of choosing which technologies to bet on. An early run of "jackpots" from one technology may cause it perfectly rationally to abandon other possibilities. Under planned intervention the fundamental problem of possibly locking in a regrettable course of development remains.

Conclusion

Under diminishing returns, static analysis is sufficient: the outcome is unique, insensitive to the order in which choices are made, and insensitive to small events that occur during the formation of the market. Under increasing returns however, static analysis is no longer enough. Multiple outcomes are possible, and to understand how one outcome is selected we need to follow step by step the process by which small events cumulate to cause the system to gravitate toward that outcome rather than the others.

To the list of already known increasing-returns properties like potential inefficiency and nonpredictability, a dynamic approach adds two new ones: *inflexibility,* in that allocations gradually rigidify, or lock-in, in structure; and *nonergodicity,* in that small events early on may decide the larger course of structural change. The dynamics thus take on an evolutionary flavor, with a "founder effect" mechanism akin to that in genetics.

Where increasing returns are present, much of the later development of an economy may depend upon "small events" beneath the resolution of an

---

11. Competition between *sponsored* technologies suffers less from this missing market. To the degree that sponsoring firms can appropriate later payoffs, they have an incentive to develop initially costly, but promising technologies. And financial markets for sponsoring investors together with insurance markets for adopters who may make the "wrong" choice, mitigate losses for the risk-averse. Of course, if a product succeeds and locks in the market, monopoly-pricing problems may arise.

observer's model and so may be impossible to predict with any degree of certainty. This suggests that there may be theoretical limits, as well as practical ones, to the predictability of the economic future.[12]

APPENDIX

The Expectations Case

We analyze here the competing standards case where adopters are affected by *future* choices as well as past choices. Assume in our earlier model that R-agents receive additional net benefits of Π_A^R, Π_B^R, if the market locks in to A or to B respectively; similarly S-agents receive Π_A^S, Π_B^S. (To preserve generality we allow variants to improve with adoption as before.) We assume that agents know the state of the market (n_A, n_B) when choosing and that they have expectations or beliefs that adoptions follow a stochastic process Ω. They choose rationally under these expectations, so that actual adoptions follow the process $\Gamma(\Omega)$. We will call this actual process a *rational expectations equilibrium process* when it bears out the expected process, that is, when

$$\Gamma(\Omega) \equiv \Omega.$$

We distinguish two cases, corresponding to the degree of heterogeneity of preferences in the market.

Case i. Suppose initially that $a_R - b_R > \Pi_B^R$ and $b_S - a_S > \Pi_A^S$ and that R and S types have beliefs that the adoption process is a random walk Ω with absorption barriers at Δ_R, Δ_S, with associated probabilities of lock-in to A, $p(n_A, n_B)$, and lock-in to B, $1 - p(n_A, n_B)$. Under these beliefs, R-type expected payoffs for choosing A or B are, respectively:[13]

$$a_R + rn_A + p(n_A, n_B)\Pi_A^R \tag{4}$$

$$b_R + rn_B + [1 - p(n_A, n_B)]\Pi_B^R. \tag{5}$$

---

12. Similar arguments apply (Leith 1966; Lorenz 1963) to the theoretical possibility of accurate meteorological forecasting. The observational net would have to be finer than the radius of the smallest eddy, else these "small events" become amplified by inherent positive feedbacks into large uncertainties.

13. Assuming agents assess probabilities given the state of the market just before they choose. An after-choice assessment would complicate the analysis, but would give similar results.

S-type payoffs may be written similarly. In the actual process R-types will switch to B when n_A and n_B are such that these two expressions become equal. Both types choose B from then on. The actual probability of lock-in to A is zero here; so that if the expected process is fulfilled, p is also zero here and we have n_A and n_B such that

$$a_R + rn_A = b_R + rn_B + \Pi_B^R$$

with associated barrier given by

$$\Delta_R = n_A - n_B = -(a_R - b_R - \Pi_B^R)/r. \tag{6}$$

Similarly S-types switch to A at boundary position given by

$$\Delta_S = n_A - n_B = (b_S - a_S - \Pi_A^S)/s. \tag{7}$$

It is easy to confirm that beyond these barriers the actual process is indeed locked in to A or B and that within them R-agents prefer A, and S-agents prefer B. Thus if agents believe the adoption process is a random walk with absorbing barriers Δ_R, Δ_S given by (6) and (7), these beliefs will be fulfilled.

Case ii. Suppose now that $a_R - b_R < \Pi_B^R$ and $b_S - a_S < \Pi_A^S$. Then (4) and (5) show that switching will occur immediately if agents hold expectations that the system will definitely lock in to A or to B. These expectations become self-fulfilling and the absorbing barriers narrow to zero. Similarly, when nonimproving standards compete, so that the only payoffs are Π_A and Π_B, again beliefs that A or B will definitely lock in become self-fulfilling.

Notice that expectations either narrow or collapse the switching boundaries—they exacerbate the fundamental market instability.

REFERENCES

Arrow, Kenneth J., and Frank J. Hahn. 1971. *General Competitive Analysis*. San Francisco: Holden-Day.
Arthur, W. Brian. 1984. "Competing Technologies and Economic Prediction," *Options* (April). I.I.A.S.A. Laxenburg, Austria.
————. 1985. "Industry Location and the Economies of Agglomeration: Why a Silicon Valley?" Mimeo, Center for Economic Policy Research, Stanford.
Arthur, W. Brian, Y. M. Ermoliev, and Y. M. Kaniovski. 1983. "On Generalized Urn Schemes of the Polya Kind" (in Russian), *Kibernetika* 19:49–56. English translation in *Cybernetics* 19:61–71 (1983).

————. 1985a. "Strong Laws for a Class of Path-Dependent Urn Processes," in *Proceedings of the International Conference on Stochastic Optimization, Kiev 1984*. Arkin, Shiryaev, and Wets (Eds.) Springer: Lecture Notes in Control and Info. Sciences.

————. 1985b. "Path-Dependent Processes and the Emergence of Macro-Structure." To appear, *European J. Operational Research*.

Beato, Paulino. 1982. "The Existence of Marginal Cost Pricing Equilibria with Increasing Returns," *Quart. J. Econ.* 97:669–87.

Brown, Donald J., and Geoffrey M. Heal. 1976. "The Existence of a Market Equilibrium in an Economy with Increasing Returns to Scale," Cowles Paper no. 425.

————. 1979. "Equity, Efficiency and Increasing Returns." *Rev. Econ. Stud.* 46:571–85.

Burton, Rodney L. 1976. "Recent Advances in Vehicular Steam Engine Efficiency." Society of Automotive Engineers, Preprint 760340.

Cipolla, Carlo M. 1967. *Clocks and Culture 1300–1700*. Norton: New York.

Conrad, Alfred, and John Meyer. 1964. "Economic Theory, Statistical Inference, and Economic History," in *The Economics of Slaving*. Aldine: Chicago.

David, Paul. 1975. *Technical Choice, Innovation, and Economic Growth*, Cambridge: Cambridge University Press.

————. 1985. "Clio and the Economics of QWERTY," *Amer. Econ. Rev. Proc.* 75:332–37.

Farrell, Joseph, and Garth Saloner. 1985. "Standardization, Compatibility, and Innovation," *Rand J. Econ.* 16:70–83.

Flaherty, M. Therese. 1980. "Industry Structure and Cost-Reducing Investment," *Econometrica* 48:1187–1209.

Fletcher, William. 1904. *English and American Steam Carriages and Traction Engines* (reprinted). Devon: David and Charles, 1973.

Guesneries, R. 1975. "Pareto Optimality in a Non-Convex Economy," *Econometrica* 43:1–30.

Hanson, Ward A. 1985. "Bandwagons and Orphans: Dynamic Pricing of Competing Systems Subject to Decreasing Costs." Ph.D. Diss., Stanford.

Hartwick, John. 1985. "The Persistence of QWERTY and Analogous Suboptimal Standards," Mimeo. Kingston, Ontario: Queen's University.

Katz, M. L., and C. Shapiro. 1983. "Network Externalities, Competition, and Compatibility." Paper no. 54. Princeton: Woodrow Wilson School.

————. 1985. "Technology Adoption in the Presence of Network Externalities." Discussion Paper no. 96. Princeton University.

Kehoe, Timothy J. 1985. "Multiplicity of Equilibria and Comparative Statics." *Quart. J. Econ.* 100:119–47.

Krugman, Paul. 1980. "Scale Economies, Product Differentiation, and the Pattern of Trade," *Amer. Econ. Rev.* 70:950–59.

Leith, Cecil. 1966. "The Feasibility of a Global Observation and Analysis Experiment." Publication 1290. Washington, D.C.: Nat. Acad. Sci.

Lieberman, Marvin. 1985. "Patents, R and D and the Learning Curve: Disentangling the Sources of Growth in the Chemical Processing Industry." Mimeo. Stanford.

Lorenz, Edward N. 1963. "The Predictability of Hydrodynamic Flow," *Transactions New York Acad. Sci.* 25:400–431.

Marshall, Alfred. 1891. *Principles of Economics,* 2d Ed. London: Macmillan.

McLaughlin, Charles C. 1954. "The Stanley Steamer: A Study in Unsuccessful Innovation," *Explorations in Entrepreneurial Hist.* 7:37–47.

Mookherjee, Dilip and Debraj Ray. 1985. "Dynamic Price Games with Learning-by-Doing," Mimeo. Stanford.

Rosenberg, Nathan. 1982. *Inside the Black Box: Technology and Economics.* Cambridge, England: Cambridge University Press.

Saxonhouse, Gary, and Gavin Wright. 1984. "New Evidence on the Stubborn English Mule," *Econ. Hist. Rev.* 37:507–19.

Scarf, Herbert E. 1981. "Production Sets with Indivisibilities—Part I: Generalities," *Econometrica* 49:1–32.

Schelling, Thomas C. 1978. *Micromotives and Macrobehavior.* Norton.

Spence, Michael A. 1981. "The Learning Curve and Competition," *Bell J. Econ.* 12:49–70.

Strack, William C. 1970. "Condensers and Boilers for Steam-Powered Cars." NASA Technical Note, TN D-5813. Washington, D.C.

Weitzman, Martin L. 1982. "Increasing Returns and the Foundations of Unemployment Theory," *Econ. J.* 92:787–804.

CHAPTER 3

Path-Dependent Processes and the Emergence of Macrostructure

W. Brian Arthur, Yuri M. Ermoliev, and Yuri M. Kaniovski

Many situations dominated by increasing returns are most usefully modeled as dynamic processes with random events and natural positive feedbacks (or nonlinearities). In this paper, Ermoliev, Kaniovski, and I introduce a very general class of such stochastic processes. We call these *nonlinear Polya processes* and show that they can model a wide variety of increasing returns and positive-feedback problems.

In the presence of increasing returns or self-reinforcement, a nonlinear Polya process typically displays a *multiplicity* of possible asymptotic outcomes. These long-run outcomes or equilibria, we show, correspond to the stable fixed points of an associated "urn function," and can easily be identified. Early random fluctuations cumulate and are magnified or attenuated by the inherent nonlinearities of the process. By studying how these build up as the dynamics of the process unfold over time, we can observe how an asymptotic outcome becomes "selected" over time.

The paper appeared in the *European Journal of Operational Research* 30 (1987): 294–303. It is a less technical version of our 1983 *Kibernetika* paper "A Generalized Urn Problem and its Applications," (which is cited at the end of this paper). For a more rigorous account of the processes described here, see chapter 10 of this volume. Yuri Ermoliev and Yuri Kaniovski are with the Glushkov Institute of Cybernetics, Kiev, Ukraine.

Of recent fascination to physical chemists, biologists, and economists are nonlinear dynamical systems of the "dissipative" or "autocatalytic" or "self-organizing" type, where positive feedbacks may cause certain patterns or structures that emerge to be self-reinforcing. Such systems tend to be sensitive to early dynamical fluctuations. Often there is a multiplicity of patterns that are candidates for long-term self-reinforcement; the cumulation of small events early on "pushes" the dynamics into the orbit of one of these and thus "selects" the structure that the system eventually locks into.

"Order-through-fluctuation" dynamics of this type are usually modelled by nonlinear differential equations with Markovian perturbations [1,2]. Showing the emergence of *structure* in the sense of long-run pattern or limiting behavior then amounts to analyzing the asymptotic properties of particular classes of stochastic differential equations. But while these continuous-time formulations work well, their asymptotic properties must often be specially studied and are not always easy to derive. Moreover, for discrete events, continuous-time formulations involve approximations. In this paper we introduce an alternative class of models (developed in previous articles [3,4,5]) that we call *nonlinear Polya processes*. These processes have long-run behavior easy to analyze, and for discrete applications they are exact. Within this class of stochastic processes we can investigate the emergence of structure by deriving theorems on long-run limiting behavior.

In this short paper we survey our recent work on the theory of *nonlinear Polya processes*. We avoid technicalities as far as possible, and present applications in industrial location theory, chemical kinetics, and the evolution of technological structure in the economy. The limit theorems we present generalize the strong law of large numbers to a wide class of path-dependent stochastic processes.

Structure and the Strong Law

If a fair coin is tossed indefinitely, the proportion heads tends to vary considerably at the start, but settles down more and more closely to 50 percent. We could say, trivially perhaps, that a *structure*—a long-run fixed pattern in the proportion of heads and tails—gradually emerges. Of course, it is perfectly *possible* that some other proportion might emerge—two heads followed by one tail repeated indefinitely, for example, would yield $2/3$ and is just as *possible* as any other sequence. But such an outcome is unlikely. Borel's strong law of large numbers tells us that repeated random variables (drawn from the same distribution) that are independent of previous ones have long-term averages that much approach their expected values. While other outcomes might in principle be possible, they have probability zero. Thus in coin-tossing, where the event "heads" is certainly independent of previous tosses, the average of heads in the total—the proportion heads—must settle down to 0.5, the expectation of each toss being a head. The emergence of a 50 percent proportion has probability one. Further, the "strong" part of the strong law tells us that once the proportion settles down it persists. If we were to repeat the coin-tossing experiment eventually all (but a zero-measure set of) repetitions would enter and remain corralled inside an arbitrarily small interval surrounding the expected 0.5 value. The standard Borel strong law then is a statement about the emergence of, the inevitability of, and the persistence of a unique structure in certain systems with independent increments subject to random fluctuations.

Coin-tossing examples are useful mainly as textbook abstractions. A more interesting dynamical system that illustrates the emergence of macrostructure under varying assumptions is the process by which firms in an industry concentrate in various regional locations [6]. Suppose that firms start up one by one, and each in sequence chooses one location from N candidate regions and settles there. Randomness enters if the firms differ in type and we do not know which type of firm will come into being next to make its locational choice.

The simplest locational dynamics would have independent increments like the coin-tossing case. Suppose that probabilities are fixed, so that the probability is p_j that the next firm to choose is of a type that will prefer location j. Thus a unit—a firm—is added to region 1, or 2, or . . . , or N at each time of choice independently of previous choices, with probabilities $p = (p_1, p_2, \ldots, p_N)$ where $\Sigma_j p_j = 1$. Starting from zero firms in any region, concentrations of the industry in the various regions will fluctuate, considerably at first; but again the standard strong law tells us that as the industry grows, proportions in the N regions must settle down to the expectation of each choice, that is, to a constant vector equal to p. Under our assumptions, a predetermined unique structure—this time a long-run fixed regional location pattern—must emerge and persist.

What happens in the more general case where firms' locational choices depend in part upon the numbers of firms in each region at the time of choosing? Here increments to the regions are not independent of previous locational choices. The standard strong law no longer applies. We now have a *path-dependent* process, where the probability p_j of an addition to region j becomes a function of the numbers of firms, or equivalently, of the proportions of the industry, in each region at each time of choice. Will such a process settle down to a fixed locational pattern of proportions? That is, will a macrostructure emerge in this path-dependent case, and if so, what will it look like? We seek, in other words, strong laws for systems of this path-dependent type.

We can see at once that path dependence can create a dynamical system of the autocatalytic or self-reinforcing type mentioned earlier. Suppose in our locational example there are now potential economies of agglomeration—so that firms choosing are attracted by the presence of other firms in a region. It will then happen that if one region by chance gets off to a good start, its attractiveness and the probability that it will be chosen become enhanced. Further firms may then choose this region; it becomes yet more attractive. If the economies of agglomeration are strong enough this region could end up with a share of the industry arbitrarily close to 100 percent [6]. Yet, by chance, a similar outcome might have been obtained with one of the other regions becoming dominant. If the process were to be replicated under different random sequences of firms choosing, different locational patterns might well emerge. With self-reinforcing path dependence, a *multiplicity* of possible structures can result.

It is not difficult to think of other examples of path-dependent systems where we might see the same phenomenon of multiple potential emergent structures. For example, chemical reactions form products at rates that depend upon current concentrations of the products. If there is more than one possible reaction product, and autocatalysis, so that products enhance their own formation, the resulting end concentrations—the macrostructure of the reaction outcome—may also have multiple possibilities. Similarly, in consumer economics, if tastes are endogenous so that people are influenced in their purchase of durable goods—cars, say—by the brands that others have purchased already, there will be path dependence. The market can "lock in" to one of a multiplicity of brands, with early events determining the brand that comes to dominate.

It turns out that it is useful to formulate path-dependent unit-increment processes of the type we are discussing as *generalized* urn processes of the Polya kind. Before we do this, however, let us pause to look at the *standard* Polya process.

The Standard Polya Case:
A Special Path-Dependent Process

In 1923 Polya and Eggenberger [7] formulated a path-dependent process that has a particularly striking outcome. Think of an urn of infinite capacity to which are added balls of two possible colors—red and white, say. Starting with one red and one white ball in the urn, add a ball each time, indefinitely, according to the rule: Choose a ball in the urn at random and replace it; if it is red, add a red; if it is white, add a white. Obviously this process has increments that are path-dependent—at any time the probability that the next ball added is red exactly equals the proportion red. We might then ask: does the proportion of red (or white) balls wander indefinitely between zero and one, or does a strong law operate, so that the proportion settles down to a limit, causing a structure to emerge? And if there is a fixed limiting proportion, what is it? Polya proved in 1931 [8] that indeed in a scheme like this the proportion of red balls does tend to a limit X, and with probability one. *But X is a random variable uniformly distributed between 0 and 1.*

In other words, if this Polya process were run once, the proportion of red balls may settle down to 22.3927 . . . percent and never change; if run again, it might settle to 81.4039 . . . percent. A third time it might settle to 42.0641 . . . percent. And so on. Moreover, the convergence is strong—given enough time the process is close to the limit, not *probably* close to it; it does not wander away from the limit from time to time.

Figure 1 shows 10 realizations of this basic process. We can see in this

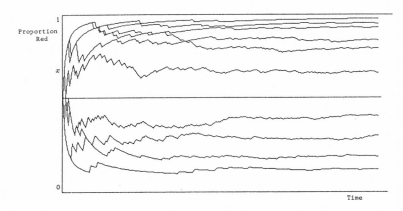

Fig. 1. Ten realizations of the standard Polya process

special case that the proportions do indeed settle down—a structure does emerge each time—but the structure that is "selected" is perfectly random. In this case an uncountable infinity of possible structures can emerge. A particularly insightful and entertaining account of this standard Polya process and how it might apply to the emergence and also to the misinterpretation of structure in biology and physics is given by Joel Cohen [9]. In the more general case where the urn starts off from an arbitrary number of red and white balls, proportions once again tend to a limit X, but now X has a two-parameter Beta distribution [10].

Here are two examples of Polya-type path dependence.

Example 1. A dual autocatalytic chemical reaction. A substrate molecule S is converted into an R-molecule if it encounters an R-molecule, or into a W-molecule if it encounters a W-molecule:

$$S + R \rightarrow 2R + \text{Waste Molecule } E,$$

$$S + W \rightarrow 2W + \text{Waste Molecule } F.$$

Thus the probability that an R-molecule is created at any time exactly equals the concentration of R-product. A standard Polya process operates. Starting with one molecule of R and W, the process settles to a fixed concentration of R-product, but one that is anywhere between 0 and 100 percent.

Example 2. Industrial location by spin-off. An industry builds up regionally from some set of initial firms, one per region say, but this time new firms are added by "spinning off" from parent firms one at a time. (David Cohen

[11] has shown that such spin-offs have been the dominant "birth" mechanism in the U.S. electronics industry.) Assume that each new firm stays in its parent location, and that any existing firm is as likely to spin off a new firm as any other. We again have Polya path dependence—firms are added to regions incrementally with probabilities exactly equal to the proportions of firms in each region. Once again, a locational structure emerges with probability one—but it is a vector of proportions that is *selected randomly* from a uniform distribution. (We could generate a representative outcome by placing $N - 1$ points on the unit interval at random, and cutting at these points to obtain N "shares" of the unit interval.)

To get some intuitive feeling for this basic Polya urn process, notice that, as in figure 2, the probability of adding a red always equals the proportion red. It is easy to show that this means, on an *expected motion* basis, that the process tends to stay where it is. There is no "drift". Of course, there are perturbations to the proportion red caused by the random sampling of balls; but unit additions to the urn make less and less difference to the proportions as the total number of balls grows, and therefore the effect of these perturbations dies away. The process then fluctuates less and less, and, since it does not drift, it settles down. Where it settles, of course, depends completely on its early random movements.

Nonlinear Path Dependence

The standard Polya framework described above is too restrictive for our purposes. It requires a highly special path dependence where the probability of adding a ball of type j exactly equals the proportion of type j. For a much wider set of applications we would want to consider a more general situation where the probability of an addition to type j is an arbitrary *function* of the proportions of all types. Moreover, to allow for realistic applications we would want more than two dimensions—two colors—and functions that may change with time. To describe our new process and the theorems that go with it, we will proceed a little more formally for a moment, drawing on our previous work [4,5], and that of Hill, Lane, and Sudderth [3].

We now take an urn of infinite capacity that may contain balls of N possible colors and allow new units to be added at each time with probabilities that are not necessarily equal to but *a function of* the proportions in the urn. Let the vector $X_n = (X_n^1, X_n^2, \ldots, X_n^N)$ describe the proportions of balls of types 1 to N respectively, at time n (after $n-1$ balls have been added). Let $\{q_n\}$ be a sequence of continuous functions mapping the proportions (of colors) into the probabilities (of an addition to each color) at time n. Thus, starting at time 1 with an *initial vector* of balls $b_1 = (b_1^1, b_1^2, \ldots, b_1^N)$, one ball is added to the urn at each time; and at time n it is of color i with probability $q_n^i(X_n)$.

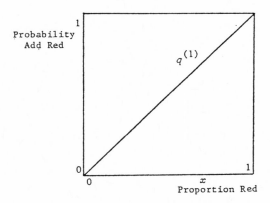

Fig. 2. Urn function: Standard Polya process

The scheme is iterated to yield the proportions vectors $X_1, X_2, X_3 \ldots$. Of interest is whether a structure emerges, chosen probabilistically from a multiplicity of possible structures—or, more technically, whether $\{X_n\}$ tends to a limit random vector X, with probability one, where X is selected from some set of possible limit vectors B.

Let the total balls initially be $w = \Sigma_i b^i_1$. At time n, define the random variable

$$\beta^i_n(x) = \begin{cases} 1 & \text{with probability } q^i_n(x), \\ 0 & \text{with probability } 1 - q^i_n(x), \\ & i = 1, \ldots, N. \end{cases}$$

Then additions of i-type balls to the urn follow the dynamics

$$b_{n+1} = b^i_n + \beta^i_n(X_n), i = 1, \ldots, N.$$

Dividing through by the total balls $(w + n - 1)$, the evolution of the proportion of i-types, $X^i_n = b^i_n/(w + n - 1)$, is described by

$$X^i_{n+1} = X^i_n + \frac{1}{(w + n)} [\beta^i_n(X_n) - X^i_n],$$

$$n = 1, 2, \ldots, \tag{1}$$

with $X^i_1 = b^i_1/w$.

We can rewrite (1) in the form

$$X_{n+1}^i = X_n^i + \frac{1}{(w+n)} \, [q_n^i(X_n) - X_n^i]$$

$$+ \frac{1}{(w+n)} \, \mu_n^i(X_n), \tag{2}$$

$$X_1^i = b_1^i/w,$$

where

$$\mu_n^i(X_n) = \beta_n^i(X_n) - q_n^i(X_n). \tag{3}$$

Equation (2) is the basic dynamic equation of our N-dimensional path-dependent process. It consists of a determinate "driving" part (the first two terms on the right of (2)) and a perturbational part (the μ-term in (2)). Notice in (3) that the conditional expectation of μ_n^i with respect to X_n is zero, so that we can show that the expected motion of X_{n+1} is given by the "driving" part of (2) as

$$E[X_{n+1}^i \mid X_n] = X_n^i + \frac{1}{(w+n)} \, [q_n^i(X_n) - X_n^i]. \tag{4}$$

Thus we see that motion tends to be directed by the term $q_n(X_n) - X_n$. In figure 3a, for example, urn function 2 shows a tendency toward 0 or 1. Urn function 3 shows a tendency toward X. In each case there is an "attraction" toward certain fixed points of q. Figure 3b shows a more complicated urn function in two dimensions, with attractions toward several fixed points.

The standard Polya process discussed earlier is represented by an urn function that is identically equal to x, and so has no expected motion driving it. Our more general process (2) has a nonlinear driving part plus the Polya perturbational part. Hence we call it a *nonlinear Polya process*.

Strong Laws for Nonlinear Path Dependence

It is tempting to conjecture from figure 3a that the dynamics must tend toward a fixed point of the urn function q. We might conjecture further from figures 3a and 3b that not any fixed point will do. Some fixed points appear to be stable ones (they attract)—while others are unstable (they repel). A moment's thought, however, shows that without formal proof, it is hard to guarantee these conjectures. Notice from (4) that the attraction toward fixed points falls off at rate $1/n$—so that the process may not have sufficient motion to be able to arrive at attracting fixed points. Notice also that while unstable points repel,

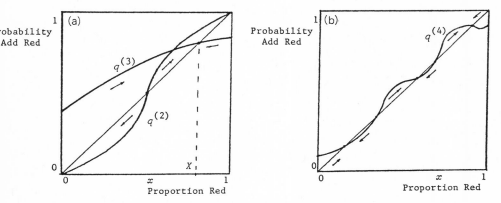

Fig. 3. Urn functions: Nonlinear Polya processes

they are nonetheless self-perpetuating—only perturbations can shake the dynamics away from them. Unless there are sufficient perturbations, and sufficient repulsion near these points, it might be the case that unstable fixed points can act as limit points for the process.

It turns out that (subject to certain technical conditions being fulfilled) our conjecture does go through. The system must indeed end up with proportions that map into the identical probabilities; and it must end up only at stable fixed points. For two-dimensional processes with stationary urn functions, this was first proved in 1980 in the elegant article of Hill, Lane, and Sudderth [3]. The present authors proved this conjecture for the *N*-dimensional processes with nonstationary urn functions described here, in articles in 1983 and 1984 [4,5].

Before we quote the relevant theorems, here are two useful definitions. We will say that $\{q_n\}$, the set of urn functions, converges *reasonably rapidly* if it converges to a function q faster than $\{1/n\}$ converges to zero. We will also say following (4), that

$$X_{n+1}^i = X_n^i + \frac{1}{(w+n)}\,[q_n^i(X_n) - X_n^i] \tag{5}$$

is the *equivalent deterministic system* corresponding to our stochastic process. Now, a deterministic system like (5) might not itself converge—it might give rise to limit cycles or other more complicated asymptotic behavior. However, we can simplify matters by restricting (5) to be a *gradient system*—so that there exists a non-negative potential function whose downhill gradient gives the movements of our deterministic system. (This rules out cycles because no process can cycle forever downhill.) Given this restriction plus a technical requirement, our first result is that *nonlinear Polya processes* have to converge to fixed points of q.

> *Theorem 1. Suppose continuous urn functions $\{q_n\}$ that converge reasonably rapidly to a function q and suppose the equivalent deterministic system is a gradient system. Suppose also that the set of fixed points of q, $B = \{x:q(x) = x\}$, contains a finite number of connected components. Then the vector of proportions $\{X_n\}$ converges, with probability one, to a point z in the set of fixed points B.*

For proof we refer the reader to [5]. The full proof is lengthy, but by way of explanation notice that in (2) we have represented the dynamics in the form of a stochastic approximation process [12]. This allows us to use the powerful machinery of stochastic approximation theory together with martingale methods. Proof then amounts to showing that, for our gradient system dynamics with perturbations, expected increments in the value of the potential are less than some negative value (of order $1/n$) at points of q which are not fixed points. Unless the system settles to a local stationary point of the potential function—a fixed point of q—cumulations of negative increments would eventually drive the potential function negative, a contradiction.

Our next two theorems show that indeed not all fixed points can emerge as the eventual structure of the process. Attracting fixed points—stable ones—are candidates for "selection" as the eventual outcome. Repelling fixed points—unstable ones—are not. Technically, given a fixed point z, we will say that it is a *stable point* if there exists a symmetric positive-definite matrix C such that

$$\langle C[x - q(x)], x - z \rangle > 0 \tag{6}$$

where x is any point in a neighborhood of z. Similarly, we will say z is an *unstable point* if there exists a symmetric positive-definite matrix C such that

$$\langle C[x - q(x)], x - z \rangle < 0. \tag{7}$$

where x is any point in a neighborhood of z. These criteria test whether expected motion is locally always toward z, or locally away from z respectively.

We will also say that point x is *reachable* if the process can arrive at it in finite time from the starting conditions with finite probability. (A sufficient condition for this is that the urn functions q_n map the interior of the unit simplex into itself.)

Theorem 2. Let the urn functions $\{q_n\}$ converge reasonably rapidly to a function q. And let z be a reachable, stable point of q. Then the process has limit point z with positive probability.

Again, we refer the reader to [4] or [5] for proof. The proof uses criterion (6) to construct a local Lyapunov function around z.

Theorem 3. Suppose the functions $\{q_n\}$ converge reasonably rapidly to some function q, and suppose z is a nonvertex unstable point of q. Then the process cannot converge to z with positive probability.

To prove this (see [5]) we use (7) to construct a suitable local Lyapunov function around z, then invoke stochastic asymptotic results of Nevelson and Hasminskii [12].

To use these theorems to study the emergence of structure—the long-run behavior of proportions or concentrations—we need then only examine the fixed points of the limiting function q that maps the proportions of each type into the probabilities of adding an increment to each type. Unstable points will not emerge as the "selected structure." And there may be a multiplicity of stable points—each candidates for "selection". Referring back to the standard Polya process earlier, we now see that all points of the urn function $q^{(1)}$ are fixed points and all are reachable, so that all points are candidates for long-run selection. The standard Polya process is in fact a highly singular special case of our more general nonlinear path-dependent process.

Notice that the conventional strong law (with unit independent increments) is a special case of our results above: Here we have $q(x) = p$ for all proportions x; the vector p is a fixed point and it is stable, reachable, and unique—p must therefore emerge as the ultimate proportions.

Here are two applications of our theorems outlined above.

Example 3. A second dual autocatalytic reaction. Consider a slightly different version of the chemical reaction given earlier.

$S + 2R \rightarrow 3R +$ Waste Molecule E,

$S + 2W \rightarrow 3W +$ Waste Molecule F.

In this case a single substrate molecule S is converted into either W- or R-form (with waste molecules E and F) according to whether it encounters *two* W-molecules before *two* R-molecules. We may think of the process of sampling the next *three* W- or R-molecules encountered and adding one to W or R

accordingly, as two out of the three molecules sampled are W or R. Now, the probability that an R-molecule is added is

$$q_n = \sum_{k=2}^{3} H(k; n, n_R, 3)$$

where H is the Hypergeometric distribution parameterized by n and n_R, the number of R-molecules where there are n R- and W-molecules in toto, and by the sample size 3. In this scheme the urn functions have an S-shape as in $q^{(2)}$ in figure 3a. There are stable fixed points at 0 and 1 and an unstable one at 0.5. Therefore, in contrast to the previous example where any intermediate concentration between 0 and 100 percent could emerge, only extreme 0 or 100 percent concentrations of R or of W can emerge.

Here is an example without multiple structures that generalizes our earlier location-through-spin-off example. This time a unique regional distribution pattern must emerge.

Example 4. Locational spin-offs: A second mechanism. There are N regions in a country. As before, firms are added to an industry by spinning off from parent firms. Again, any existing firm is as likely to spin off a new firm as any other. Now suppose that a firm in region j spins off a new firm that settles in region i with some positive probability $q(i, j)$ where $\sum_{i=1}^{N} q(i, j) = 1$ for all j. In this case we can write the vector of probabilities q_n given the proportions x as

$$q_n(x) = Qx$$

where Q is the matrix $Q = [q(i, j)]$.

Our theory tells us that the regional structure that will emerge corresponds to a fixed point $z = Qz$. And from our condition that all $q(i, j)$ elements are greater than zero, we can show that there is a unique, stable, fixed point. Therefore, in contrast to the previous stay-put spin-off case where any locational shares are possible, in this case the regional shares of the industry must converge to a unique pre-determined structure.

Some remarks are necessary at this stage.

1. We can see from (3) that nonlinear Polya processes have the property that initially they are dominated by stochastic motions—random unit increments early in the process make a large difference—but that later these dissolve away and the deterministic expected motions come to the fore. In fact, the possible structures that may emerge are com-

pletely given by the equivalent deterministic system—it is the role of the perturbations to "select" from these. It is this property that makes these processes natural models for the emergence of (determinate) structure through (stochastic) fluctuation.

2. It is possible to generalize this nonlinear Polya process further, to discontinuous urn functions, to cases where the equivalent deterministic system has limit cycles or more complex behavior, and to non-unit increments. But that is beyond the scope of this paper.

3. Notice that in the theory and examples given above, we are dealing with pure birth processes—only increments are allowed. A corresponding theory could be developed where decrements are allowed (that is, where balls may be taken from the urn). But in this case, in general we would no longer have strong laws: usually we would have convergence in distribution to the emergent structure.

4. We could usefully distinguish between processes that have a single stable fixed point, so that a unique structure or limit must emerge, and processes that have more than one reachable stable fixed point, where structure is "selected" partly randomly. The former we can call *ergodic* —there is one possible outcome, and perturbations "wash away." The latter are *nonergodic*—there are multiple outcomes and early perturbations become all-important in the "selection" of structure.

An interesting and instructive case of nonergodic path dependence seems to determine the technological structure that emerges in the economy [13,14]. We briefly summarize this case now.

Path-Dependence and the Emergence of Technological Structure

Very often, individual technologies show increasing returns to adoption—the more they are adopted the more is learned about them; in turn the more they are improved, and the more attractive they become [15]. Very often, too, there are several *technologies* that *compete* for shares of a "market" of potential adopters. (In the 1890s, for example, the steam engine, the electric motor, and the gasoline engine competed—albeit unconsciously—as power sources for the new automobile.)

Adoption of technologies that compete can be usefully modelled as a nonlinear Polya process. A unit increment—an individual adoption—is added, each time of choice, to a given technology with a probability that depends on the numbers (or proportions) holding each technology at that particular time. We can use our strong-law theorems to show circumstances under which *increasing returns to adoption* (the probability of adoption rises with the share of the market) may drive the adopter "market" to a single dominant technology, with small events early on "selecting" the technology that takes over [13,14,16].

Asymptotic theory is also important in showing three key features of the dynamics that arise in this nonergodic "increasing returns" case. First, *a priori* we cannot say with accuracy *which* technological structure will "win" the market. In fact, gasoline was held to be the least likely option in the 1890s [14] and yet it emerged as the dominant technological structure for automobile propulsion. Second, the technology that comes to dominate—the structure that emerges—does not necessarily have to be the "best" or most efficient; events early on can lock the system in to an inferior technological path. It has certainly been argued in the engineering literature that, had steam been developed to the same degree as gasoline, it might conceivably have been superior [17]. (The 1950s programming language FORTRAN, the U.S. color television system, and the QWERTY typewriter keyboard [18] are demonstrably inferior structures that seem to be locked in.) Third, once a single-technology structure emerges and becomes self-reinforcing, it is difficult to change it. If it were desirable to re-establish an excluded technology—say steam propulsion—an ever-widening technical changeover gap would have to be closed.

For nonergodic systems—like competing technologies with sufficient increasing returns to adoption—these properties of the macrostructure that emerges—*nonpredictability,* potential *nonsuperiority,* and *structural rigidity* —appear to be common and to some degree inevitable [13].

Conclusion

We have defined "structure" for the purposes of this brief survey as the long-run pattern in eventual proportions, concentrations, or shares of a market that emerges from a dynamic process. The conventional strong law of large numbers makes statements about the emergence of structure in processes where additions to the possible categories occur with independent, fixed probabilities. In the more general "nonlinear Polya" case we have examined, where additions to categories are influenced at each time by the proportions in each category—the process has dependent increments. We have shown that the Borel strong law (under certain technical conditions) can be generalized to this important dependent-increment case: such processes do indeed settle down, with probability one, to proportions that are fixed.

In certain simple cases nonlinear Polya processes settle to unique predeterminable proportions. But more generally they possess the familiar property of nonlinear systems: a multiplicity of structures may be possible of which one will be eventually, dynamically "selected." We can identify these candidate structures as represented by the set of stable fixed points in the mapping from proportions into probabilities. Thus nonlinear Polya processes may offer a useful alternative to the usual differential-equation formulations. And for particular, discrete path-dependent systems—in chemical kinetics, industrial location, and technological choice, for example—we can construct exact models that demonstrate how small fluctuations at the outset can cause quite different eventual structures to emerge.

REFERENCES

1. Nicolis, G., and I. Prigogine. 1971. *Self-Organization in Nonequilibrium Systems: From Dissipative Structures to Order through Fluctuations.* New York: Wiley.
2. Mansour, M. M., C. Van den Broek, G. Nicolis, and J. W. Turner. 1981. "Asymptotic properties of Markovian master equations." *Annals Phys.* 131:1–30.
3. Hill, B. M., D. Lane, and W. Sudderth. 1980. "A strong law for some generalized urn processes." *Annals Prob.* 8:214–26.
4. Arthur, W. B., Y. M. Ermoliev, and Y. M. Kaniovski. 1983. "A generalized urn problem and its applications." *Kibernetika* 19:49–57 (in Russian). Translated in *Cybernetics* 19:61–71.
5. Arthur, W. B., Y. M. Ermoliev, and Y. M. Kaniovski. 1984. "Strong laws for a class of path-dependent stochastic processes, with applications." In: *Proc. Conf. on Stochastic Optimization, Kiev 1984*, Arkin, Shiryayev, Wets. (eds.). Springer, Lecture Notes in Control and Information Sciences.
6. Arthur, W. B. 1984. "Industry location pattern and the importance of history: Why a Silicon Valley?", Stanford University, Center for Econ. Policy Research.
7. Polya, G., and F. Eggenberger. 1923. "Ueber die Statistik verketteter Vorgaenge." *Z. Angew. Math. Mech.* 3:279–89.
8. Polya, G. 1931. "Sur quelques Points de la Théorie des Probabilités." *Ann. Inst. H. Poincaré.* 1:117–61.
9. Cohen, J. 1976. "Irreproducible results and the breeding of pigs (or nondegenerate limit random variables in biology)." *Bioscience* 26:391–94.
10. Johnson, N., and S. Kotz. 1977. *Urn Models and their Application.* New York: Wiley.
11. Cohen, D. 1984. "Locational patterns in the electronics industry: A survey." Mimeo, Econ. Dept., Stanford University.
12. Nevelson, M. B., and R. Z. Hasminskii. 1972. *Stochastic Approximation and Recursive Estimation.* Amer. Math. Soc. Translations of Math. Monographs. Vol. 47. Providence, RI.
13. Arthur, W. B. 1985. "Competing technologies and lock-in by historical small events: The dynamics of allocation under increasing returns." C.E.P.R. Research Publication no. 43. Stanford University.
14. Arthur, W. B. 1984. "Competing Technologies and Economic Prediction." *Options* (April). Laxenburg, Austria: IIASA.

15. Rosenberg, N. 1982. *Inside the Black Box: Technology and Economics*. Cambridge: Cambridge University Press.
16. Hanson, W. 1985. "Bandwagons and orphans: Dynamic pricing of competing systems subject to decreasing costs", Ph.D. diss., Economics, Stanford University.
17. Burton, R. L. 1976. "Recent advances in vehicular steam engine efficiency." Soc. of Automotive Eng. Preprint no. 760340.
18. David, P. A. 1985. "Clio and the economics of QWERTY." *Am. Econ. Rev. Proc.* 75:332–37.

CHAPTER 4

Industry Location Patterns and the Importance of History

In the 1920s and 1930s several members of the great German industry-location school argued that the geographical location of industry was not fully determinate: Where economies of agglomeration existed, so that firms found benefits to being near other firms (a form of locational increasing returns), industry could end up heavily clustered in places chosen by historical accident. But though intuitively appealing, this argument foundered for lack of a theoretical foundation. In the presence of agglomeration economies, a high multiplicity of candidate locational clusters was typically possible. Missing was a rigorous exposition of how "historical accidents" could act over time to "select" the eventual outcome from the many patterns possible.

This paper, written in 1986, attempts to provide a sound basis for the dynamics of industry location under agglomeration economies. It examines industrial location using a model in which firms benefit from the local presence of other firms, and where they sequentially choose locations in an order of choice that is subject to "historical accidents."

The paper appeared in its present form as Center for Economic Policy Research (Stanford) Publication No. 84, June 1986. A revised version "'Silicon Valley' Locational Clusters: When Do Increasing Returns Imply Monopoly" was published in *Mathematical Social Sciences* 19 (1990): 235–51. The mathematical part of this paper is taken from the latter version.

Two different world-views exist, interwoven, in the spatial economics literature. The first, which we might associate with the names of von Thünen (1826), the early Weber (1909), Predöhl (1925), Christaller (1933), Lösch (1944), and Isard (1956) tends to see the spatial ordering of industry as preordained—by geographical endowments, transport possibilities, and firms' needs. It stresses geographical differences, shipment costs, market interactions, and the spatial distribution of rents and prices that these induce. The locational pattern that results is an equilibrium outcome. In this view, locational history does not matter: to the extent that the equilibrium outcome

I am grateful to the Committee on Economic Policy Research at Stanford for financial support, and to Paul David and Yuri Kaniovski for discussions.

is unique, it is inevitable; and therefore early events in the configuration of the industry cannot affect the outcome. We might call this view *stasis*. The locational system is determinate, therefore it is predictable. From any beginning it leads to a single outcome, therefore it is ergodic.

The second world-view, which is nowhere stated very explicitly but runs through the writings of the later Weber, Engländer (1926), Ritschl (1927), and Palander (1935), sees spatial order as process-dependent, almost geologically stratified, with new industry laid down layer by layer upon inherited, previous locational formations. Again geographical endowments and transport possibilities are important, particularly to Weber, but the main driving forces here are agglomeration economies—benefits to being close to other firms or to concentrations of the industry. In the simplest formulation of this view (Maruyama 1963), an industry starts off on a uniform, featureless plain; early firms put down by "historical accident" in one or two locations; others are attracted by their presence, and others in turn by *their* presence. The industry ends up clustered in the early-chosen places. But this spatial ordering is not unique: a different set of early events could have steered the locational pattern into a different outcome, so that settlement history is crucial. We might call this view *historical dependence*.[1] Here the locational system generates structure as it goes. It is fundamentally dynamic. It can follow divergent paths, therefore it is nonergodic. It possesses a multiplicity of outcomes, therefore it is nonpredictable.

The two world-views would explain observed spatial patterns somewhat differently.[2] Stasis would see the electronics industry in the United States as spread over the country, with a substantial part of it in Santa Clara County in California (Silicon Valley) because that location is close to Pacific sources of supplies, and because it has better access to skilled labor and to advances in academic engineering research than elsewhere. Historical dependence would see "Silicon Valley" and similar concentrations as largely the outcome of chance. Certain key people—the Hewletts, the Varians, the Shockleys of the industry—happened to set up near Stanford University in the 1940s and 1950s, and the local labor expertise and inter-firm market they helped to create in Santa Clara County made subsequent location there extremely advan-

---

1. Similar historical-dependence arguments appear in the regional-disparity literature: Myrdal (1957), Kaldor (1970), Faini (1984); and in the "growth pole" theories of Perroux (1955) and others in the 1950s. Allen and Sanglier (1981) use simulation techniques to investigate the importance of small events in determining locational patterns.

2. They also lie behind many of the debates in regional economics. Ontarians sometimes see Toronto's preeminence in Canada's financial service industry as the pre-ordained consequence of the superior entrepreneurship of Canada's English-speaking people. Québecois, understandably, tend to see it as the result of bad historical luck, together with the subsequent agglomeration pull of massed resources in Toronto.

tageous for the thousand or so firms that followed them (see Cohen [1984]). If these early entrepreneurs had had other predilections, "Silicon Valley" might well have been somewhere else.

There are no insuperable difficulties in modeling industry location under the stasis assumptions. Endowments, possibilities, and preferences are given. Therefore the industry configuration can be determined as the solution to the appropriate equilibrium model. The historical dependence-agglomeration argument is more problematical. Agglomeration economies introduce an indeterminacy: when firms will want to congregate where other firms are, one or a few locations may end up with the entire industry. But *which* locations "win," as Isard (1956) noted, is not answerable in advance. If we bypass this indeterminacy by arguing "historical accident" for the dominant locations, we must then define "historical accidents" and how they act to "select" the winning locations. In the absence of such theory, to date the argument has remained nebulous.

This paper attempts to provide a sound theoretical basis for the historical-accident-plus-agglomeration viewpoint. In particular, it examines the dynamics of industrial location and the selection of an asymptotic location pattern using a model that permits a simple notion of historical accident by assuming that firms differ slightly in their locational tastes and that they make their locational choice one by one in an order that is "random" as far as an observer is concerned. It examines how the presence of agglomeration economies influences locational patterns, and the degree to which "history" can be held responsible.

I show that where there is no ceiling to economies of agglomeration, industry will indeed cluster in one dominant location, but *which* one depends both on geographical attractiveness and accidental historical order of choice. I show that the presence of agglomeration economies does not guarantee a "Silicon Valley" outcome: Where there are upper limits to agglomeration benefits, certain combinations of "historical accident" can produce a single dominant location; others can produce locational dispersion of the industry exactly as if agglomeration effects were absent. And I show that, paradoxically, agglomeration effects can easily *cause* regional separation of the industry.

A Model

First, some preliminaries. I will say there are *economies of agglomeration* (Weber 1909; Hoover 1937) if net benefits to being in a location together with other firms increase with the number of firms in the location. The sources are several: as a location gains firms, it also gains useful infrastructure. Its labor markets deepen (David 1984a). Specialized legal and financial services appear. Spare parts and out-of-stock items become locally available, reducing inventory costs. And social networks come into being where information, expertise, and contracts can be easily exchanged. *Diseconomies of agglomeration*—net benefits that decrease with increasing numbers of other firms—may also occur. The location may become congested; land may become expensive; or firms that sell locally may find themselves in monopolistic competition with nearby firms as in Lösch (1941). And of course, besides agglomeration effects, there may be benefits or costs due to geographical differences—in transportation cost, in the availability of raw materials, in factor prices, in climate, or in proximity to markets.

I now set up a model where firms in an industry decide on locating in one of N possible regions, or sites, or cities. Each firm is well informed on profits or returns—the net present value of siting in each location—at the time of its choice; each chooses what, for it, is the maximum return location and then stays there. I assume that new firms are added slowly and the future is discounted so that initially we can ignore expectational problems and assume that new firms decide to locate at their sites of *present* maximum return.

The firms in an industry differ in product mix or in manufacturing process—hence in locational needs. In this simple model I condense all benefits or returns, r_j^i, to firm i for locating in site j, into two components:

$$r_j^i = q_j^i + g(y_j), \tag{1}$$

where q_j^i is the *geographical benefit* to firm i for siting in location j (returns in the absence of other firms); and $g(y_j)$ is the net *agglomeration benefit* from having y_j firms already located there at the time of choice. (I will speak of firm *tastes*, understanding these to be geographical preferences in the absence of other firms' settlement. Where the agglomeration function, g, is increasing, we have economies of agglomeration; where decreasing, diseconomies of agglomeration.)

Firms enter the industry at different times. Thus, we may think of them as arriving in sequence to make their choice. I introduce "historical accident" by supposing that the sequence of firm types that enter is unknown to an observer. Thus, we can represent each new firm as a random "drawing," of a vector $q = (q_1, q_2, \ldots, q_N)$ which denotes that firm's locational tastes for each possible site, from a given distribution F of potential firms over locational tastes. (Thus, F determines the frequency of arrival of different firm types, and in general there is a continuum of possible firm types.) I assume that the vector of tastes, q, has finite support. Note that since we can add a positive constant to all q's without changing location decisions, we can treat q as always positive. Sites that are frequently preferred (in the absence of agglomeration economies) I will call *attractive* and I include in the analysis only sites that would be chosen with positive probability.

This model has been kept deliberately simple so as not to complicate the subsequent analysis. It could be modified to specify how new firms are generated and how other industries might affect locational returns. A later section discusses several extensions.

Given the above assumptions, we can compute the probability that an entering firm chooses location j. Suppose there are $y_1, y_2, \ldots, y_N$ firms already in locations 1 through N, respectively. Then the probability that the next firm "drawn" prefers j over all other sites is:

$$p_j = \text{Prob}\{[q_j + g(y_j)] > [q_i + g(y_i)] \text{ all } i \neq j\}. \tag{2}$$

We can calculate this probability as the (Lebesgue-Stieltjes) integral:

$$p_j = \int_{V_1} \cdots \int_{V_j} \cdots \int_{V_N} dF(z_1, \ldots, z_j, \ldots, z_N), \tag{3}$$

where the region of integration $V_i = [-\infty, z_j + g(y_j) - g(y_i)]$ for $i \neq j$ and $V_j = (-\infty, \infty)$. I will call $p = (p_1, p_2, \ldots, p_N)$ the probability vector of locational choice. Notice that through the agglomeration function g these probabilities p of an addition to locations 1 through N are a function of the current configuration of the industry, as we would expect.

The problem is now to derive and examine the locational pattern—the proportion of the industry in regions 1 through N—under different assumptions about geographical benefits and increasing returns due to agglomeration economies.

Dynamics of the Locational Process

We proceed by tracing the locational pattern of the industry as it forms, and as firms of different types enter it. We would expect this pattern to fluctuate somewhat because of the randomness in entry of firm type; and we would expect its movement to depend upon its present state, because locational choices depend on the current placement of firms.

Starting from a given number of firms in each location (which, for convenience, we set at zero), the industry forms by the addition of one firm at a time, distributed to one and only one location. We can describe the spatial configuration of the industry at "time" n, after n firms in total have located, by the vector of firms in the N locations $Y_n = [y_1(n), \ldots, y_N(n)]$. An equivalent but more convenient description is the vector of *locations' shares* or proportions of the industry, $X_n = [x_1(n), \ldots, x_N(n)]$, where $X_n = Y_n/n$. The vector of probabilities of locational choice, p, is a function of Y or, equivalently, a (continuous) function of the locational shares of the industry, X, and of n.

Now, the industry forms by the addition of one firm at a time, so that the vector of firm numbers in the potential locations evolves as:

$$Y_{n+1} = Y_n + b(n; X_n); \quad Y(0) = 0, \tag{4}$$

where b is the jth unit vector with probability $p_j(n; X_n)$.

Then, dividing (4) by $n + 1$, the vector of proportions of the industry in sites 1 through N, or locational shares, evolves as:

$$X_{n+1} = X_n + \frac{1}{n+1} [b(n; X_n) - X_n]; \quad X_0 = 0. \tag{5}$$

We can rewrite (5) in the form:

$$X_{n+1} = X_n + \frac{1}{n+1} [p(n; X_n) - X_n] + \frac{1}{n+1} \mu(n; X_n), \quad X_0 = 0, \tag{6}$$

where μ is defined as the random vector:

$$\mu(n; X_n) = b(n; X_n) - p(n; X_n).$$

Equation (6) is the description of the dynamics of locational shares that we want. Mathematically it has the form of a stochastic approximation.

Notice that the conditional expectation of μ with respect to the current state X_n is zero, hence we can derive the *expected motion* of the locational shares as:

$$E(X_{n+1}|X_n) - X_n = \frac{1}{n+1} [p(n; X_n) - X_n]. \tag{7}$$

We see that, if the probability $p_j(X_n)$ of an addition to location j is greater than the current proportion of the industry $x_j(n)$ in location j, this location's share should increase—at least on an expected basis. Conversely, if the probability is less than the current proportion, it should decrease.

Equation (6) therefore tells us that locational shares are driven by an expected motion effect (the second term on the right) that derives from locations' relative attractiveness and current agglomeration pull, together with a perturbation effect (the third term) that derives from randomness in entry.

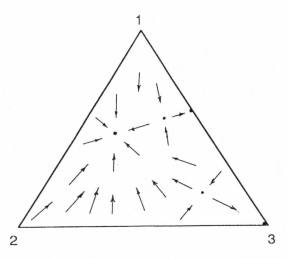

Fig. 1. Expected motions for a given locational probability function

Both expected motions and fluctuations have less effect on shares as the industry grows. Both die away at the rate $1/n$; hence we might expect locational shares to settle down as the industry becomes large.

We can get some idea of how locational shares might settle down, for a given locational probability function p, if we plot expected motions on the unit simplex of locations' shares (as in fig. 1).

Depending upon the function p—and ultimately on the distribution of firm tastes and the agglomeration function—there may be several points x (several locational patterns) at which expected motion is zero. These are the fixed points of p, where $p(x) = x$. Some of these are attractor points, some are repellor points. We might conjecture that, if choices in a given problem are "driven" by a locational probability-of-choice function p, the locational pattern will converge to a fixed point of p on the simplex of locational shares, and to one that is an attractor. Furthermore, if there are multiple attractors, they might all be candidates for the limiting locational pattern, with the locational distribution of the industry falling into the orbit of one of these by "historical accidents" of sequence of entry.

A recent set of theorems for path-dependent processes like (6), due to Arthur, Ermoliev, and Kaniovski (1983, 1986) (referred to here as AEK and applicable to a broad variety of nonconvex problems in economics and physics) confirms these conjectures. Under certain technical conditions: (i) X_n converges with probability one to a fixed point where $p(x) = x$; (ii) X_n can converge to "attractor" or stable fixed points (points on the simplex that expected motions are toward); and (iii) X_n cannot converge with positive probability to "repellor" or unstable fixed points (points on the simplex that expected motions lead away from). Where the function p varies with time n as in our locational case, this generalized strong-law theorem still goes through, provided that the dynamics "settle down" to stationarity—that is, provided that the set of "driving" probabilities $\{p_n\}$ tends to a limit function p.

Notice that the standard strong law of large numbers makes statements about limiting shares when increments are added independently of present state of the process. AEK is thus a generalization of the strong law of large numbers for the case of path-dependent increments.

Locational Patterns in Several Cases

I have described the spatial formation of the industry as a process where unit increments (firms) are added to one of N categories (candidate locations) with a probability vector p (of an addition to category 1 through N) that in general is a function of the current proportions X_n in the N categories: $p = p(x; n)$. We now seek limiting vectors of locational shares, and we start with a trivial but useful benchmark case.

Suppose agglomeration economies are absent, so that g is zero and only geographical considerations q count. We see from (3) that the probabilities of choice p are constant and are therefore independent of locational shares at all times. Thus, increments are added independently of current proportions, and we can invoke the standard strong law of large numbers to show that the locational shares X_n converge to p. We then have

> *Theorem 1. Where there are no economies or diseconomies of agglomeration (that is, $g \equiv 0$), then, with probability one, locational shares tend to be fixed, predictable proportions in the limit as the industry becomes large.*

In this "pure attractiveness" case, locational dispersion of the industry takes place to the degree the industry is heterogeneous in taste. If all firms are alike, each will choose the same maximal location and the industry will cluster. Thus, dense concentrations of the film industry near Los Angeles may not necessarily be evidence of the presence of agglomeration economies. They may simply reflect homogeneity of early needs—for cheap real estate, dry weather, and good outdoor lighting. Agglomeration economies are not a necessary condition for spatial clustering.

Unbounded Agglomeration Economies

In our more general case where agglomeration economies *are* present, increments to locations are *not* independent—the probability of adding firms depends upon past additions—so that the standard strong law is not usable. We now examine this case assuming first that additions of firms always confer net benefits on a location, without upper limit. We might expect that if one location gets sufficiently ahead in industry share by "historical accident," it will build up an unassailable advantage and eventually monopolize the industry. This indeed happens.

Theorem 2. Where there are unbounded economies of agglomeration such that the agglomeration function increases at least at the rate $\partial g/\partial y > \epsilon y^\mu$, where $\mu > -1$, then, with probability one, in the limit as the industry becomes large, one location takes all but a finite set of firms. Locational shares tend to zero in all but one location.

Proof. The argument consists in showing that if n is large enough, for points in the simplex of locational shares the location of highest share must be chosen with probability one. Thereafter that location is repeatedly chosen; the process is locked-in to it and its share of the industry goes to 100 percent.

Consider the set $B = \{x \in S^N: \text{two or more elements of } x \text{ are maximal}\}$ (see fig. 2); and B_ϵ, its ϵ-neighborhood. Points in $S^N \backslash B_\epsilon$ then represent locational shares with a unique maximal element, with index J say (of the nearest vertex). Partition $S^N \backslash B_\epsilon$ into separate sets C^J designated by the nearest vertex J. Now consider a given point z in C^J. The fact that g is increasing and unbounded guarantees that there exists a finite time $n(z)$ such that returns $\{q_J + g[n(z) \cdot z_J]\} > \{q_I + g[n(z) \cdot z_I]\}$, all $I \neq J$. Furthermore, it is easy to show that $n(z)$ has an upper bound n^J in C^J. Therefore, if the process X_n is in C^J at a time n greater than n^J, location J will have maximal returns for all firm types; it will then be chosen with probability one; it will continue to be chosen with probability one; the process will never exit C^J and it will converge to 100 percent share for location J.

Alternatively, the process might not enter a set C^J; it could stay within B_ϵ forever. Consider "balanced" points θ_K defined to be points in the simplex where locations outside the subset K have zero proportion and those inside K have equal proportions. No "unbalanced points" in B_ϵ can be sustained: beyond some finite time locations with least share will be shut out as before. Furthermore, the process cannot cycle: unbalanced points cannot be recovered once they are shut out. X_n can then stay within B_ϵ indefinitely only by converging to a "balanced point" θ_K. However, direct calculation shows that, under the condition stated for g in the theorem, balanced points θ_K are *unstable*. That is to say, we can show that as long as $\partial g/\partial y > \epsilon y^\mu$, with $\mu > -1$, then any given θ_K satisfies the instability criterion that there exists within K a symmetric matrix C, and parameters λ and $v > 0$, such that $\langle C_{p_n}(z), z - \theta_K \rangle \geq \lambda$

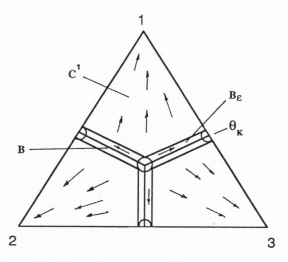

Fig. 2. Expected motions under unbounded agglomeration economies

$\langle C(z - \theta_K), z - \theta_K \rangle^{1+v} + \delta_n$, where $\Sigma_n\, \delta_n < \infty$, for z in a neighborhood of θ_K. By Theorem 3 of Arthur, Ermoliev, and Kaniovski (1989), the instability of θ_K ensures that $\text{Prob}\{X_n \to \theta_K\} = 0$.[3] The process cannot converge to θ_K. It must exit B_ϵ in finite time and must therefore converge to some vertex J. The theorem follows. Notice that the limiting probability function p becomes a step function (with element $p_J = 1$ for points with nearest vertex J and with each vertex an attracting fixed point). ■

In reality, of course, industries do not grow forever. It is best to construe this theorem as a law-of-large-numbers result in the usual sense that the larger the eventual size of the industry, the more likely locational shares will tend to 100 percent domination of a locality.

In this unbounded-agglomeration case the locational process eventually "locks in" to a "Silicon Valley" outcome—a monopoly of one location. *Which* location this is, of course, depends on the order of entry of firm types and very much on early locators' relative preferences for locations. The process is path-dependent (more precisely, nonergodic) in that a slightly different order-of-choice history early on could sway the outcome to a different location becoming predominant. An attractive location will likely be favored by many firms early in the choice order, and therefore it has a larger probability of predom-

---

3. I have updated the mathematical material here to correspond to the 1990 *Math Soc. Sciences* version of this paper. The reference here is to Arthur, Ermoliev, and Kaniovski, "A generalized urn scheme with arbitrary increments," Santa Fe Inst. mimeo, 1989.

inating. Attractiveness, interacting with historical accidents of choice-order, determines the outcome.

It may seem obvious that monopoly must result in this unbounded agglomeration case. Yet it is easy to construct entry-sequences that lead to locations sharing the industry indefinitely; and to show that there is an infinity of such sequences. The power of this theorem lies in its showing that such nonmonopoly outcomes have measure zero in the sample space of all possible outcomes.

REMARK 1. Where the density function f of geographical preferences has infinite "tails" in all directions instead of bounded support, it is easy to check that the vertices remain the only stable attractors, and the above theorem again goes through: a single location again monopolizes.

Bounded Agglomeration Economies

In our next case, where the increasing returns—the agglomeration economies —are *bounded,* monopoly no longer occurs with probability one. In this case, locations could, with positive probability, share the industry exactly as if agglomeration economies were absent.

To see why this should be so, suppose agglomeration economies g are increasing but bounded above by the constant $h:$ thus, adding firms enhances a location's advantages, but not without limit. Suppose two regions only. Now it may happen that if enough firms that prefer region A occur early in the queue of entries, A will move sufficiently ahead to dominate B for all subsequent choosers. As before, one location will take all. Suppose, however, that firms preferring A and firms preferring B arrive more or less evenly in the sequence. Then regions A and B will be bid upward in tandem; both regions will reach the agglomeration upper bound and neither will be sufficiently ahead to shut out the other (see fig. 3). But now the agglomeration economies realized will be equal; they will cease to matter in locational choice and so eventually both regions will share the industry, with shares that will equal the proportion of firm types that prefer A and B in the absence of agglomeration economies. Whether monopoly or locational sharing takes place depends, of course, on "historical accident" of the entry sequence.

Our N location case is more complicated. We must first determine the "candidate" sets of locations that if bid upward together could shut the other locations out and thus together dominate the industry.

Consider the (random) vector of returns $\pi = q + g(y)$, for a given vector y of firms. Important in what follows is the *support* of these returns, which we will designate Q_y. (The support Q_y indicates the region in N-dimensional preference (or returns) space over which firm types are spread.) As settlement

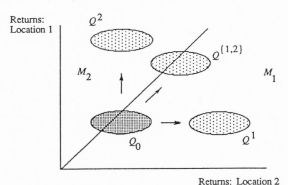

Fig. 3. Support sets of firms' returns for a two-location problem

takes place and agglomeration economies accrue to locations that are chosen, the returns support Q_y will shift. If it enters a region where some subset of locations always have maximum returns, all firms will choose locations in this subset, other locations will never be chosen, and the process will be then locked-in to this subset of locations.

Now, let K be a set of locations, and let M_K be the cone of vectors in $\mathfrak{R}^N$ with maximal element in the set K. Let Q^K be the support of the returns vector $q + \gamma_K$, where the vector γ_K has 0-elements for locations not in K and h-elements for locations in K. (This is where returns would eventually lie if locations in set K only were to receive firms.) We will say that K is a potential *lock-in set* if (i) $Q^K \subset M_K$ and (ii) $Q^K \not\subset M_{K'}$ for any $K' \subset K$. We will say that K is a *potentially dominant* set if there also exists some finite sequence of arrivals that causes Q_y to belong to $Q_\epsilon^K \subset M_K$, where Q_ϵ^K is any given ϵ-neighborhood of Q^K.

> *Theorem 3. Suppose economies of agglomeration g are increasing and bounded above. Then in the limit as the industry becomes large, one set of locations from the collection of potentially dominant sets will take 100 percent of the industry, with probability one, and each such set K has positive probability of being this monopolizing set. Furthermore, locations in the monopolizing set share the industry exactly as if no agglomeration economies had been present and they were the only locations available at the outset.*

Proof. First, the process must converge with probability one to non-zero proportions in some subset J. One firm is added each time, and so some set J of locations must continue to receive firms ad infinitum. Locations in this set are bid to their agglomeration ceiling. Probabilities of additions to locations in J therefore become independent of current proportions; and by the strong law of large numbers, the process must converge.

Now suppose the process converges to non-zero proportions in a nonpotentially-dominant set J. The nondominance of J implies either that some locations in J receive firms when their locational probability is zero, or that choices outside J occur with positive probability. Either way convergence to J is contradicted.

Finally, consider a set K of locations that is *potentially dominant*. By definition, there may occur with positive probability a finite sequence of arrivals that causes returns Q_y to lie within Q_ϵ^K in the cone M_K. Once returns lie within this set, locations other than those in K cannot be preferred and the process locks in to this set K. Therefore the set K can monopolize the locational process with positive probability, with location proportions X_n converging to the relative proportions of firms that prefer each location K. The theorem follows.   ∎

In this bounded agglomeration case, industry can be shared by several locations. The reason is not so much that agglomeration is overpowered by heterogeneity, but rather that certain choice-orders cause several locations to accumulate firms at more or less the same rate, and therefore agglomeration forces remain balanced enough as the industry forms for heterogeneity of tastes to spread the firms over these locations. Thus, the monopolizing tendencies of increasing-return effects may be overcome by even a small degree of heterogeneity. Historical choice-order once again matters greatly here—it "selects" the set of dominant locations that will share the industry. But once this set is decided and "locked-in," the locational process proceeds as if the agglomeration effects were entirely absent. There are two extreme cases worth mentioning. First, agglomeration forces may be too weak to cause any monopolizing of the industry by subsets of locations at all:

Corollary 1. If $h < \mathrm{Min}_K[d(Q_0, M_K)]$ then all *locations share the industry, with probability one, in the proportions that would have occurred if agglomeration economies were absent.*

(Here d is the set-distance operator.) In this case potential agglomeration economies are not great enough to overcome heterogeneity of preferences. Equivalently, there are always some firm types that do not switch their "natural" choice to the populated locations. All locations eventually reach the agglomeration ceiling, and so agglomeration forces may as well not be present at all. In this special case history does not matter.

Second, conditions might exist under which a single location *must* monopolize the industry even though agglomeration effects are bounded. To illustrate this, let Q_e^j be the support of the returns when one firm only has chosen and is in location j.

Corollary 2. If $Q_e^j \subset M_{\{j\}}$ for all j, then one location takes all the industry with probability one.

In this extreme illustrative case agglomeration economies drive the support straight into the dominance region of the location that receives the first firm. Practically speaking, this can happen when preferences are tightly clustered, and when agglomeration effects at the outset are strong.

In the results above, it was crucial that firms' tastes had bounded support. Suppose now they have unbounded support—that is, that the distribution function F of geographical preferences has infinite tails in all directions.

Theorem 4. Where preferences F have unbounded *support, and the agglomeration function g is bounded above, then* all *locations share the industry, with probability one, in the proportions that would have occurred if agglomeration economies were absent.*

Proof. In this case no subset can ever become dominant—there is always a positive probability of a location outside the subset being chosen. Locations are added until all have been bid up to their agglomeration bound. We may subtract this agglomeration advantage equally from all locations; the dynamics then proceed as if no agglomeration component were present, and all locations share the industry according to their natural probabilities of being chosen.   ∎

Locational Orphaning and Spatial Separation

Many industries are not concentrated, Silicon Valley fashion, into a dominant location. Firms are spread out with some spatial regularity. The usual, Löschian explanation for spreading and separation invokes spatial monopolistic competition: firms distance themselves from their rivals for local markets. That is, *diseconomies* of agglomeration cause firms to separate spatially.

Strangely enough, *economies* of agglomeration can also cause separation and spreading. The reason is that locations with large numbers of firms are preferred to geographically similar, neighboring locations with few firms. Locations with large numbers of firms therefore cast an "agglomeration shadow" in which little or no settlement takes place. This causes separation of the industry.

To see this in more detail, consider now a two-dimensional landscape with returns q for any given firm-type varying continuously over the surface—reflecting climate variation or transportation costs, say. (To preserve finiteness of the number of locations we can treat potential locations as points on a fine grid. The industry is still heterogeneous, so that tastes q are distributed as before in the density function f.) Tastes are uniformly continuous in the sense that (for all firm types) tastes for two neighboring sites always differ by less than some ϵ.

Consider two locations, a and a', separated by d units (under a suitable metric), having k and k' firms respectively. Location a, with more firms, will dominate location a' for *all* firm types if $g(k) + q(a) > g(k') + q(a') + \epsilon \cdot d$, so that site a' will not receive any future firms. When attractiveness varies smoothly over the landscape, then places near a location with a larger number of firms are similar to this location geographically; and they are not sufficiently more attractive to overcome the agglomeration advantage of their dominant neighbor. These places have become dynamically *orphaned,* and we can say that they lie within the *agglomeration shadow* of their dominant neighbor.

As a location receives firms its agglomeration shadow grows; it shuts out further neighbors and it thereby enlarges the domain of tastes—the "gravitational region"—from which it receives further firms. The result of this, in the realistic case where agglomeration economies are bounded, is that neighboring locations cannot share the industry but that sufficiently separated regions can.

Agglomeration economies have *caused* separation and dispersion. And once again *which* locations gain the industry and which become orphaned is a matter of historical accident.

Remarks and Extensions

I have shown in a simple model that where agglomeration economies are present, historical "accidents" of choice-order select a limiting spatial pattern from a possibly large collection of candidate spatial patterns. The following are brief remarks on various possible extensions:

1. Suppose there were eventual net *diseconomies* of agglomeration, so that disamenities of industry ultimately outweighed agglomeration benefits. In this case g would eventually decrease and be unbounded below. Locations would fill up, partly by historical accident, the attractive ones first, until diminishing returns set in. Then industry would begin to site in the less attractive locations, and still less attractive, until all locations showed diminishing returns. I leave it to the

reader to confirm that the point $x = (1/N, \ldots, 1/N)$ would be the only attractor of the limiting locational probability function, and therefore that the industry would eventually be shared equally between all locations, with probability one. Under diseconomies of agglomeration, historical accident would not count.

2. Suppose firms were affected not just by the presence of other firms only in the same locality but by the entire configuration of firms in *all* other locations. Total returns would then become:

$$r_j^i = q_j^i + g(y_1, y_2, \ldots, y_N), \tag{8}$$

with the wider agglomeration function g also possibly location- or firm-type-specific if necessary. This form would allow cases of more general agglomeration or deglomeration effects (such as the Löschian monopolistic-competition case where neighboring competitors cut into a firm's demand to a degree that varies with distance). Analysis in this entire-configuration framework would be similar to that above—the AEK strong law for example handles this case directly—but calculation of the probabilities of locational choice would now be more complicated. I would expect findings similar to the above.

3. Suppose transaction costs to moving were zero, so that firms could move, and thus "recontract" their locational decisions. Now after each new entrant's choice there would be a round of relocations of settled firms that could improve their returns. Firms would tend to move, from places they settled in that received firms early on but which have now by "chance" become orphaned or left behind in agglomeration, to places that are currently heavily populated with firms. Again there would be multiple potential outcomes, with "accidents" of choice-order in moving as well as in entry selecting an ultimate locational pattern. "Historical accident" would still count.

4. Suppose entering firm-types were not independent, but that there was sequence "linkage": certain entrants might attract complementary producers; later entrants might differentiate their firm-type to fit with earlier entrants; and particular stages of an industry's technological development might be associated with the entry of a characteristic type of firm. Firm-type arrivals would then be serially correlated; and path dependence would extend now to firm-types and to recent arrivals, as well as to previous locational choices. It would be simple to formulate this case, but analysis would require more general path-dependent techniques than the ones used here.

5. Suppose present choosers were affected by future firms' location decisions. We might then assume that firms form beliefs about the type of

stochastic process they find themselves in, in the shape of conditional probabilities of future states of the locational process. Expectations would therefore change as the settlement process worked itself out. In choosing, firms would create an *actual* stochastic process, which would be in rational expectations equilibrium if it were identical to the *believed* stochastic process (cf. Lucas 1972). Preliminary results show that expectations would exacerbate monopoly tendencies (cf. Arthur 1985). An unattractive location that was lucky early on could come to dominate as choosing firms increasingly enhanced their beliefs of that location's success.

Conclusion

Two decades or so after Alfred Weber's sophisticated demonstration of the unique location pattern that minimizes costs under economies of agglomeration, Engländer and Palander both objected that it could be achieved only by a single, coordinating entrepreneur acting *de novo;* that in reality historical events would have provided a locational structure already in place; and that this inherited structure combined with agglomeration tendencies would determine future settlement. Engländer and Palander were right. But while the historical argument appealed to the intuition, it remained vague, plagued by indeterminacy problems.

This study shows that it is indeed possible to put a theoretical basis under the historical-accident-plus-agglomeration argument. Agglomeration economies do indeed bring into being a multiplicity of potential location patterns. And inherited structures and the "historical accidents" that caused them do indeed determine the pattern that industry settles into. This much confirms the historical-dependence viewpoint. But contrary to conventional beliefs, agglomeration economies—increasing returns in spatial form—are not sufficient for one location to establish a locational monopoly. If agglomeration economies are bounded, even a small amount of heterogeneity can cause locations to share the industry as if agglomeration economies were absent. They are not necessary either. Dense concentrations of an industry are no evidence of the presence of agglomeration economies. Concentrations may trivially reflect homogeneity of needs.

If agglomeration economies are present in the industry location problem, static equilibrium analysis is not enough. Settlement patterns can proceed down different paths; we are forced to follow the locational structure as it forms, and this requires dynamic analysis. Interestingly, the picture that emerges is more Darwinian than equilibrational in nature, with geographical attractiveness bestowing selectional advantage; locations "selected" early on by chance becoming locked-in or "fixed"; and some locations exercising "competitive exclusion" on others by appropriating the available agglomeration economies.

Our analysis of the validity of the historical-dependence viewpoint does not imply that the conventional viewpoint, the unique-equilibrium-outcome *stasis* one, is wrong. The two *Weltanschauungen* are complementary. The validity of each depends on the degree to which agglomeration economies are present or absent.

REFERENCES

Allen, P., and M. Sanglier. 1981. "Urban Evolution, Self-Organization, and Decision-Making." *Environment and Planning A,* 13:167–83.

Arthur, W. B. 1985. "Competing Technologies and Lock-In by Historical Small Events: The Dynamics of Choice under Increasing Returns." C.E.P.R. Paper 43. Stanford.

Arthur, W. B., Y. M. Ermoliev, and Y. M. Kaniovski. 1983. "A Generalized Urn Problem and Its Applications." *Cybernetics* 19:61–71.

———. 1985. "Strong Laws for a Class of Path-Dependent Urn Processes." In *Procs. International Conf. on Stochastic Optimization, Kiev 1984*. Arkin, Shiryayev, and Wets (eds.). Springer: Lecture Notes in Control and Info. Sciences 81.

———. 1986. "Path-Dependent Processes and the Emergence of Macro-Structure." Forthcoming *European Journal of Operations Research.*

Christaller, W. 1933. *Central Places in Southern Germany.* Prentice-Hall, 1966.

Cohen, D. L. 1984. "Locational Patterns in the Electronic Industry: A Survey." Mimeo. Stanford.

David, P. 1984. "The Marshallian Dynamics of Industrialization: Chicago, 1850–1890." Mimeo. Stanford.

———. 1984. "High Technology Centers and the Economics of Locational Tournaments." Mimeo. Stanford.

Engländer, O. 1926. "Kritisches und Positives zu einer allgemeinen reinen Lehre vom Standort." *Zeitschrift für Volkswirtschaft und Sozialpolitik,* Neue Folge 5.

Faini, R. 1984. "Increasing Returns, Non-Traded Inputs and Regional Development." *Econ. Journal* 94:308–23.

Hill, B., Lane, D., and W. Sudderth. 1980. "Strong Convergence for a Class of Urn Schemes." *Annals of Probability* 8:214–26.

Hoover, E. M. 1937. *Location Theory and the Shoe and Leather Industries.* Harvard.

Isard, W. 1956. *Location and Space-Economy.* Wiley.

Ljung, L. 1978. "Strong convergence of a Stochastic Approximation Algorithm." *Annals of Statistics* 6:680–96.

Lösch, A. 1941. *The Economics of Location.* Yale University Press, 1954.

Maruyama, M. 1963. "The Second Cybernetics: Deviation Amplifying Mutual Causal Processes." *American Scientist* 51:164–79.

Myrdal, G. 1957. *Economic Theory and Underdeveloped Regions.* Duckworth.

Palander, T. 1935. *Beiträge zur Standortstheorie.* Almqvist and Wicksell.

Perroux, F. 1955. "Note sur la Notion de Pôle de Croissance." *Économie Appliquée* 7:307–20.
Predöhl, A. 1925. "Das Standortsproblem in der Wirtschaftslehre." *Weltwirtschaftliches Archiv* 21:294–331.
Ritschl, H. 1927. "Reine und historische Dynamik des Standortes der Erzeugungszweige." *Schmollers Jahrbuch* 51:813–70.
Thuenen, J. H. von. 1826. *Der Isolierte Staat in Beziehung auf Landwirtschaft und Nationalökonomie*. Hamburg.
Weber, A. 1909. *Theory of the Location of Industries*. University of Chicago Press, 1929.

CHAPTER 5

Information Contagion

W. Brian Arthur and David A. Lane

This paper explores a positive feedback mechanism quite different from the ones discussed earlier in this book. It works through the way information is transmitted in a typical technical-product market.

When prospective buyers are making purchasing decisions among several available technically-based products, choosing among different computer workstations, say, they often augment whatever publicly available information they can find by asking previous purchasers about *their* experiences— which product they chose, and how it is working out for them. This is a natural and reasonable procedure; it adds information that is hard to come by otherwise. But it also introduces an "information feedback" into the process whereby products compete for market share. The products new purchasers learn about depend on which products the previous purchasers "polled" or sampled and decided to buy. They are therefore likely to learn more about a commonly purchased product than one with few previous users. Hence, where buyers are risk-averse and tend to favor products they know more about, products that by chance win market share early on gain an information-feedback advantage. Under certain circumstances a product may come to dominate by this advantage alone.

We call this phenomenon *information contagion* and explore it in depth in this paper. The paper appeared in working paper form in 1991 as Santa Fe Institute Paper 91-05-026 under the title "Information Constriction and Information Contagion." The version here is the published one; it is from *Economic Dynamics and Structural Change,* 1993. David A. Lane is with the School of Statistics, University of Minnesota, Minneapolis.

This work was prepared under the auspices of the Santa Fe Institute's Economics Research Program which includes grants from Citicorp/Citibank Research Corp., the Alex C. Walker Foundation and the Russell Sage Foundation; and of grants to SFI from the John D. and Catherine T. MacArthur Foundation, the National Science Foundation (PHY-8714918), and the U.S. Department of Energy (ER-FG05-88ER25054). Lane also received support from National Science Foundation grant DMS-8911548. We also thank Nicola Dimitri, Ed Green, Larry Gray, Francesco Corelli, Marcel Fafchamps, Ashok Maitra, and participants in the Stanford mathematical economics seminar for helpful comments and conversations about the ideas presented here.

1. Introduction

For the potential purchaser, a new technically based product can be a source of considerable uncertainty. Specifications, advertising brochures, and consumer reports may be available, and the cost of purchase precisely known. Yet the purchaser may still be unsure about how the product will perform for him: how smoothly it can be integrated into his existing operations; how much maintenance or "down time" the product will require; whether the product in fact is suited to the particular uses he has in mind. For example, in choosing among computer programs that create environments for "doing mathematics" or statistical data analysis on desktop computers, the prospective user may be well-informed about prices and technical features; but typically he does not know in advance the various practical difficulties and unexpected advantages that will inevitably emerge after he takes up a given program. In cases like these, usually the potential purchaser tries to reduce this uncertainty by asking previous purchasers about how *they* have fared with the products *they* bought and subsequently used.

This sampling or "polling" of the experiences of past purchasers is natural and reasonable: it helps fill in information that is otherwise missing. But it also introduces an "informational feedback" into the process whereby the products compete for market share. Which product the prospective purchaser decides to buy depends on information obtained from previous purchasers; but the information he encounters depends on which of the products these purchasers decided to buy. Under certain circumstances this informational feedback can cause market shares to become self-reinforcing. Prospective purchasers are more likely to learn about a commonly purchased product than one with few previous users; so that, if they are risk averse, products that by chance win market share early on are at an advantage. Under certain circumstances, in fact, a product may come to dominate by this advantage alone. This informationally generated linkage between a product's prevalence and its likelihood of purchase we call *information contagion*.

Notice of course that, even though private information is added to the public information by this "polling" of previous users, in sampling only a small subset of all past purchasers much of the available information about the competing products must be missed. Information about performance from *all* past purchasers would be valuable to prospective purchasers, but in most circumstances there is no means by which to collect it. Thus much of the available information in the market is not accessed by prospective purchasers. The market is subject to a *constriction* of information.

In this paper we investigate the effects that feedback from sampling previous purchasers may have in determining the market shares that emerge over time. The model on which our analysis is based is described in detail in

Section 2 below. To isolate the effects of informational feedback, the model excludes other feedback processes that would operate jointly with information contagion to determine the allocation dynamics in real economic situations— for example, network externalities, learning effects, and the strategic manipulation of prices and information by producers of the competing products.[1]

We use the model to address the following two questions:

- Need a stable market share for each product emerge over time? If so, what are the possible limit shares?
- Under what circumstances will informational feedback drive the market to domination by a single product?

Our model of information contagion specifies how the prospective purchaser chooses which previous purchasers to interrogate, what he finds out from them, and how he uses the information he obtains. Here we want to highlight two of the model's key features:

1. *Agent-Oriented Sampling:* Ideally, a prospective purchaser would like to get "sufficient" information about each product, and, to do this efficiently he would like to take into account which products previous purchasers had bought and used when he selects them for inclusion in his sample. Unfortunately, it is generally difficult to know which product someone used without asking him directly. Consequently, we suppose that the prospective purchaser samples previous purchasers without knowing in advance which product they bought. That is, the sampling is on agents, not products.

2. *Bayesian Information Processing:* It is possible to imagine that prospective purchasers simply *imitate* the decisions taken by previous purchasers: for example, they might decide to buy the product used by a majority of those whom they poll. It is fairly obvious how information contagion may come about from an imitative strategy like this, but the psychology thus imputed to purchasers seems to us both unrealistic and uninteresting. In contrast, we will suppose an equally

---

1. The assumption that no strategic manipulation of price or information takes place during the course of the market process is primarily motivated by our desire to focus on purely informational effects. Nonetheless, there are some circumstances under which the assumption is plausible. For example, the two products might be unsponsored technologies (like public domain software), in which case no one has an interest in strategic manipulation; or, there may be many producers of each product, so that no one has sufficient market power to affect price; or, the market may be so structured that the time scale on which pricing responses to market signals operate may be sufficiently slower than the rate of purchase in the market that the asymptotic structures described below may be attained before price changes can go into effect.

extreme but opposite psychological point of view: that purchasers process in a "rational" way what they learn about the performance of the competing products from the agents they sample. That is, a purchaser assimilates this privately obtained information with that which is publicly available by Bayesian updating of his probability distribution on the relevant product performance characteristics—and then he chooses the product that maximizes his posterior expected utility.

We put "rational" above in quotes because this processing of information still falls short of *complete* rationality. To be completely rational, our agents would also use the information about product quality that is *implied* by the choice of product made by each sampled previous purchaser. But to do so, they would have to model the process whereby other agents gather information and use it to guide their choice between products, and we believe it is both unrealistic and needlessly complicating to consider this process as common knowledge. We assume simply that our agents learn from sampling previous purchasers which product each purchased and obtain some information about how that product performed: the latter information is rationally processed, while the evidential content of the former is ignored.

A word or two on how this study fits into the literature on uncertainty in economics. The classic literature on search or sampling in economics (see for example the surveys of Diamond and Rothschild 1978; Lippman and McCall 1981; and Rothschild 1973) concentrates on the problem of optimal information gathering. But it assumes an environment being searched that is unchanging. In this paper we allow that the population being searched—the distribution being sampled—may *itself* change endogenously as a result of the information gathering process; and we study the phenomena that may arise as a result. As such, we are concerned more with the self-reinforcing effects of the information gathering and decision process than with the standard problems of optimal sampling.[2]

In what follows, we consider what happens when a sequence of "Bayesian information processing" purchasers must each choose between two new products A and B. These purchasers share a fund of public information about the products, which they may augment by agent-oriented sampling of previous purchasers.

---

2. Thus besides adding to the literature on uncertainty, the paper fits squarely into the new body of work on allocation under increasing returns (see Arthur 1988, 1989). Note that other mechanisms that can introduce positive feedback into the market allocation process, such as network externalities or learning-by-doing, change the utility of a competing product to prospective purchasers, as a function of the number of previous purchasers of that type of product. In contrast, information contagion does not affect the actual utilities of the products, only what the prospective purchaser is able to learn about them.

The paper is organized as follows. Section 2 describes the general information contagion model. To provide a background for the effects of informational feedback, section 3 discusses what can be said about eventual market shares in two informationally extreme cases: when agents have no access to information about the experiences of previous purchasers, and when observations on product performance for each purchaser immediately become public knowledge. Section 4 then analyzes the dynamics of the market process that results from the informational feedback: each product asymptotically obtains a stable share of the market; the set of possible limit shares depends on psychological characteristics of the agents and on their sampling rules; and these limit shares can be calculated as the fixed points of a certain function. In certain cases there are multiple possible limit shares, and in these, *which* limit share emerges over time may depend on "chance"—that is, on who learns what from whom early on. Section 5 explores in more detail what market structures can result when each purchaser samples a fixed number of previous purchasers. In particular, two factors that can result in extreme market shares are identified and discussed: agents' risk aversion and the degree to which they underestimate how effective new products really are. Section 6 presents an example that illustrates another such mechanism, which may operate when purchasers use more complicated, sequential sampling rules. Finally, section 7 discusses some possible modifications of the model. Proofs of the mathematical results are given in an appendix at the end of the paper.

2. The Information Contagion Model

Agents enter a market sequentially and choose between two new products, A and B, that have similar functions. The products have performance characteristics c_A^* and c_B^* that determine their performance in practice. We suppose that neither these performance characteristics nor the price of the products change over the course of the market process described by the model.

We begin with a general description of the process whereby each agent decides which product to buy. We then introduce five assumptions whose primary purpose is to render the model analytically tractable. The consequences of some variations of these assumptions are discussed in sections 3 and 7.

Information Acquisition and Product Choice

The value of product i ($i = A, B$) to a prospective purchaser is determined by his utility function, u, which has as arguments c_i^* and p_i, the price of i. However, since price is supposed known and unchanging, we can suppress the dependence of u on price in expected utility expressions. Thus, we will suppose that the prospective purchaser chooses the product i that maximizes $E[u(c_i^*)]$.

The prospective purchaser encodes his opinion about product i, based on publicly available information, as a probability distribution π_i. He then *randomly samples* τ previous purchasers where τ is a *stopping rule* (that is, a well-defined decision rule for terminating sampling that depends only on the information gathered, the cost of gathering it, and model parameters). For each sampled individual, the purchaser determines which product the individual bought and an estimate X of the performance characteristic for the relevant product. The information in these estimates is then incorporated via Bayes' Theorem into posterior distributions for c_A^* and c_B^*. The expected utilities of these quantities are then calculated with respect to their posterior distributions.

Assumptions

1. The structure of the observations X

   $X = c_i^* + \epsilon$, *where* i (= A, B) *is the product-type used by the sampled purchaser and* ϵ *is a Normal random variable with mean 0 and standard deviation* σ_{ob}.

   The error random variables ϵ *are independent within a single potential purchaser's sample and between the samples of different potential purchasers.*

   These assumptions imply in particular that ϵ has the character of "pure" measurement error; it does not depend on attributes of the sampling or the sampled agents. An interesting alternative would be to assume that each user experiences a different realized value of c_i^*, corresponding to his unique skills and requirements with respect to the use of the product. With this assumption, each time a particular purchaser is sampled, the same product information is obtained. The resulting model is somewhat more complicated to analyze, but the main qualitative conclusions described in Sections 4 and 5 also hold for it; see Section 7 for some comments on how the two models differ.

2. Homogeneous agents

   All purchasers have the same priors π_A, π_B, *stopping rules* τ *and utility functions* u.

   That the purchasers have the same prior distributions reflects more than just an assumption of psychological homogeneity. It also depends on the presumption that they have access to the same public information about the products' performance characteristics and, in particular, that no additional information becomes publicly available as more and more agents purchase and use one or another of the products. This last point is of course an idealization, but may be reasonable in a number of situations: when purchasers have a strategic interest in secrecy, as with oil exploration technology; when there are prohibitive information acquisition costs, as with information about the effectiveness of drugs after they have been introduced on the market; or when the time scale of the adoption process is faster than the relevant information diffusion process, as with new computer programs for scientists that are reviewed in scientific journals.

3. The structure of prior beliefs

   π_A *and* π_B *are independent normal distributions, with means* μ_A *and* μ_B *and standard deviations* σ_A *and* σ_B

4. Constant risk aversion

   Agents possess a constant-risk utility function, u_λ, *with parameter* λ (≥ 0):

$$u_\lambda(c) = \begin{cases} - \exp(-2\lambda c) & \text{if } \lambda > 0 \\ c & \text{if } \lambda = 0 \end{cases}$$

5. Bounded stopping rule

   The stopping rule τ *is essentially bounded: that is, there exists an integer* N *such that* $P[\tau \leq N] = 1$.

With Assumptions 1–5, the decision model is completely specified by selecting a bounded stopping rule τ and values for the six parameters μ_A, μ_B, σ_A, σ_B, σ_{ob}, and λ. The dynamics of the market-share allocation process are determined by these parameters, plus the true product performance characteristics c_A^* and c_B^*.

In this model, the expected utility of product i, U_i, is given by

$$U_i = \mu_{post,i} - \lambda \sigma_{post,i}^2$$

$$= \frac{1}{n_i + \alpha_i} (n_i \bar{X}_i + \alpha_i \mu_i - \lambda \sigma_{ob}^2)$$

where the subscript "post" refers to the distribution of c_i^* posterior to the information obtained from sampling, n_i is the number of sampled purchasers who selected product i, $\bar{X}_i$ is the average value of their observed performance characteristics, and α_i is σ_{ob}^2/σ_i^2.

3. Market Shares in Two Extreme Models

To appreciate the role information can play in structuring the dynamics of market share allocation, it is helpful first to consider two simple informationally extreme models of product adoption. The first—which we will refer to as the *full constriction* model—is a trivial special case of the general information contagion model. Here information is completely constricted, so that agents obtain no private information—that is, $\tau = 0$. In this model, the product with higher prior expected utility will be purchased by all the agents. If the distributions have the same priors, the problem is ill-posed: the resulting market shares depend on how agents resolve ties. However we resolve this indeterminacy, we can certainly conclude that the resulting market share allocation is highly sensitive to any imaginable perturbation of the model— for example, changing one of the distributions slightly, or admitting tiny differences in how the agents encode the publicly available information into their prior distributions π. If the products differ in priors, the one with higher expected utility will trivially achieve complete market domination; so that knowledge of how the agents encode the available information (that is, of π_A and π_B) is then sufficient to predict the outcome of the allocation process.

In the second extreme model there is no constriction of information whatever. Information about product performance from each purchaser becomes publicly available; therefore agents need not sample previous purchasers. In this *full-public-knowledge* model we can think of each purchaser as contributing a normal observation on the performance characteristics of the product he purchased to a "bulletin board" to which all successive purchasers have access (as in Assumption 2). Purchasers then form their posterior distributions on performance characteristics based on the data on this bulletin board and priors as described in Assumption 3 above, and then choose the product that maximizes their expected utility, with utility as in Assumption 4. (Note that this model differs from the standard information contagion model of section 2 in the way information is gathered; hence it is not a special case.)

With full public knowledge, it is possible to imagine that sufficient information about the products will be generated so that eventually it will be clear which one is better, and then that one will achieve market domination. The same intuition would suggest that when the products are actually the same, that too would become publicly evident, and the ultimate market shares would, as in the full constriction model with identical priors, depend on how agents break ties.

According to Theorem 1 below, however, these intuitions are misplaced. Only one type of limiting market structure is possible in the full-public-knowledge model: market domination by one of the products. This is true even if in fact the two products are the same (that is, c_A^* equals c_B^*). And, if the products differ in their performance, the best product need not win. While it is certain *a priori* in the full-public-knowledge model that one product will eventually dominate the other, which product emerges triumphant depends on "chance," through the observation error sequence.

To state Theorem 1, we introduce the following definition:

Definition.

a) Product *A* achieves *strong market domination* over product *B* if there exists an *N* such that every purchaser after the *N*th chooses *A*.
b) Product *A* achieves *weak market domination* over product *B* if the proportion of *A*-purchasers among the first *n* purchasers converges to 1 as *n* goes to infinity.
c) Product *A* achieves ϵ-*weak market domination* over product *B* if the proportion of *A*-purchasers among the first *n* purchasers eventually exceeds $1 - \epsilon$ as *n* goes to infinity.

Theorem 1. In the full-public-knowledge *model, one product achieves strong market domination over the other with probability one. For any values of the model parameters, both products have positive probability of dominating the other.*

We give a formal proof in the Appendix. To see intuitively why this should be true, suppose first that no domination occurs. If one product is genuinely better in performance than the other, both products would be purchased indefinitely and agents' beliefs about their performances would then converge to their true values. But then the better product would eventually shut out and dominate the inferior one—a contradiction. In the more subtle case in which the true performances are the same, randomness in the observations means that (with probability one) beliefs about one of the products' performances will sooner or later "wander" below c^* leaving the other to converge to c^*—resulting once again in strong domination. Finally, whatever the parameter values, there is positive probability of a sequence of low-valued observations on one of the products, bad enough to terminate subsequent choices of that option even if its true performance is superior, and lock in the other for all subsequent time. The arguments here, and the possibility of shutting out a superior option, are analogous to those given in the well-known case of the two-armed bandit (see Rothschild 1974).

4. Information Contagion and Market Share Allocation

Let us return to the general information contagion model presented in Section 2. Recall that we can fully parameterize it by specifying the stopping rule τ and the model parameters μ_A, μ_B, σ_A, σ_B, σ_{ob}, λ, c_A^*, and c_B^*. We show in Theorem 2 below that whatever the parameters, market shares for the competing products converge asymptotically to stable limiting values. Further, for any given parameterization of the model, these possible limiting shares are determined by the fixed points of a polynomial that is derived by computing the conditional probability of selecting a product of type A, given the proportion of A purchases among all previous purchases. When there is more than one possible limiting share for product A—more than one fixed point—which one obtains is of course history-dependent, with "accidents" of sampling or observation having greater effects on the evolution of market structure the earlier they occur in the process.

The information contagion model admits a richer set of possibilities for the dynamics of the market share allocation process than do the full-constriction and full-public-knowledge models. Here we state three interesting differences between them, which will be illustrated by examples in Section 5:

First, some parameterizations of the information contagion model allow either stable market sharing with, say, equal shares to both products or nearly complete market domination by one or the other of the products. Thus, in these cases, whether a "competitive" or "monopolistic" market structure will emerge may depend on accidents of sampling and need not be knowable *a priori* to an observer who knows all the relevant psychological characteristics of the agents and the true performance characteristics of the competing products.

Second, in contrast to the full-public-knowledge model, certain other choices of parameters allow only one possible limiting market share for each product. Moreover, these "asymptotically deterministic" parameterizations may occur arbitrarily close in parameter space to parameterizations that permit multiple possible limit shares. For example, in certain cases a small increase in the degree of agents' risk aversion can change a "deterministic" structure in which both products necessarily garner 50 percent market share to one in which both have the possibility of nearly sweeping the market.

Third, in the general information contagion model, neither strong nor weak market domination can occur. This is because it is always possible for an agent to obtain abominable observations from all (up to N, the bound on τ) sampled purchasers of the better (or merely currently dominant) product, and thus opt for the alternative. However, it is easy to find parameters that will allow ϵ-weak domination for one or both of the products, for any value of ϵ.

To state Theorem 2, we introduce the following notation:
Consider two variants of the random sampling assumption: agents sample with replacement; and agents sample without replacement. (These induce two different probability distributions on the allocation process. Theorem 2 asserts that they yield the same qualitative limiting behavior.)

For $j = 1, 2, \ldots,$ let $T_j = \begin{cases} 1 & \text{if the } j\text{th purchase is } A \\ 0 & \text{otherwise} \end{cases}$

and

$$a(j) = \sum_{k=1}^{j} T_k$$

Lemma 4.1. In an information contagion model (with replacement sampling)

$$P[T_{n+1} = 1 \mid T_1, \ldots, T_n] = f\left(\frac{a(n)}{n}\right),$$

where f is a polynomial of degree at most N, whose coefficients depend on the stopping rule τ and the model parameters μ_A, μ_B, σ_A, σ_B, σ_{ob}, λ, c_A^*, and c_B^*.

That is, given the model parameters and Assumptions 1–5, the probability of A- or B-purchases depends only on their current proportion.

Definition. Given an information contagion model (τ, μ_A, μ_B, σ_A, σ_B, σ_{ob}, λ, c_A^*, c_B^*), the associated *urn function*[3] *f* is the function defined on rationals x in [0,1] by

$$f(x) = P\left[T_{n+1} = 1 \mid \frac{a(n)}{n} = x\right],$$

where *P* is calculated assuming replacement sampling, and extended by continuity to all x in [0,1].

Definition. Suppose *f* is a function on [0,1] and $f(x) = x$. Then x is an *upcrossing* if for some $\epsilon > 0$, $f(y) < y$ for y in $(x - \epsilon, x)$ and $f(y) > y$ for y in $(x, x + \epsilon)$.

Theorem 2. In an information contagion model (with or without replacement sampling), the proportion of purchasers who choose products of

---

3. The term *urn function* comes from the fact that we can represent our allocational process as a generalized urn process (see Hill, Lane, and Sudderth 1980; and Arthur, Ermoliev, and Kaniovski 1983, 1986, 1987). These are processes in which one ball of several possible types (or colors) is added to an urn at each event time, where each type has a probability of being added that depends only on the current proportions of ball types in the urn. In our process, purchase of product A (or B) corresponds to an addition of a ball of type A (or B) to the urn. Since Lemma 4.1 shows that the probability of A- or B-purchases depends only on their current proportion, our process is a generalized urn process, and the theory developed for these becomes available to us.

type A converges with probability 1. The limit points attained with positive probability are the elements of

$$L = \{x \text{ in } [0,1]: f(x) = x, \, x \text{ not an upcrossing}\},$$

where f is the urn function associated with the model.

The theorem tells us that if, for a given specification of the model, we can compute the function that maps A's market share into the probability of purchase of A, we can identify the limiting market shares as the stable (non-upcrossing) fixed points of this mapping.

As stated above, there is always a positive probability of a sequence of low values on all sampled observations on a product. Hence we have:

Corollary. In an information contagion model, neither product can weakly (and hence also strongly) dominate the other.

5. Market Shares under Risk Aversion and Unanticipated Effectiveness

Having established that market shares converge to limiting values given by the stable fixed points of the corresponding urn function, our next step is to investigate how these limiting values are affected by risk aversion, prior information, and other aspects of the model. At this stage we might impose the restriction that agents sample according to optimal stopping rules. But this would be problematic for two reasons. "Optimal" information gathering has neither been assumed nor defined above; and if fully defined, it would greatly complicate an already complicated analysis.[4] Hence in this section we restrict our attention to fixed-budget stopping rules—a family for which we can obtain analytical results.[5] In the next section, we do go part way toward

---

4. How to define "optimal" information gathering is by no means obvious in this setting. Unlike the standard problems of searching for maximum wage or lowest price, this problem of choice between sequentially-sampled objects inherits many of the difficulties of statistical decision theory. For example, we might reasonably specify that agents sample so as to maximize expected utility. But then if it became obvious in the sampling that one product was undeniably better than the other, so that sampling should stop, it might yet pay to continue to sample just to lower the variance on the chosen product, even though this would in no way affect the choice. To explore optimal stopping properly, we would need to model the *consequences* of making the decision. This might entail a criterion of minimum regret; or of maximum probability of correct choice; or of some other maximand. We would also need to specify the costs of gathering information, agents' assumptions about the distributions of observations they receive, and their knowledge of current market share.

5. We have explored by computer calculation limiting market shares under some simple versions of optimal stopping. We find that the results of this section (Theorem 3) do not qualitatively change.

optimality by considering the consequences of several illustrative, sequential-stopping rules.

Assume now that agents follow a fixed-budget stopping rule, so that $\tau \equiv k$ a constant, for some positive integer k. With stopping rules in this class, we can explicitly compute the associated urn functions and thus illustrate with particular examples some of the dynamic behavior of market share allocation under information contagion. In particular, with Theorem 3 and the examples that follow it, we show that both the agents' risk aversion and the unanticipated effectiveness of new products can drive the market to domination by one of the competing products.

We begin by introducing the class of symmetric information contagion models. For models in this class, agents are presumed to have the same prior beliefs about the two products and, moreover, the products do in fact perform identically. Thus, any differences in market share will come about solely because of the information agents manage to obtain from previous purchasers and how they process this information, not because of differences in the quality of the products or the "pre-release" public information about them.

Definition. An information contagion model $(\tau, \mu_A, \mu_B, \sigma_A, \sigma_B, \sigma_{ob}, \lambda, c_A^*, c_B^*)$ is *symmetric* if:

(i) $\mu_A = \mu_B = \mu$ and $\sigma_A = \sigma_B = \sigma$;

(ii) $c_A^* = c_B^* = c^*$

We denote by SC symmetric information contagion models with constant stopping times.

We can obtain a succinct reparameterization of SC models as follows. First, normalize units by setting σ_{ob} equal to 1. Next, introduce two new parameters: $\alpha = 1/\sigma^2$ and $e = \alpha(c^* - \mu)$. We call e the "unanticipated effectiveness" parameter, since it measures how much better the products actually are than the agents initially believe them to be. According to Lemma 5.1, a parameterization sufficient to generate the dynamical behavior of the allocation process is (n, λ, e, μ), where n is the number of previous purchasers sampled by each agent:

Lemma 5.1. For a SC model with $\tau \equiv n$, the associated urn function f is given by

$$f(x) = \sum_{k=0}^{n} p(k) \binom{n}{k} x^k (1 - x)^{n-k}$$

with

$$p(k) = (1 - \Phi)\left((\lambda + e) \, \frac{n - 2k}{r(k)}\right),$$

where Φ is the standard normal c.d.f. and

$$r(k) = \sqrt{k[\alpha + (n - k)]^2 + (n - k)(\alpha + k)^2}$$

Theorem 3 (Bifurcation Theorem). Consider the family of SC models with fixed parameters α and n, $n \geq 3$. Then:

1. *There exists a value $r > 0$ such that, for $\lambda + e < r$, A and B asymptotically attain 50 percent market shares with probability one.*
2. *Fix $\epsilon > 0$: There exists a value $R < \infty$ such that, for $\lambda + e > R$, either A or B achieves ϵ-weak market domination with probability one.*

According to Theorem 3, then, if both λ and e are sufficiently small, products A and B will end up sharing the market equally, while if either of these parameters is sufficiently large, domination by one product must result, with the dominant product determined solely by the vagaries of sampling. Why should this be so?

It is not difficult to see why high risk aversion might drive the market to domination by a single product. The more risk averse agents are, the more value they place on how much they know about a product, compared to how good they believe that product to be. If one product currently enjoys a market lead, an agent is more likely to sample its previous purchasers and so to learn more about it than about its competitor—and hence, as an increasing function of his degree of risk aversion, to purchase it.

High values of the unanticipated effectiveness parameter produce market domination as a byproduct of the agents' rationality. Suppose e is large: that is, the products are in fact much better than agents initially believe them to be. Certainly, if the agents only paid attention to the positive news they received from previous purchasers, their miscalibration *a priori* would have no consequences for their choice between the products. However, because they merge this news with their prior beliefs according to Bayes' formula, their prior under-appreciation of the benefits of the new products weighs more heavily against the product less represented in their sample, resulting in an advantage to the product currently in the lead that can amplify until that product sweeps the market.

Is it plausible to imagine that either of these information contagion mechanisms might actually operate in real allocation processes? Certainly, agents in the real world may be risk averse enough to induce a strong enough contagion effect that domination occurs.[6] But it is also reasonable to believe that under certain circumstances they might tend to systematically underestimate how good new products actually are. In particular, when the new products arise from a recent scientific or technological breakthrough, agents may tend to anchor their expectations about how well the new products will work on their experience with older products that performed some of the same functions. But these older products are based on a now outmoded technology, and they may well perform substantially less well than the new products. But how much less well is difficult to conceive of *a priori*. That is, it is difficult to anticipate the effects of a revolution. In such circumstances, the value of the unanticipated-effectiveness parameter may be relatively high.

Theorem 3 describes the possible market structures for small and large values of λ and e. To characterize completely the asymptotic behavior of SC models, we would like to describe the possible limit distributions for all such models as a function of their parameters. We cannot yet carry out such an analysis, but we have discovered only two kinds of bifurcation behavior and we conjecture that they are in fact the only possible. Because of the symmetry of the urn functions given in Lemma 5.1 with respect to λ and e, we can represent the bifurcation behavior by diagrams in a single parameter, λ or e, with the other parameters (n, α, and e or λ) held fixed.

Figure 1 gives a typical such bifurcation diagram for $n = 3$: the horizontal axis represents λ and the vertical axis gives the possible limiting market shares for A. Here, there is a single critical value λ_c, which depends of course on α and e. For $\lambda < \lambda_c$, the only possible long-run market structure is equal shares; for $\lambda > \lambda_c$, there are two possible limit shares, $a(\lambda)$ and $1-a(\lambda)$, where a is a continuous function of λ. In the example, with $\alpha = 1$ and $e = 0$, the critical value equals 1.788.

For $n > 5$ (at least up to 150, the highest integer for which we have carried out the relevant computations), the typical bifurcation diagram is given in figure 2. Here, there are two critical values, λ_{c1} and λ_{c2}. For $\lambda < \lambda_{c1}$, the only possible limiting market share is $1/2$. At λ_{c1}, two new possibilities appear, $a(\lambda_{c1})$ and $1 - a(\lambda_{c1})$, $a(\lambda_{c1})$ near 0. Between λ_{c1} and λ_{c2}, there are three possibilities: $1/2$, $a(\lambda)$ and $1 - a(\lambda)$. The probability that $1/2$ is the limit decreases continuously on this interval, from 1 to 0. Beyond λ_{c2}, the only possibilities are $a(\lambda)$ and $1 - a(\lambda)$. The function a is continuous and increasing on (λ_{c1}, ∞). Note in particular that if the agents' risk aversion parameter

---

6. Recent carefully conducted experimental-economic tests using the context we describe (Narduzzo and Warglien 1992) show that aggregate choices of human subjects do indeed tilt the "market" into domination of one of the objects of choice. Whether A or B corners the market varies from experiment to experiment as predicted, reflecting chance events in the sampling process.

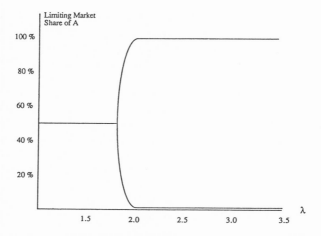

Fig. 1. This plot gives the possible limiting market shares for product A as a function of λ, for the SC model with $n = 3$, $e = 0$, $\alpha = 1$. λ is plotted on the x-axis and the values on the y-axis represent the possible limit points. Limiting values were calculated and plotted for λ-increments of 0.01; thus, though the possible limiting values vary continuously after λ_c, the information contagion limit is reached very rapidly.

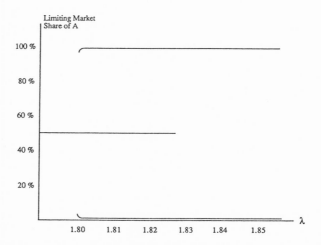

Fig. 2. This plot gives the possible limiting market shares for product A as a function of λ, for the SC model with $n = 5$, $e = 0$, $\alpha = 1$. Limiting values were plotted for λ-increments of 0.01, in an interval including the two critical values.

happens to lie between the two critical values, then even with full knowledge of the model parameters, it is indeterminate *a priori* whether the two competing products will end up sharing the market or one will essentially dominate the other. In the example, with $\alpha = 1$ and $e = 0$, λ_{c1} equals 1.80069 and λ_{c2} equals 1.82704.

We conclude this section by constructing an example of an information contagion model in which the only possible limiting market structure is ϵ-weak domination by one of the two competing products, say A. Clearly, this cannot happen within the class of symmetric models. Suppose, however, that while agents have the same prior distributions for c_A^* and c_B^*, in fact $c_A^* > c_B^*$. In this case, the urn function given in Lemma 5.1 has to be modified by changing the coefficients $p(k)$ as follows:

$$p(k) = \Phi \left[\frac{(2k - n)[\alpha(c_B^* - \mu) + \lambda] + k(n - k + \alpha)(c_A^* - c_B^*)}{r(k)} \right].$$

If c_A^* is sufficiently larger than c_B^*, the associated urn function will have only a single intersection with the diagonal, which can be made arbitrarily close to 1, and so the associated allocation process must result in ϵ-weak domination by product A. Figure 3 gives an example of such an urn function.

6. Sequential Stopping Rules

In the previous section, we considered only constant stopping rules, primarily because of their computational simplicity. More realistically, agents would continue sampling until they had obtained "sufficient" information, where the criteria defining sufficiency might be modelled in a number of different ways, or until further sampling exceeded some budget constraint. In general, such considerations would lead to random, sequential stopping times: that is, different agents would sample different numbers of previous purchasers, depending on what they had observed.

Of course, sequential stopping times can be thought of simply as mixtures of constant stopping rules (indeed, finite mixtures, by Assumption 5). It is perhaps tempting to suppose that the asymptotic behavior of the allocation process resulting from a sequential stopping time could be thought of in some sense as the "mixture" of the asymptotic behaviors resulting from the allocation processes associated with the relevant constant times. In particular, if τ is a stopping time such that $n \leq \tau \leq N$, and if for each constant stopping time between n and N, the corresponding information contagion model produced only one type of limiting market structure, one might conjecture that the same ought to be true for the model with stopping time τ. Examples 1 and 2 below show that this conjecture is false.

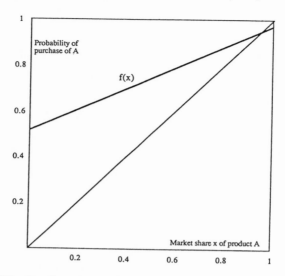

Fig. 3. This plot gives the urn function *f* associated to the asymmetric constant stopping rule information constriction model with parameters $n = 3$, $e = 0$, $\alpha = 1$, $\lambda = 0$, and $c_A^* - c_B^* = 1$. The only possible limiting share for product *A* is 0.943. (By contrast, if $c_A^* - c_B^* = 2$, the possible limiting share for *A* is 0.999712.)

Example 1. Consider a symmetric information contagion model with parameters $\lambda = 1.785$, $e = 0$ and $\alpha = 1$. Since λ is less than the critical value for $n = 3$ and for $n = 4$, the SC models corresponding to these two constant stopping times can only result in equal market sharing. Consider, however, the stopping rule: stop at 3 if all three sampled agents purchased the same type of product; otherwise sample a fourth previous purchaser and then stop. The urn function associated with this model is given by

$$f(x) = \Phi(\lambda\sqrt{3})x^3 + \Phi(-\lambda\sqrt{3})(1 - x)^3 + 3\Phi(\lambda/\sqrt{7})x^3(1 - x)$$

$$+ 3x^2(1 - x)^2 + \Phi(-\lambda/\sqrt{7})x(1 - x)^3,$$

and the limiting market shares for *A* computed from this function are .0039 and .9961. That is, if agents stop sampling (at 3) just when they perceive that one of the products has a substantial lead over the other, market domination will result.

Example 2. Now consider a symmetric information contagion model with parameters $\lambda = 2$, $e = 0$ and $\alpha = 1$. Here the risk aversion parameter is above the critical value for $n = 3$ and $n = 4$, so the SC models for these constant stopping times produce ϵ-weak market domination by one of the competing products (with $\epsilon = .005$ and $.0004$ for $n = 3$ and $n = 4$ respectively). However, consider the model with stopping rule: stop at 3, unless all three sampled agents purchased the same type of product, in which case sample a fourth previous purchaser and then stop. By calculating the urn function for this model, it can be shown that the resulting allocation process necessarily leads to equal market sharing.

The stopping rules in Examples 1 and 2 depend only on the products purchased by the sampled agents, not on the observations of these products' performance characteristics. The urn functions associated with stopping rules that also depend on these observations are typically difficult to compute. However, Example 1 suggests a mechanism that can produce market domination in models employing such rules: a rule designed to stop when a "sufficient" difference between the competing products is detected may be able to "find" such a difference, even when it does not actually exist; and it might do so in such a way as to confer an advantage to the competitor currently ahead.

7. Comments and Extensions

In this paper we have introduced the idea of information contagion and used it to explore how learning about new products from previous purchasers can affect the dynamics of market shares. Learning in this context does not take place in an unchanging environment, but instead causes the population being sampled to change endogenously, thereby inducing an informational feedback. We described several ways in which this informational feedback could drive this process towards market domination by one of the competing products, even when the products were in fact the same and publicly available information did not distinguish between them.

In this final section, we will sketch some possible variants and extensions of our information contagion model and speculate on the extent to which our conclusions are robust to these changes:

A Random Effects Model

Our model assumed fixed performance characteristics for each product that, in particular, did not depend on the intended uses or skills of the purchaser. In many situations, it is more reasonable to suppose that performance is specific to each purchaser, but that the experiences of different purchasers are still relevant to inferences about how well the product will perform for someone else. Thus, one might suppose that to each product is associated a distribution, and each potential purchaser experiences as his performance characteristic a draw from this distribution. Further suppose that, should a purchaser be sampled by another agent, the value he experienced can be observed by that agent without error.

With this random effects model, a bad experience with a particular product persists: anyone who samples the agent who had a bad experience with a product receives bad news about that product. Thus, the random effects model induces even more history dependence than did the model we analyzed in this paper, and in particular it is clear that it is easier to obtain conditions that lead to market dominance with the random effects model than with our model.

If it is assumed that the distributions for performance characteristics have finite support, the random effects model can be analyzed using the theory of generalized urn process with many values, as developed by Arthur, Ermoliev, and Kaniovski (1983, 1986, 1987). In principle, more complex dynamics for the allocation process are possible in the multi-value context. We have not yet determined whether this can actually happen with the particular urn functions associated with a random effects information contagion model.

Distributional Assumptions

The assumptions of normality for prior and sampling distributions and exponential forms for risk aversion were adopted to facilitate closed-form analysis. It seems very unlikely to us that any of our qualitative conclusions depends on these functional forms, and indeed we have developed examples with simple discrete distributions for all the dynamic phenomena described in Section 4. Neither is the assumption of homogeneity of agents essential to produce the effects we describe, although marked inhomogeneities can by themselves prevent market domination if the products actually differ and each is much better suited to one of the segments of the population of potential purchasers. Thus, we believe that our model is robust under the kind of perturbation that might completely change conclusions from the full-constriction model as described in Section 3.

Strategic Manipulation

If producers of the competing products were to strategically manipulate either price or information in response to market signals, a strategic overlay would be added to the allocation process we have described. We can formulate this strategic version of the information contagion problem fairy easily as a stochastic duopoly game in which producers face a tradeoff between raising prices (and hence short-term profits) and lowering them to increase probability of purchase (and hence long-term market share with its positive contagion effects). We have not carried out a full analysis of limiting market shares here. But from studies along these lines for other positive-feedback models (Arthur and Ruszczynski 1992; Dosi, Ermoliev, and Kaniovski 1992) we would expect, other things equal, if the competing firms' discount were sufficiently high, market sharing would result. (If only the present counted, the problem would collapse to a standard Bertrand duopoly, with competition in pricing "convexifying" the dynamics and maintaining a shared market.) If on the other hand discount rates were low so that the long term counted heavily, and there was significant information contagion (positive feedback), then typically strategic firms would cut prices early on to obtain market share; but once a firm began to achieve dominance, possibly in part as a result of chance, it would raise prices and take monopoly profits while keeping the other firms on the contestable margin. Market shares closer to 0 or 100 percent would then result.

Spatial Sampling

When agents obtain private information, they typically do not sample randomly from all previous adopters, but instead interrogate previous purchasers that are "close" to them, geographically, professionally, or in some other appropriate sense. Various models could be constructed, taking this "spatial" aspect of sampling into account. These models could explore such interesting possible phenomena as the emergence of regions of domination by different products.

APPENDIX

Section 3: Proofs

Consider the following families of random variables:

1. $\{X_{ij}\}$, $i = A, B; j = 1, 2, \ldots$

   X_{ij}'s independent, $X_{ij} \sim N(c_i^*, \sigma_{ob}^2)$
   (X_{ij} is the observation generated by the jth purchaser of product i.)

2.
$$V_{i,n} = \frac{1}{(n + \alpha_i)} \left[\sum_{j=1}^{n} X_{ij} + \alpha_i \mu_i - \lambda \sigma_{ob}^2 \right],$$

   where $\alpha_i = \sigma_{ob}^2/\sigma_i^2$ and $i = A, B; n = 1, 2, \ldots$
   (If exactly n previous purchasers have selected product i, $V_{i,n}$ gives the expected utility of i to the next purchaser.)

3. $\{T_j\}, j = 1, 2, \ldots,$ defined as follows:

$$T_1 = \begin{cases} 1 & \text{if } \mu_A - \lambda\sigma_A^2 > \mu_B - \lambda\sigma_B^2 \\ 0 & \text{otherwise} \end{cases}$$

$$T_k = \begin{cases} 1 & V_{A,\Sigma_{j=1}^k T_j} > V_{B,k-\Sigma_{j=1}^k T_j} \\ 0 & \text{otherwise} \end{cases}$$

4. For $n = 1, \ldots, \infty$ set $a(n) = \Sigma_{j=1}^n T_j$ and $b(n) = \Sigma_{j=1}^n [1 - T_j]$. For $N = 1,$ $2, \ldots, B(N) = \{a(\infty) \leq N\}$ and $A(N) = \{b(\infty) \leq N\}$.

(Of the first n purchases, $a(n)$ were of product A and $b(n)$ of product B. On $\cup_{N=1}^\infty B(N)$, B achieves strong market domination, while A does so on $\cup_{N=1}^\infty A(N)$.)

Lemma 3.1. *For $i = A, B$, $P[V_{i,n} \to c_i^*$ as $n \to \infty] = 1$.*

Proof. Strong law of large numbers.

Lemma 3.2. *Suppose $c_A^* = c_B^*(= c^*)$. Then:*

a. (*) $P[\cap_{m>n}\{V_{j,m} > r\} \mid V_{j,n} = r]$
   *does not depend on j ($= A, B$) or n, but only on r. Denote * by $f(r)$:*
b. *f is a decreasing function of r.*
c. *$f(r) > 0 \;\; \forall r < c^*$.*

Proof. For $m > n$,

$$V_{j,m} = \frac{1}{m + \alpha_j} \sum_{n+1}^m X_{jk} + \frac{\alpha_j + n}{\alpha_j + m} \; (V_{j,n}).$$

Thus, on $\{V_{j,n} = r\}$,

$$V_{j,m} > r \text{ iff } \frac{1}{m - n} \sum_{n+1}^m X_{jk} > r.$$

Hence,

$$f(r) = P\,[\cap_{m>n}\{V_{j,m} > r\} \mid V_{j,n} = r]$$

$$= P[\cap_{m\geq 1} \left[\frac{\Sigma_{k=1}^m X_{jk}}{m} > r \right\}] \tag{1}$$

$$=P\left[\cap_{m\geq 1}\left\{\frac{S_m}{m}>r\right\}\right]$$

where S_m is the mth partial sum of a $N(c^*, \sigma^2)$-random walk. Conclusions (a) and (b) of the lemma follow immediately from Eq. (1), while (c) is an easy consequence of the strong law of large numbers.   ■

Lemma 3.3. *Suppose* $c_A^* = c_B^* = c^*$. $P[\exists\ n \ni V_{j,n} < c^*] = 1$ *for* $j = A, B$.

Proof:

$$V_{j,m} \geq c^* \quad \text{iff} \quad \sum_{k=1}^{m} X_{j,k} - mc^* > \alpha_j(c^* - \mu) + \lambda\sigma^2$$

or

$$S_m > b,$$

where S_m is the mth partial sum of a $N(0, \sigma_{ob}^2)$-random walk, and $b = \alpha_j(c^* - \mu) + \lambda\sigma_{ob}^2$. Thus, $P[V_{j,m} \geq c^* \forall m] = P[S_m > b \forall m] = 0$, since $P[\limsup S_m = \infty, \liminf S_m = -\infty] = 1$.   ■

Proof of Theorem 1:
    Case 1: $c_A^* \neq c_B^*$

Fix δ: we show there exists $N < \infty$ such that $P[A(N)] > 0$, $P[B(N)] > 0$, and $P[A(N) \cup B(N)] > 1 - \delta$. This will imply the conclusions of Theorem 1.
    Suppose $c_A^* > c_B^*$, and choose $\epsilon > 0$ such that $c_A^* - \epsilon > c_B^* + \epsilon$. By Lemma 3.1 and the independence of $\{X_{Aj}\}$ and $\{X_{Bj}\}$, it is possible to select N so that

$$P[S = \cap_{m\geq N} \cup_{\epsilon=A,B}\{c_i^* - \epsilon \leq V_{i,m} \leq c_i^* + \epsilon\}] > 1 - \delta.$$

Note that for $\omega \epsilon S$, if $a(\infty)(\omega) > N$, then $b(\infty)(\omega) \leq N$. Thus, $A(N) \cup B(N) \supset S$. Clearly, both $A(N)$ and $B(N)$ have positive probability.
    Case 2: $c_A^* = c_B^*$
    By Lemma 3.3, without loss of generality we can suppose that for some n and $r < c^*$,

$$V_{A,a(n)} < V_{B,b(n)} = r.$$

Let $\tau_1 = \inf\{t > n: V_{B,b(t)} < V_{A,a(t)}\}$, and for $k \geq 1$

$$\tau_{2k} = \inf\{t > \tau_{2k-1}: \quad V_{A,a(t)} < V_{B,b(t)}\}$$

$$\tau_{2k+1} = \inf\{t > \tau_{2k}: \quad V_{B,b(t)} < V_{A,a(t)}\}$$

By Lemma 3.2, for all j,

$$P[\tau_j = \infty \mid \tau_{j-1} < \infty] \geq f(r).$$

Thus, by the Borel 0-1 Law,

$$P[\exists j \ni \tau_j = \infty] = 1.$$

But $\{\exists j \ni \tau_j = \infty\}$ is precisely the set on which one of the two products achieves strong market domination. ∎

Section 4. Proofs

Proof of Lemma 4.1: Consider the set of ordered samples

$$S = \{0, 1\}^N.$$

The interpretation is that for $s = (s_1, \ldots, s_N)$ in S, $s_i = 1$ if the ith sampled agent purchased a product of type A. We suppose N agents are sampled, with observations obtained from the first $\tau \leq N$ of them. For s in S, set

$$S = \Sigma_{k=1}^N s_k.$$

$$P[T_{n+1} = 1 \mid T_1, \ldots, T_n] = \sum_{s \text{ in } S} P[T_{n+1} = 1 \mid s, T_1, \ldots, T_n]$$

$$P[s \mid T_1, \ldots, T_n].$$

Since observations are obtained only from sampled agents, T_{n+1} and $(T_1, \ldots, T_n)$ are independent given s. Under WITH,

$$P(s \mid T_1, \ldots, T_n) = \left(\frac{a(n)}{s}\right)^s \left(1 - \frac{a(n)}{n}\right)^{N-S}$$

Thus,

$$P[T_{n+1} = 1 \mid T_1, \ldots, T_n] = \sum_{s \text{ in } S} P[T_{n+1} = 1 \mid s]$$

$$\left(\frac{a(n)}{n}\right)^s \left(1 - \frac{a(n)}{n}\right)^{N-S},$$

and $P[T_{n+1} = 1 \mid s]$ depends on the stopping rule τ and the model parameters.

Proof of Theorem 2:

Under WITH, Lemma 4.1 implies that the process $\{a(n)/n\}_{n=1,2,...}$ is a generalized urn process as defined by Hill, Lane, and Sudderth (1980). The a.s. convergence of the process and the characterization of the limit set follow from Theorems 4.1, 4.2, and 5.1 of that paper and the Corollary to Theorem 1 of Pemantle (1991). The proofs of these results are easily modified to imply the same conclusions under WITHOUT. ∎

Proof of Corollary:

The corollary follows from the fact that $f(0) > 0$ and $f(1) < 1$ for all associated urn functions f. ∎

Section 5. Proofs

Proof of Lemma 5.1: Let $s(k)$ be the event that k of the n sampled agents purchased A. By the argument in the proof of Lemma 4.1,

$$f(x) = \sum_{k=0}^{n} P_{\text{WITH}}[T_{n+1} = 1 \mid s(k)] \binom{n}{k} x^k (1-x)^{n-k}.$$

$\{T_{n+1} = 1\} = \{U_A > U_B\}$, and on $s(k)$,

$$U_a > U_B \text{ iff } Y = \frac{k}{\alpha + k} \bar{X}_a - \frac{n-k}{\alpha + (n-k)} \bar{X}_B$$

$$> (\lambda - \alpha) \frac{n - 2k}{(\alpha + k)(\alpha + n + k)}.$$

Since

$$\bar{X}_a \sim N[c^*, 1/k] \text{ and } \bar{X}_B \sim N\left[c^*, \frac{1}{n-k}\right],$$

$$Y \sim N\left[\frac{\alpha(2k - n)}{(\alpha + k)\alpha(n - k)} c^*, \frac{k}{(\alpha + k)^2} + \frac{n-k}{[\alpha + (n-k)]^2}\right].$$

Thus,

$$p(k) = P_{\text{WITH}}[\cup_A > \cup_B \mid s(k)]$$

$$= (1 - \Phi)\left[(\lambda + e) \frac{n - 2k}{\sqrt{k[\alpha + (n-k)]^2 + (n-k)(\alpha + k)^2}}\right].$$

For the SC model (n, λ, e, α), denote the associated urn function by $f_{(n,\lambda,e,\alpha)}$ and the corresponding coefficients (the $p(k)$ of Lemma 5.1) as $p_k(n, \lambda, e, \alpha)$. To prove Theorem 3, we require the following three lemmas.

Lemma 5.2: For all n and α

1. as

$$\lambda + e \to \infty,$$

$$p_k(n, \lambda, e, \alpha) \to p_k(n, \infty) = \begin{cases} 1 & k > \dfrac{n}{2} \\ \dfrac{1}{2} & k = \dfrac{n}{2} \\ 0 & k < \dfrac{n}{2} \end{cases}$$

and
2. as $\lambda + e \to 0$

$$p_k(n, \lambda, e, \alpha) \to \frac{1}{2}.$$

Proof. Note that $p_k(n, \lambda, e, \alpha) = (1 - \Phi)[(\lambda + e)(n - 2k)R(n, \alpha, k)]$ and $R(n, \alpha, k) > 0$ for $k = 0, \ldots, n$.

Now set $f_n(x) = \sum_{k=0}^n p_k(n, \infty) \binom{n}{k} x^k (1 - x)^{n-k}$.

Lemma 5.3: For all n and α, as $\lambda + e \to \infty$, $f_{(n,\lambda,e,\alpha)}$ converges to f_n and $f'_{(n,\lambda,e,\alpha)}$ converges to f'_n, uniformly in $[0,1]$.

Proof Immediate from Lemma 5.2.

Lemma 5.4: For $n \geq 3$,

1. $f_n(x) > x$ for all x in $(1/2,1)$

2. $\{x \text{ in } [0,1]: f_n(x) = x\} = \{0,1/2,1\}$

Proof of 1: $f_1(x) = f_2(x) = x$ for all x in $[0,1]$. We show: for all *even* integers n, and x in $(1/2,1)$,

a. $f_{n+1}(x) > f_{n-1}(x)$

b. $f_n(x) = f_{n-1}(x)$.

(a) and (b) imply conclusion (1) of the lemma.

Proof of (a): Fix x in $(1/2,1)$. Let $X_1, \ldots$ be independent bernoulli random variables with parameter x, and $S_1, \ldots$ the corresponding random walk. For n an even integer, note that

$$\{S_{n-1} > n - 1\} = \left\{ S_{n+1} > \frac{n}{2}, S_n \neq \frac{n}{2} \right\} \cup \left\{ S_n = \frac{n}{2}, X_n = 0 \right\}$$

Therefore,

$$P\left[S_{n+1} > \frac{n}{2} \right] = P\left[S_{n-1} > \frac{n}{2} - 1 \right] - P\left[S_n = \frac{n}{2}, X_n = 0 \right]$$

$$+ P\left[S_n = \frac{n}{2}, X_{n+1} = 1 \right]$$

$$= P\left[S_{n-1} > \frac{n}{2} - 1 \right] - P\left[S_n = \frac{n}{2} \right] P\left[X_n = 0 \mid S_n = \frac{n}{2} \right]$$

$$+ P\left[S_n = \frac{n}{2} \right] P\left[X_{n+1} = 1 \mid S_n = \frac{n}{2} \right]$$

$$= P\left[S_{n-1} > \frac{n}{2} - 1 \right] - P\left[S_n = \frac{n}{2} \right] \frac{1}{2} + P\left[S_n = \frac{n}{2} \right] x$$

$$= P\left[S_{n-1} > \frac{n}{2} - 1 \right] + \left(x - \frac{1}{2} \right) P\left[S_n = \frac{n}{2} \right]$$

$$> P\left[S_{n-1} > \frac{n}{2} - 1 \right].$$

Finally, note that $f_{n+1}(x) = P[S_{n+1} > n/2]$, $f_{n-1}(x) = P[S_{n-1} > n/2 - 1]$.
Proof of (b):

$$f_n(x) = P\left[S_n > \frac{n}{2} \right] + \frac{1}{2} P\left[S_n = \frac{n}{2} \right]$$

and

$$P\left[S_n > \frac{n}{2} \right] = P\left[S_{n-1} > \frac{n}{2} - 1 \right] - P\left[S_{n-1} = \frac{n}{2}, X_n = 0 \right],$$

But the events $\left\{ S_{n-1} = \frac{n}{2}, X_n = 0 \right\}$ and $\left\{ S_{n-1} = \frac{n}{2} - 1, X_n = 1 \right\}$ have the same probability, and their union is $\left\{ S_n = \frac{n}{2} \right\}$. Thus,

$$f_n(x) = P\left[S_{n-1} > \frac{n}{2} - 1\right] = f_{n-1}(x).$$

Proof of 2:

Conclusion (2) follows from (1) and evaluation of f_n at $\{0, 1/2, 1\}$.   ∎

Proof of Theorem 3:

Fix $n \geq 3, \alpha$. Since $f_n'(0) < 1, f_n'(1) < 1, f_n'(1/2) > 1$, it is possible to choose δ such that $0 < \delta < \epsilon$, and

i. on $[0, \delta] \cup [1 - \delta, 1], f_n' < 1$, while on $[1/2 - \delta, 1/2 + \delta], f_n' > 1$.

Since, by Lemma 5.4, $f_n(x) > x$ for x in $(1/2, 1)$, and, by symmetry, $f_n(x) < x$ on $(0, 1/2)$,

ii. on $[\delta, 1/2, -\delta] \cup [1/2 + \delta, 1 - \delta], f_n(x) - x > 0$.

By Lemma 5.3, there exists $R < \infty$ such that (i) and (ii) also hold for $f_{(n,\lambda,e,\alpha)}$ with $\lambda + e > R$. Clearly, for all (n, λ, e, α)

$$f_{(n,\lambda,e,\alpha)}'(1/2) = 1/2, f_{(n,\lambda,e,\alpha)}(0) > 0, f_{(n,\lambda,e,\alpha)} < 1.$$

For $\lambda + e > R$,

$$f_{(n,\lambda,e,\alpha)}'(1/2) > 1.$$

Thus, for all (n, λ, e, α) with $\lambda + e > R$, there must exist a unique $c(n, \lambda, e, \alpha)$ in $[0, \delta]$ such that

$$f_{(n,\lambda,e,\alpha)}(c_{(n,\lambda,e,\alpha)}) = c_{(n,\lambda,e,\alpha)}.$$

Similarly, $1 - c_{(n,\lambda,e,\alpha)}$ is the only root of $f_{(n,\lambda,e,\alpha)}(x) - x = 0$ in $[1 - \delta, 1]$. Hence,

$$\{x \text{ in } [0,1]: f_{(n,\lambda,e,\alpha)}(x) = x \text{ and } f_{(n,\lambda,e,\alpha)}'(x) < 1\}$$

$$= \{c_{(n,\lambda,e,\alpha)}, 1 - c_{(n,\lambda,e,\alpha)}\}.$$

Together with Theorem 2, this establishes conclusion (2). The argument for conclusion (1) is similar, based on the fact that $f_{(n,\lambda,e,\alpha)}(x) \equiv 1/2$.   ∎

REFERENCES

Arthur, W. B. 1988. "Self-Reinforcing Mechanisms in Economics," in *The Economy as an Evolving Complex System,* Anderson, P. W., Arrow, K. J. and Pines, D. Eds., Addison-Wesley.

————. 1989. "Competing Technologies, Increasing Returns, and Lock-In by Historical Events," *Econ. Journal* 99:116–31.

Arthur, W. B., Y. M. Ermoliev, and Y. M. Kaniovski. 1983. "A Generalized Urn Problem and Its Applications," *Kibernetika* (trans. in *Cybernetics*) 19, 61–71.

————. 1986. "Strong Laws for a Class of Path-Dependent Urn Processes," in Springer: Lect. Notes in Control and Info. Sciences, No. 81.

————. 1987. "Non-Linear Urn Processes: Asymptotic Behavior and Applications," I.I.A.S.A. Working Paper:87–85, Laxenburg, Austria.

Arthur, W. B. and A. Ruszczynski. 1992. "Dynamic Equilibria in Markets with a Conformity Effect," *Archives of Control Science* 37:7–31.

Diamond, P. and M. Rothschild. 1978. *Uncertainty in Economics,* Academic Press, New York.

Dosi G., Y. M. Ermoliev, and Y. M. Kaniovski. 1992. Mss. in preparation.

Hill, B. M., D. A. Lane, and W. D. Sudderth. 1980. "A Strong Law for Some Generalized Urn Processes," *Annals of Probability* 8:214–26.

Lippman, S. A. and J. J. McCall. 1981. "The Economics of Uncertainty," Chap. 6 in *Handbook of Mathematical Economics, Vol. 1.* Arrow, K. J. and M. D. Intriligator (eds.). North-Holland, Amsterdam.

Narduzzo, A. and M. Warglien. 1992. "Learning from the Experience of Others: First Report on an Aggregate Choice Experiment," mss. in preparation, Università degli Studie di Venezia, Italy.

Pemantle, R. 1991. "When are Touchpoints Limits for Generalized Polya Urns?," *Proceedings of the American Mathematical Society.*

Rothschild, M. 1973. "Models of Market Organization with Imperfect Information: A Survey," *Journal of Political Economy* 81:1283–1308.

————. 1974. "A Two-Armed Bandit Theory of Market Pricing," *Journal of Economic Theory* 9:185–202.

CHAPTER 6

Urban Systems and Historical Path Dependence

When does history make a difference in the formation of economic structures? Under some circumstances the small events of history are averaged away and an unavoidable outcome or structure is reached. Under other circumstances, differences in these chance events can steer the economy into potentially very different structures.

This paper—a variation on the locational themes of chapter 4—explores the importance of history by contrasting three mechanisms or models of industry location. In the first (called *pure necessity*) chance events influence location but are averaged away, so that history does not count. In the second (called *pure chance*) *any* locational pattern can arise, and history is all-important. In the third (called *chance and necessity*) geographical attractions interact with chance events, and history is partially responsible for the outcome.

The paper was written in 1987 and appeared as chapter 4 in *Cities and Their Vital Systems*, edited by Jesse H. Ausubel and Robert Herman, National Academy Press, Washington D.C. 1988, 85–97. In the version here, I have made small changes in the introduction.

If small events in history had been different, would the pattern of cities we have inherited be different in any significant way? Could different "chance events" in history have created a different formation of urban centers than the one that exists today?

To a great degree, cities form around and depend upon clusters of industry, so that without doing too much injustice to the question we can ask whether the patterns of location of industry follow paths that depend upon history. The German Industry Location School debated this question in the earlier part of this century, but it was never settled conclusively. Some theorists[1] saw the spatial ordering of industry as preordained—by geographical endowments, shipment possibilities, firms' needs, and the spatial distribution of rents and prices that these induced. In their view, history did not matter: the observed spatial pattern of industry was a unique "solution" to a well-defined spatial economic problem. Therefore, early events in the configuration of an

---

1. Von Thünen (1826), the early Weber (1909), Predöhl (1925), Christaller (1933), and Lösch (1944).

industry could not affect the result. Others[2] saw industry location as path-dependent—as an organic process with new industry laid down upon and very much influenced by inherited, locational patterns already in place. Again geographical differences and transport possibilities were important, but here the main driving forces were agglomeration economies—the benefits of being close to other firms or to concentrations of industry. In this view, early firms arriving by "historical accident" might put down in locations they were attracted to for geographical reasons. Later firms might be attracted to these same places by the presence of these early locators, rather than geography. Still later firms might be attracted in turn by *their* presence. The industry ends up clustered in the early-chosen places. But this spatial ordering is not unique: a different set of early choosers could have steered the locational pattern into quite a different outcome, so that settlement history would be crucial.

These two viewpoints—determinism versus history dependence, or "necessity" versus "chance"—are echoed in current discussions of how modern industrial clusters have come about. The determinism school, for example, would tend to see the electronics industry in the United States as spread over the country, with a substantial part of it in Santa Clara County in California (Silicon Valley) because that location is close to Pacific sources of supply and because it has better access there than elsewhere to airports, skilled labor, and advances in academic engineering research. Any "small events" that might affect location decisions are overridden by the "necessity" inherent in the equilibration of spatial economic forces; and Silicon Valley is part of an inevitable result. Historical dependence, on the other hand, would see Silicon Valley and similar concentrations as largely the outcome of "chance." Certain key persons—the Packards, the Varians, the Shockleys of the industry—happened to set up near Stanford University in the 1940s and 1950s, and the local labor expertise and interfirm markets they helped to create in Santa Clara County made subsequent location there extremely advantageous for the thousand or so firms that followed them. If these early entrepreneurs had had other predilections, Silicon Valley might well have been somewhere else. In this argument, "historical chance" is magnified and preserved in the locational structure that results.

Although the historical dependence-agglomeration argument is appealing, it has remained problematical. If history can indeed steer the spatial system down different paths, there are multiple "solutions" to the industry location problem. Which of these comes about is indeterminate. In the 1920s, analysts could not cope with this difficulty, and the historical chance argument did not gain enough rigor to become completely respectable.

---

2. The later Weber, Engländer (1926), Ritschl (1927), and Palander (1935). See also Maruyama (1963).

This chapter investigates the importance of "chance" (as represented by small events in history) and "necessity" (as represented by determinate economic forces) in determining the pattern of industry location. It contrasts three highly stylized locational models in which small events and economic forces are both present and allowed to interact. In each model an industry is allowed to form, firm by firm, and build up into a locational pattern. In each model we will examine whether historical chance can indeed alter the locational pattern that emerges. Insights gained from the three models will be used to derive some general conditions under which long-run locational patterns may be affected by small historical events.

The Evolution of Locational Patterns: Three Models

Model 1. Pure Necessity: Location under Independent Preferences

Let us begin with a very simple model of the emergence of an industry location pattern. Starting from zero firms, we allow an industry to form firm by firm, with each new firm that enters deciding "at birth" which of N possible regions (or sites) it will locate in. Once located, each firm will stay put. Firms in this industry are not all alike; there are I different types. The net present value or payoff to a firm of type i for locating in region j is Π_j^i; each firm choosing selects the location with the highest return for its type. In this model, firms are independent: the presence or absence of other firms does not affect what they can earn in each region.

We now inject a small element of "chance" by assuming that the particular historical circumstances that lead to the next firm's being of a particular type are unknown. We do know, however, that a firm of type I will occur next with probability p_i. The question is: What pattern of industrial settlement will emerge in this model, and can it be affected by a different sequence of historical events in the formation of the industry?

It is not difficult to work out the probability that at any time of choice, region j will be chosen. This is simply the probability, q_j, that the newest firm is of a type that has its highest payoff in region j, which is given by $q_j = \Sigma p_k$ for $k \in K$, where K is the set of firm types that prefer j. Repeating this calculation for each of the N regions, we have a set of probabilities of choice $q = (q_1, q_2, \ldots, q_N)$ that are constant no matter what the current pattern of location is. Starting from zero firms in any region, concentrations of the industry in the various regions will fluctuate, considerably at first. But the strong law of large numbers tells us that as the industry grows, the proportions of it in the N regions must settle down to the probabilities of an addition being made to each region. That is, regions' shares of the industry must converge to the constant vector q. In this simple model then, even though well-defined "chance historical events" are present, a unique, predetermined locational pattern emerges and persists.

Figure 1 shows a simple three-region simulation of this process, with three possible firm types that prefer (clockwise from the top) region 1, region 2, and region 3, respectively, with probabilities of occurrence .5, .25, and .25. After 16 firms have located, the regions' share of the industry are 0.75, 0.125, and 0.125, respectively—not yet close to the long-run predicted pattern. After 197 firms have located, however, the shares are 0.528, 0.221, and 0.251—much closer to the predetermined theoretical long-run shares.

In this model, chance events, represented as randomness in the sequence of firm types that enter the industry, are important early on. But they are progressively averaged away to become dominated by the economic forces represented by firms' payoffs in each region. Different sequences of firm types caused by different historical events would, with probability one, steer the system into the same locational pattern. Here, historical chance cannot affect the outcome. Necessity dominates.

Model 2. Pure Chance: Location by Spin-off

We now assume a quite different mechanism driving the regional formation of an industry—one in which chance events become all-important. Once again the industry builds up firm by firm, starting with some set of initial firms, one per region, say. This time new firms are added by "spinning off" from parent firms one at a time. (David Cohen [1984] has shown that such spin-offs have been the dominant "birth mechanism" in the U.S. electronics industry.) We assume that each new firm stays in its parent location and that any existing firm is as likely to spin off a new firm as any other. With this mechanism we have a different source of "chance historical events": the sequence in which firms spin off daughter firms.

It is easy to see that in this case firms are added incrementally to regions with probabilities exactly equal to the proportions of firms in each region at that time. This random process, in which unit increments are added one at a time to one of N categories with probabilities equal to current proportions in each category, is known in probability theory as a *Polya process*. We can use this fact to examine the long-term locational patterns that might emerge. From Polya theory we know that once again the industry will settle into a locational pattern (with probability one) that has unchanging proportions of the industry in each region. But although this vector of proportions settles down and becomes constant, surprisingly it settles to a constant vector that is *selected randomly* from a uniform distribution over all possible shares that sum to 1.0. This means that each time this spin-off locational process is "rerun" under

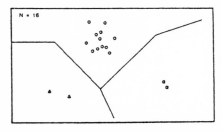
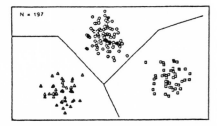

Fig. 1. A three-region example of the independent preferences location model

different historical events (in this case a different sequence of firms spinning off), it will in all likelihood settle into a different pattern. We could generate a representative outcome by placing $N - 1$ points on the unit interval at random and cutting at these points to obtain N "shares" of the unit interval.

Figure 2 shows four realizations of this location-by-spin-off mechanism starting from the same three original firms in a three-region case. Each of the four "reruns" has settled into a pattern that will change but little in regional shares with the addition of further firms. But each pattern is different from the others. In this model, industry location is highly path-dependent. Although we can predict that the locational pattern of industry will indeed settle down to constant proportions, we cannot predict what proportions it will settle into. Any given outcome—any vector of proportions that sum to 1.0—is as likely as any other. "History," in the shape of the early random sequence of spin-offs, becomes the sole determining factor of the regional pattern of industry. In this model, "chance" dominates completely.

Model 3. Chance and Necessity: Location under Agglomeration Economies

Firms that are not tied to raw material localities and that do not compete for local customers are often attracted by the presence of other firms in a region. More densely settled regions offer better infrastructure, deeper labor markets (David 1984), more specialized legal and financial services, better local availability of inventory and parts, and more opportunity to do business face to face. For our third model we go back to model 1 and extend it by supposing that new firms gain additional benefits from local agglomerations of firms.

Suppose now that the net present value or payoff to a firm of type i for locating in region j is $\Pi_j^i + g(y_j)$, where the "geographical benefits," Π_j^i, are enhanced by additional "agglomeration benefits," $g(y_j)$, from the presence of y_j firms already located in that region. We can recalculate the probability that

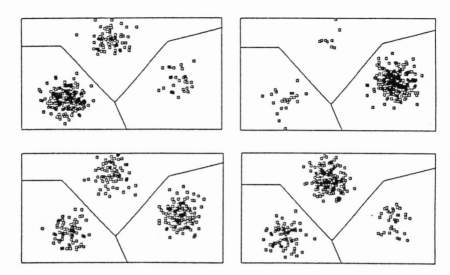

Fig. 2. Four realizations of location by spin-off

region j is chosen next, given that $y_1, \ldots, y_N$ firms are currently in regions 1 through N, once again as $q_j = \Sigma p_k$ for $k \in K$, where K is now the set of firm types for which $\Pi_j^i + g(y_j) > \Pi_m^i + g(y_m)$ for all regions $m \neq j$. Notice that in this case the probability that region j is chosen is a function of the number of firms in each region at the time of choice.

Starting from zero firms in the regions, once again we can allow the industry to grow firm by firm, with the appearance of firm-types subject to known probabilities as in model 1. Again, the pattern of location of the industry will fluctuate somewhat; but in this model, if by a combination of luck and geographical attractiveness a region gets ahead in numbers of firms, its position is enhanced. We can show (see Arthur 1986, for proof) that if agglomeration benefits increase without ceiling as firms are added to a region (that is, if the function g is monotonically increasing without upper bound), then eventually (with probability 1.0) one of the regions will gain enough firms to offer sufficient locational advantages to shut the other regions out in all subsequent locational choices.[3] From then on, each entering firm in the industry will choose this region, and this region's share of the industry will tend to 100 percent with the others' shares tending to 0 percent.

---

3. In the case where g is bounded, several locations can share the industry in the long run. But again, typically, there are multiple possible outcomes, so that chance events matter here too (see Arthur 1983, 1984, 1986, 1987).

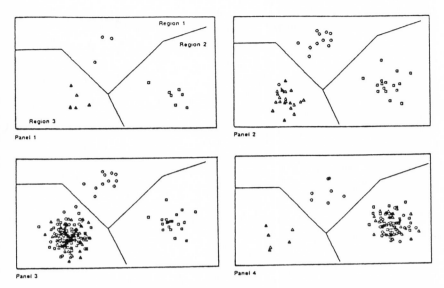

Fig. 3. Two realizations of a locational process with agglomeration economies

Figure 3 shows two realizations of a three-region example with agglomeration economies. The first three panels show the buildup of firms, with geographical preferences dominating in panel 1 but with region 3 in panel 2 by good fortune in the sequence of arrival of firm-types just gaining enough firms to cause another firm-type to favor it instead of its pure geographical preference. In panel 3, region 3 has come to dominate the entire industry in a Silicon Valley-like cluster. Panel 4 shows the outcome of an alternative run. Here the industry is locked in to region 2.

In this model of unbounded agglomeration economies, monopoly of the industry by a single region must occur. But which region achieves this "Silicon Valley" locational monopoly is subject to historical luck in the sequence of firm-types choosing. Chance, of course, is not the only factor here. Regions that are geographically attractive to many firm-types—regions that offer great economic benefits—will have a higher probability of being selected early on. And this will make them more likely to become the single region that dominates the industry. To use an analogy borrowed from genetics, chance events act to "select" the pattern that becomes "fixed"; but regions that are economically attractive enjoy "selectional advantage," with correspondingly higher probabilities of gaining dominance. In this third model the long-run locational pattern is due both to chance and necessity.

Path Dependence and Convexity

Each of our three stylized industry location models includes both determinate economic forces and some source of chance events. Yet each behaves differently. Determinate forces, or historical chance, or a mixture of the two are in turn responsible for the long-run pattern of industry settlement that emerges.

To explain these results and to provide some precise conditions under which historical chance can be important, it is useful to introduce a general framework that encompasses all three models (as well as many others). In this general framework, suppose there are N regions and that industry locates, one firm at a time, starting from a given number of firms in each region. Different economic forces, different sources of chance events, and different mechanisms of locational choice would be possible within this framework, but we do not need to know these. What we do need to know are the probabilities that region 1, region 2, . . . , region N will be chosen next, as a function of current regional shares of the industry x_1, x_2, . . . , x_N. Plotting this function (as in fig. 4 for the two-region case), we might expect that where the probability of a region's receiving the next firm exceeds its current proportion of the industry, it would tend to increase in proportion; and where the probability is less than its current proportion, it would tend to decrease in proportion. Moreover, as firms are added, each new addition changes proportions or shares by an ever smaller magnitude. Therefore proportions should settle down, and fluctuations in proportions should die away. In the long run then, we might expect that regions' proportions (the industry's location pattern) ought to converge to a point—to a vector of locational shares—where proportions equal probabilities, a point that expected motions lead toward (point x in fig. 4). That is, this process ought to end up at a stable fixed point of the proportions-to-probabilities function. It takes powerful theoretical machinery to prove this conjecture, but it turns out to hold under unrestrictive technical conditions (see Hill, Lane, and Sudderth 1980; and Arthur, Ermoliev, and Kaniovski 1983, 1986, 1987).[4] Further, and significantly for us, where there are multiple stable fixed points, each of these would be a candidate for the long-run locational pattern, with different sequences of chance events steering the process toward one of the multiple candidates.

We can now see what happened in our three locational models (fig. 5). The first model, "independent-preferences," has constant probabilities of choice and thus a single fixed point. Therefore, it has a unique, predetermined

---

4. The set of fixed points needs to have a finite number of components. Where the proportions-to-probabilities function itself changes with the number of firms located, as in the agglomeration case, the theorem applies to the limiting function of these changing functions, providing it exists. (See Arthur et al. 1986, 1987.)

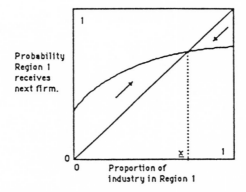

Fig. 4. Proportion-to-probability mapping (arrows indicate expected motions)

outcome. The second model, "spin-off," with probabilities equal to proportions, has every point a fixed point, so that "chance" could drive this locational process to any outcome. The third model, "agglomeration economies," has 0 and 1 as two candidate stable fixed points. Thus, the outcome is not fully predetermined, and one of the candidate solutions is "chosen" by the accumulation of chance events.

When does history matter in the determination of industry location patterns? We can now answer this question, at least for the broad class of models that fit our general framework. History—that is, the small elements outside our economic model that we must treat as random—becomes the determining factor when there are multiple solutions or multiple fixed points in the proportions-to-probabilities mapping. More intuitively, history counts when expected motions of regions' shares do not always lead the locational process toward the same share.

It is useful to associate with each probability function a potential function *V* whose downhill gradient equals the expected motion of regions' shares (see fig. 6).[5] Intuitively, we can think of the process as behaving like a particle attracted by gravity to the lowest points on the potential, subject to random fluctuations that die away. If this potential function is convex (looking upward at it), it has a unique minimum; therefore, the locational process that corresponds to it has a unique determinate outcome which expected motions lead toward and which historical chance cannot influence. If, on the other hand, this potential function is nonconvex, it must have two or more minima with a

---

5. For dimension $N > 2$, a potential function may not exist. This would be the case if there were cycles or more exotic attractors than the single-point cycles considered here.

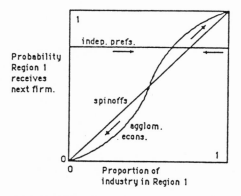

Fig. 5. Probability mappings for the three models

corresponding split in expected motions and with "historical chance" determining which of these is ultimately selected.[6]

To establish nonconvexity, all we need is the existence of at least one unstable point, a "watershed" share of the industry, above which the region with this share exerts enough attraction to increase its share and below which it tends to lose its share. Yet in a way, this is another definition of the presence of agglomeration economies: if above a certain density of settlement a region tends to attract further density, and if below it it tends to lose density, there must be some agglomeration mechanism present. The underlying system will then be nonconvex, and history will count.

Conclusions

Whether small events in history matter in determining the pattern of spatial or regional settlement in the economy reduces, strangely enough, to a question of topology. It reduces to whether the underlying structure of locational forces guiding the locational pattern as it forms is convex or nonconvex. And for this structure to be nonconvex, so that history will matter, some mechanism of agglomeration must be present.

Our models were highly stylized. They considered populations of firms, not people; they assumed that firms lived forever and never moved; and they dealt with the formation of only one industry over time, not several. Neverthe-

---

6. For some early discussion of nonconvexity's importance for the role of history, see David (1975).

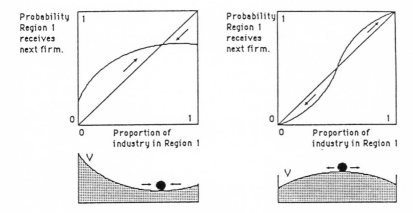

Fig. 6. Convex and nonconvex potential functions

less, even if the mechanisms creating urban systems in the past and present are a great deal more complex, it is still likely that a mixture of economic determinism and historical chance—and not either alone—has formed the spatial patterns we observe. Certain firms, such as steel manufacturers, need to be near sources of raw materials; for them, spatial economic necessity dominates historical chance. Certain other firms, such as gasoline distributors, need to be separated from their competitors in the same industry; for them, the necessity to spread apart again dominates historical chance. But most firms need to be near other firms—if not firms in their own industry, then firms in other industries that act as their suppliers of parts, machinery, and services, or as consumers of their products and services. For this reason, firms are attracted to existing and growing agglomerations. After all, it is this need of firms to be near other firms that causes cities—agglomerative clusters—to exist at all.

Thus, it is highly likely that the system of cities we have inherited is only partly the result of industries' geographical needs, raw material locations, the presence of natural harbors, and transportation costs. It is also the result of where immigrants with certain skills landed, where early settlers met to market foods, where wagon trains stopped for the night, where banking services happened to be set up, and where politics dictated that canals and railroads be built. We therefore cannot explain the observed pattern of cities by economic determinism alone without reference to chance events, coincidences, and circumstances in the past. And without knowledge of chance events, coincidences, and circumstances yet to come, we cannot predict with accuracy the shape of urban systems in the future.

REFERENCES

Arthur, W. B. 1983. Competing technologies and lock-in by historical small events: The dynamics of choice under increasing returns. Center for Economic Policy Research Paper 43. Stanford University.

―――. 1984. Competing technologies and economic prediction. Options. I.I.A.S.A. Laxenburg, Austria, April: 10–13.

―――. 1986. Industry location patterns and the importance of history. Center for Economic Policy Research Paper 84. Stanford University.

―――. 1987. Self-reinforcing mechanisms in economics. In The Economy as an Evolving Complex System. P. W. Anderson and K. J. Arrow, eds. New York: Addison-Wesley.

Arthur, W. B., Y. M. Ermoliev, and Y. M. Kaniovski. 1983. A generalized urn problem and its applications. Cybernetics 19:61–71.

―――. 1986. Strong laws for a class of path-dependent urn processes. In Proceedings of the International Conference on Stochastic Optimization, Kiev 1984, Arkin, Shiryayev, and Wets, eds. New York: Springer, Lecture Notes in Control and Information Sciences 81.

―――. 1987. Path-dependent processes and the emergence of macro-structure. European Journal of Operational Research 30:294–303.

Christaller, W. 1933. Central Places in Southern Germany. Englewood Cliffs, N.J.: Prentice-Hall.

Cohen, D. L. 1984. Locational patterns in the electronics industry: A survey. Stanford University. Mimeo.

David, P. A. 1975. Technical choice, innovation and economic growth. New York: Cambridge University Press.

―――. 1984. High technology centers and the economics of locational tournaments. Stanford University. Mimeo.

Engländer, O. 1926. Kritisches and Positives zu einer allgemeinen reinen Lehre vom Standort. Zeitschrift für Volkswirtschaft und Sozialpolitik. Neue Folge 5.

Hill, G., D. Lane, and W. Sudderth. 1980. Strong convergence for a class of urn schemes. Annals of Probability 8:214–26.

Lösch, A. 1944. The Economics of Location. New Haven, Conn.: Yale University Press, 1954.

Maruyama, M. 1963. The second cybernetics: Deviation amplifying mutual causal processes. American Scientist 51:164–79.

Palander, T. 1935. Beiträge zur Standortstheorie. Stockholm: Almqvist and Wicksell.

Predöhl, A. 1925. Das Standortsproblem in der Wirtschaftslehre. Weltwirtschaftliches Archiv 21:294–331.

Ritschl, H. 1927. Reine und historische Dynamik des Standortes der Erzeugungszweige. Schmollers Jahrbuch 51:813–70.

Thünen, J. H. von. 1826. Der Isolierte Staat in Beziehung auf Landwirtschaft und Nationalökonomie. Hamburg.

Weber, A. 1909. Theory of the Location of Industries. Chicago: University of Chicago Press, 1929.

CHAPTER 7

Self-Reinforcing Mechanisms in Economics

This paper was written for the 1987 conference on the economy as an evolving, complex system that brought together physicists and economists at the Santa Fe Institute for the first time. It surveys the increasing returns and positive feedback literature in economics as it stood in the late 1980s. Some of the material overlaps that of other chapters. But much of it is sufficiently different to warrant including the paper in this volume. I have lightly edited this version to minimize overlap with other chapters.

The paper appeared in *The Economy as an Evolving, Complex System*, edited by Philip Anderson, Kenneth Arrow, and David Pines, in the series *Studies in the Sciences of Complexity*, Addison-Wesley, Reading, Mass., 1988, 9–31.

Dynamical systems of the self-reinforcing or autocatalytic type—systems with local positive feedbacks—in physics, chemical kinetics, and theoretical biology tend to possess a multiplicity of asymptotic states or possible "emergent structures." The initial starting state combined with early random events or fluctuations acts to push the dynamics into the domain of one of these asymptotic states and thus to "select" the structure that the system eventually "locks into."

My purpose in this paper is to look at corresponding dynamical systems in economics. The literature covers a wide range of topics; therefore, I will not claim to give a complete survey. My aim is to show that the presence of self-reinforcing mechanisms, in very different problems drawn from different sub-fields of economics, gives rise to common themes, common features. I will note analogies with physical and biological systems; and I will illustrate with theory wherever it is available.

Conventional economic theory is built largely on the assumption of diminishing returns on the margin (local negative feedbacks); and so it may seem that positive feedback, increasing-returns-on-the-margin mechanisms ought to be rare. Yet there is a sizeable literature on such mechanisms, much of it dating back to the 1920s and 1930s, particularly in international trade theory, industrial organization, regional economics, and economic develop-

The author is grateful to the Guggenheim Foundation for financial support, and to Kenneth Arrow and Stuart Kauffman for comments on an earlier draft.

ment. Self-reinforcement goes under different labels in these different parts of economics: increasing returns; cumulative causation; deviation-amplifying mutual causal processes; virtuous and vicious circles; threshold effects; and nonconvexity. The sources vary. But usually self-reinforcing mechanisms are variants of or derive from four generic sources: large set-up or fixed costs (which give the advantage of falling unit costs to increased output); learning effects (which act to improve products or lower their cost as their prevalence increases) (Arrow 1962; Rosenberg 1982); coordination effects (which confer advantages to "going along" with other economic agents taking similar action); and self-reinforcing expectations (where increased prevalence on the market enhances beliefs of further prevalence).

To fix ideas, consider a concrete example. The video technology Sony Betamax exhibits market self-reinforcement in the sense that increased prevalence on the market encourages video outlets to stock more film titles in Betamax; there are coordination benefits to new purchasers of Betamax that increase with its market share. If Betamax and its rival VHS compete, a small lead in market share gained by one of the technologies may enhance its competitive position and help it further increase its lead. There is positive feedback. If both systems start out at the same time, market shares may fluctuate at the outset, as external circumstances and "luck" change, and as backers maneuver for advantage. And if the self-reinforcing mechanism is strong enough, eventually one of the two technologies may accumulate enough advantage to take 100 percent of the market. Notice however we cannot say in advance *which* one this will be.

Of course, we would need a precise formulation of this example to be able to show that one technology or the other *must* eventually take all of the market. But for the moment, let us accept that conditions exist under which this happens. Notice four properties:

> *Multiple equilibria*. In this problem two quite different asymptotic market-share "solutions" are possible. The outcome is indeterminate; it is not unique and predictable.
>
> *Possible inefficiency*. If one technology is inherently "better" than the other (under some measure of economic welfare), but has "bad luck" in gaining early adherents, the eventual outcome may not be of maximum possible benefit. (In fact, industry specialists claim that the actual loser in the video contest, Betamax, is technically superior to VHS.)
>
> *Lock-in*. Once a "solution" is reached, it is difficult to exit from. In the video case, the dominant system's accrued advantage makes it difficult for the loser to break into the market again.
>
> *Path dependence*. The early history of market shares—in part the conse-

quence of small events and chance circumstances—can determine which solution prevails. The market-share dynamics are nonergodic.

Economists have known that increasing returns can cause multiple equilibria and possible inefficiency at least since Marshall (1891; bk. 4, chap. 13, and app. H). Modern approaches to multiple equilibria and inefficiency can be found in Arrow and Hahn 1971, chap. 9; Brown and Heal 1979; Kehoe 1985; Scarf 1981; among others. In this paper I will concentrate on the less familiar properties of lock-in and path dependence.

Besides these four properties, we might note other analogies with physical and biological systems. The market starts out even and symmetric, yet it ends up asymmetric: there is "symmetry breaking." An "order" or pattern in market shares "emerges" through initial market "fluctuations." The two technologies compete to occupy one "niche" and the one that gets ahead exercises "competitive exclusion" on its rival. And if one technology is inherently superior and appeals to a larger proportion of purchasers, it is more likely to persist: it possesses "selectional advantage."

Why should self-reinforcement (or increasing returns or nonconvexity) cause multiple equilibria? If self-reinforcement is not offset by countervailing forces, local positive feedbacks are present. In turn, these imply that deviations from certain states are amplified. These states are therefore unstable. If the vector field associated with the system is smooth and if its critical points—its "equilibria"—lie in the interior of some manifold, standard Poincaré-index topological arguments (see Dierker 1972; Varian 1975, 1981; Kehoe 1985) imply the existence of other critical points or cycles that *are* stable, or attractors. In this case multiple equilibria must occur. Of course, there is no reason that the number of these should be small. Schelling (1978) gives the practical example of people seating themselves in an auditorium, each with the desire to sit beside others. Here the number of steady-states or "equilibria" would be combinatorial.

Many sub-fields of economics that allow self-reinforcing mechanisms recognize the possibility of multiple "solutions" or equilibria, and are able to locate these analytically. Here are three examples:

1. *International Trade Theory.* The standard example here is that of two countries that each can undertake production in two possible industries (say, aircraft and cars) with large set-up costs or some other source of increasing returns. Statically, a (local minimum) least-cost arrangement would be for one country to produce all of one commodity, the other to produce all of the other. The countries could then trade to arrive at their preferred consumption mixture. But there are two such arrangements. *Which* commodity is produced in which country is

indeterminate. (When the countries differ in size, these two "solutions" or equilibria can have different welfare consequences.) Statically, increasing returns trade theory has demonstrated and located multiple equilibria under a variety of increasing returns mechanisms (for example, Graham 1923; Ohlin 1933; Matthews 1949; Helpman and Krugman 1985). But as yet it does not address the question of how a *particular* trade pattern comes to be selected.

2. *Spatial Economics.* In 1909 Alfred Weber showed that where firms benefit from the local presence of other firms or agglomerations of industry, several configurations of industry can be local-minimum-cost "solutions" to the optimal location problem. Engländer (1926), Palander (1935), and Ritschl (1927) used this to argue that observed industry location patterns might not necessarily be the unique "solution" to a problem of spatial economic equilibrium, but rather the outcome of a process that is subject in part to "historical accident." One "solution"—not necessarily the optimal one—might be "selected" dynamically, in part by the historical sequence of early settlement. Thus, one region might draw ahead in concentration of industry at the expense of the others. Kaldor (1970) argued that regional *prosperity* can also be self-reinforcing, if a region's productivity is tied to its economic growth (as in Verdoorn's "law"). Similarly endowed regions can diverge in income over the long-run. Because of their intuitive appeal, these verbal arguments have had some influence, but until recently (Allen and Sanglier 1981; Faini 1984; Arthur 1986) there have been few attempts to formalize them.

3. *Industrial Organization.* As one example from several possibilities here, Katz and Shapiro (1985, 1986) showed that a combination of "network externalities" (coordination effects) and expectations could lead to multiple market-share equilibria. If, *ex ante,* sufficient numbers of consumers believe that a product—the IBM personal computer, say—will have a large share of the market, and if there are advantages to belonging to a prevalent product's "network" of users, then they will be willing to purchase this product, and the producer will be induced to put a large quantity on the market, fulfilling their beliefs. But the same statement could be made for a competing product. There are therefore multiple "fulfilled-expectation equilibria" that is, multiple sets of eventual (Cournot-equilibrium) market shares that fulfill prior expectations. Here expectations are given and fixed; this is a static model with multiple solutions.

In these three sub-fields the absence of an accepted dynamics means that what I call the *selection problem*—the question of *how* a particular equilibrium comes to be selected from the multiplicity of candidates—is left unresolved.

Other areas of economics that admit self-reinforcing mechanisms do have an accepted, if simple, dynamics that shows how equilibria or steady-states are reached. An example is the neoclassical growth theory of the 1960s. Self-reinforcement occurs here for example when a threshold capital-labor ratio exists, above which sufficient savings are generated that the ratio rises, below which it falls (Solow 1956). There are multiple equilibria. Similarly, recent attempts at an aggregate macrodynamics (Heal 1986), with Walrasian dynamics and unit costs falling with increased output, exhibit two long-run outcomes. One—corresponding to economic health—has high output coupled with high demand and low prices. The other—corresponding to stagflation—has low output coupled with low demand and high prices. In these parts of economics, the presence of multiple steady states is typically analyzed by standard phase-plane methods, often with demonstrations of local stability. Attractors are typically point attractors; only recently has economics begun to analyze richer possibilities.

Lock-in

When a nonlinear physical system finds itself occupying a local minimum of a potential function, "exit" to a neighboring minimum requires sufficient influx of energy to overcome the "potential barrier" that separates the minima. There are parallels to such phase-locking, and to the difficulties of exit, in self-reinforcing economic systems. Self-reinforcement, almost by definition, means that a particular outcome or equilibrium possesses or has accumulated an economic advantage. This advantage forms a potential barrier. We can say that the particular equilibrium is *locked in* to a degree measurable by the minimum cost to effect changeover to an alternative equilibrium.

In many economic systems, lock-in happens dynamically, as sequential decisions "groove" out an advantage that the system finds it hard to escape from. Here is a simple case that recurs in many forms.

Suppose an economic agent—the research and development department of a firm perhaps—can choose each time period to undertake one of N possible activities or projects, $A_1, A_2, A_3, \ldots, A_N$. Suppose activities improve or worsen the more they have been undertaken. A_j pays $\Pi_i(n)$ where n is the number of times it has been previously chosen. Future payoffs are discounted at the rate β.

Theorem. If the payoffs $\Pi_i(n)$ increase monotonically with n, then the activity A_j that is chosen at the outset is chosen at each time thereafter.

Proof. An inductive proof is straightforward.

Thus if activities increase in payoff the more they are undertaken (perhaps because of learning effects), the activity that is chosen first, which depends of course on the discount rate, will continue to be chosen thereafter. The decision sequence "grooves out" a self-reinforcing advantage to the activity chosen initially that keeps it locked in to this choice.

Notice that at each stage, an optimal choice is made under conditions of certainty; and so there can be no conventional economic inefficiency here. But there may exist *regret*. Consider the case of a person who has the choice of practising medicine or law each year. Each activity pays more, the more previous experience has been accumulated. Suppose the rewards to practising law rise rapidly with experience but then flatten out; and those to practising medicine are small initially but eventually surpass those of law. According to the theorem, whichever activity the person chooses, he will continue to choose thereafter. If he has a high discount rate, he will choose law. And this choice will at all stages continue to be rational and superior to the alternative of first-year payoff as a doctor. Yet there may exist *regret,* in the sense that after N years in the law, an equivalent time served in medicine would have paid more at each time into the future. Self-reinforcement can lock a single, rational economic agent in to one activity, but not necessarily the one with the best long-run potential.

Sequential-choice lock-in occurs in the economics of technology (Arthur 1983, 1984). When a new engineering or economic possibility comes along, often several technologies are available to carry it through. Nuclear power, for example, can be generated by light-water, or gas-cooled, or heavy-water, or sodium-cooled reactors. Usually technologies improve with adoption and use. In the case of several initially undeveloped technologies available for adoption, each with the potential of improvement with use, the sequence in which adoptions occur may decide which technologies improve. This time choice is by *different* agents each time—adopters acting in their own individual interest. Where adopters are exactly alike in their preferences, the outcome is trivial. If one of the embryo technologies offers a tiny advantage over the others, it is chosen by the first adopter-developer. It is used and improved. It is therefore chosen by the next developer; it is further improved. And so on. Thus, the adopter sequence can trivially lock in to the development of a technology that shows initial success in partially developed form, but that later turns out inferior in the sense that an equally developed alternative might have eventually delivered more.

Lock-in in a Stochastic Model

It might be objected that this scenario is unrealistic in that lock-in is completely predetermined and razor-edged. The technology with the slightest initial advantage becomes the one that dominates. More reasonably, we might suppose that each technology stands some chance of early development and that "luck" in the form of "random events" can influence the outcome.

As a simple example of this approach (see Arthur 1983), consider two technologies, *A* and *B*, available to a large "market" of potential adopters, both of which improve with adoption. Assume two types of adopters, *R* and *S*, each type equally prevalent, with "natural" preferences for *A* and *B* respectively. For each adopter type, payoffs-to-adoption of *A* or *B* increase linearly with the number of previous adoptions of *A* or *B*. We can inject randomness by assuming that the order of arrival of *R* and *S* types is unknown, and that it is equally likely that an *R* or an *S* will arrive next to make his choice. Once an adopter has chosen, he holds his choice.

Initially at least, if an *R*-agent arrives at the "adoption window" to make his choice, he will adopt *A*; if an *S*-agent arrives, he will adopt *B*. Thus the difference-in-adoptions between *A* and *B* moves up or down by one unit depending on whether the next adopter is an *R* or an *S*; that is, it moves up or down with probability one-half.

However, if by "chance" a sufficient number of *R*-types cumulates in the line of choosers, *A* will be improved in payoff over *B* enough to cause future *S*-types choosing to switch to *A*. From then on, both *R*- and *S*-types will adopt *A*, and only *A*. The adoption process is then locked-in to technology *A*. Similarly, if a sufficient number of *S*-types by "chance" arrives to adopt *B* over *A*, *B* will improve sufficiently to cause future *R*-types to switch to *B*. The process instead locks in to *B*. These dynamics form a random walk with absorbing barriers on each side, the barriers corresponding to the lead in adoption it takes for each agent-type to switch its choice.

In a random walk with absorbing barriers, absorption occurs eventually with probability one. Therefore, in the model I have described, the adoption process *must* lock in to monopoly of one of the two technologies, *A* or *B*. But with the presence of random events, *which* technology is not predictable in advance. The order of arrival of agent types—the source of randomness here—"decides" the eventual outcome.

This lock-in-by-fluctuation to one pattern or structure out of several possible has parallels in thermodynamics, ferromagnetism, laser theory, and chemical kinetics, and in allele fixation through genetic drift. (For example, see Nicolis and Prigogine 1976; Haken 1978; and Roughgarden 1979.)

Does the economy sometimes lock in to a technology that is inferior in development potential, because of small, random events in history? It appears that it does. Cowan (1987) argues that a series of minor circumstances acted to favor light-water nuclear reactors in the mid-1950s over potentially superior competing alternatives, with the result that learning and construction experience gained early on locked the nuclear reactor market in to light water. David, who noted in 1975 "that marked divergences between ultimate out-

comes may flow from seemingly negligible differences in remote begin-
nings," examines (1985) the historical circumstances under which the (probably inferior) QWERTY typewriter keyboard became locked in.

Exit from Lock-in

If an economic system is locked in to an inferior local equilibrium, is "exit" or
escape into a superior one possible? There is rarely in economics any mechanism corresponding to "annealing" (injections of outside energy that "shake"
the system into new configurations so that it finds its way randomly into a
lower cost one). Exit from an inferior equilibrium in economics depends very
much on the source of the self-reinforcing mechanism. It depends on the
degree to which the advantages accrued by the inferior "equilibrium" are
reversible or transferable to an alternative one.

Where learning effects and specialized fixed costs are the source of
reinforcement, usually advantages are not reversible and not transferable to an
alternative equilibrium. Repositioning the system is then difficult. For example, in most countries road and rail are to some degree substitutes as alternative modes of transportation. Each mode is self-reinforcing in that the more
heavily it is used, the more funds become available for investment in capital
improvements that attract further users. Therefore, one mode may achieve
dominance at the expense of the other. But reversing this or trying to assure a
balance may require a significant subsidy to the weaker mode to bring it level
with the advantage accumulated by the dominant mode. Capital assets—the
source of advantage here—are not transferable or easily reversed, and here
repositioning is costly.

Where coordination effects are the source of lock-in, often advantages
are transferable. For example, users of a particular technological standard
may agree that an alternative would be superior, provided everybody
"switched." If the current standard is not embodied in specialized equipment
and its advantage-in-use is mainly that of commonality of convention (like the
rule against turning right on a red light in many states), then a negotiated or a
mandated changeover to a superior collective choice can provide exit into the
new "equilibrium" at negligible cost. Coordination *is* transferable—and possibly by fiat. Even if there is no outside "standard setting" agency, and users
are restricted to noncooperative behavior, Farrell and Saloner (1985, 1986)
show that as long as each user has certainty that the others also prefer the
alternative, each will decide independently to "switch." But where users are
uncertain of others' preferences and intentions, there can be "excess inertia":
each user would benefit from switching to the other standard, as long as the
others go along, but individually none dare change in case others do not
follow. To use Kauffman's terminology (1987), an "adaptive walk to an adja-

cent peak" by nearest neighbor transitions (single-agent switches) is not possible here.

The theme of "exit" by coordination from an inferior low-level equilibrium—a locked-in position—runs through the economic development literature. Examining Eastern Europe's post-war development prospects in 1943, Rosenstein-Rodin argued that, because of increasing returns caused by indivisibilities and complementarities in demand, industries or the firms within them may not find it profitable to expand separately; but if all could expand together via a coordinated effort, the expansion might be profitable to each. Hence development calls for coordinated expansion and investment— for what Rosenstein-Rodin called a "Big Push" on the part of government. These ideas, stimulated by Young's analysis of 1928, influenced a generation of development economists, in particular Hirshman (1958) who further examined "synergistic" or linkage effects between industries; Chenery (1959) who formalized this argument using linear programming; and Myrdal (1957) who pointed to further mechanisms of cumulative causation. A remarkably similar set of ideas has independently emerged in the recent macroeconomic literature (Weitzman 1982). In the presence of increasing returns, large suppliers cannot create sufficient demand to make independent expansion profitable. The economy tends to "stick" below full capacity. Economy-wide coordinated stimulation is needed for exit to full employment.

Path Dependence: Allocation Processes

So far I have given examples of multiple equilibria and the dynamics of lock-in under very particular self-reinforcing mechanisms. Is there a general analytical framework that encompasses problems like these? The answer of course is no. But we might be able to design broad classes of analytical systems that encompass large numbers of examples. In thinking what such systems should look like, we might usefully be guided by three considerations that emerge from the discussion so far:

1. To be able to examine and track how one particular "equilibrium" or "solution" comes to be "selected" from a multiplicity of alternatives requires a dynamic approach. Therefore, we need to allow for the sequence in which actions occur or economic choices are made.
2. Many of the problems that interest us can be cast as problems of allocation or sequential choice between alternatives, where these allocations or choices are affected by the numbers or proportions of each alternative present at the time of choice.
3. Self-reinforcing systems often start off in a "balanced" but unstable position, so that their end-states may be determined by small events

outside the model, as well as by initial conditions. If we treat these small events as perturbations, we need to allow for well-defined sources of randomness. In practice this means that the "state" of the system may not determine the next economic action, but rather the *probability* of the next economic action.

Allocation Processes

Let us consider one general class of dynamical systems that allows for these considerations. I will call these *allocation processes*.

Suppose a unit addition or allocation is made to one of K categories at each time, with probabilities that are a function of the proportion of units currently in the K categories. Time here is event time, not clock time. (In practice we might be considering the build-up of market shares by observing "allocations" of adopters, one at a time, to K technologies; or consumers to K product brands; or, in regional economics, firms to K locations.) Thus, the next unit is added to category i with probability $p_i(x)$ where x is the vector of current proportions or market shares. (The vector of probabilities $p = [p_1(x), p_2(x), \ldots, p_K(x)]$ is a function—the *allocation function*—that maps the unit simplex S^K of proportions into the unit simplex of probabilities). In practice p could be obtained, at least implicitly, from the particular mechanism under consideration. Figure 1 shows two illustrative allocation functions in the case where $K = 2$.

We are interested in how market shares, or equivalently, the numbers or proportions in each category, build up. Our question is what happens to the long-run proportions in such a system. What limiting steady-states can emerge? The standard probability-theory tool for this type of problem is the Borel Strong Law of Large Numbers which makes statements about long-run proportions in processes where increments are added at successive times. But we cannot use the standard Strong Law in our process—we do not have *independent* increments. Instead we have increments—unit allocations to 1 through K—that occur with probabilities influenced by past increments. We have something like a multidimensional coin-tossing problem, where the probability of a unit addition to the category Heads changes with the proportion of Heads tossed previously.

To anticipate results somewhat, we can show that under nonrestrictive technical conditions proportions *must* converge to one of the fixed points of the allocation function p. And where there are self-reinforcing mechanisms, typically there are multiple fixed points of p. We therefore have a useful way to identify the possible "structures" that can "emerge."

Let us look at the dynamics of this process. The process starts at time 1, with an initial vector of allocations $y = (y_1, y_2, \ldots, y_K)$, and initial total

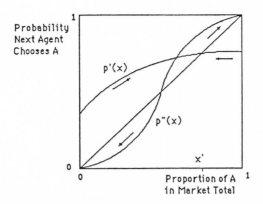

Fig. 1. Two illustrative allocation functions for dimension $K = 2$

$w = \Sigma y_i$. Let Y_n be a vector that describes the number of units in categories 1 through K at time n (when $w + (n - 1)$ units in total have been allocated). Then

$$Y_{n+1} = Y_n + b(X_n); \qquad Y_1 = y; \tag{1}$$

where b is the jth unit vector with probability $p_j (X_n)$.

Dividing Eq. (1) by the total units $w + n$, the vector of proportions in categories 1 through K, or shares, evolves as

$$X_{n+1} = X_n + \frac{1}{n + w} [b(X_n) - X_n]; \qquad X_1 = y/w. \tag{2}$$

We can rewrite Eq. (2) in the form

$$X_{n+1} = X_n + \frac{1}{n + w} [p(X_n) - X_n] + \frac{1}{n + w} \xi(X_n);$$

$$\tag{3}$$

$$X_1 = y/w.$$

where ξ is defined as the random vector

$$\xi(X_n) = b(X_n) - p(X_n).$$

Eq. (3) is the description of the dynamics of shares that we want.

Notice that the conditional expectation of ξ with respect to the current state X_n is zero; hence, we can derive the *expected motion* of the shares or proportions as

$$E(X_{n+1} \mid X_n) - X_n = \frac{1}{n + w} [p(X_n) - X_n]. \tag{4}$$

We will call

$$X_{n+1} = X_n + \frac{1}{n + w} [p(X_n) - X_n] \tag{5}$$

the *equivalent deterministic system* corresponding to our stochastic process. We see that, if the probability $p_j (X_n)$ of an addition to category j is greater than the current proportion $x_j(n)$ in category J, this category's share should increase—at least on an expected basis. Conversely, if the probability is less than the current proportion, it should decrease. Eq. (3) therefore tells us that shares are driven by the equivalent deterministic system (the first and second term on the right), together with a perturbation effect (the third term).

Depending upon the function p—and ultimately on the distribution of preferences and possibilities that defines p—there may be several points x (several market share patterns) at which deterministic motion is zero. These are the fixed points of p, where $p(x) = x$. Some of these are attractor or stable points (defined in the usual way), some are repellant or unstable points. We have the following Strong Law:

Theorem.
i.   Suppose $p : S^K \to S^K$ is continuous, and that the equivalent deterministic system possesses a Lyapunov function v whose motion is negative outside a neighborhood of the set fixed points of p, $B = \{x : p(x) = x\}$. Suppose B has a finite number of connected components. Then the vector of proportions $\{X_n\}$ converges, with probability one, to a point z in the set of fixed points B.
ii. Suppose p maps the interior of the unit simplex into itself and that z is a stable point. Then the process has limit point z with positive probability.
iii. Suppose z is a nonvertex unstable point of p. Then the process cannot converge to z with positive probability.
   Proof. See Arthur, Ermoliev, and Kaniovski (1983, 1986). (For the case $K = 2$ with p stationary, see Hill, Lane, and Sudderth 1980.)

In other words, if allocation processes converge, they must converge to a vector of proportions (shares) represented by one of the attracting fixed points of the mapping from proportions into the probabilities of allocation. Thus in

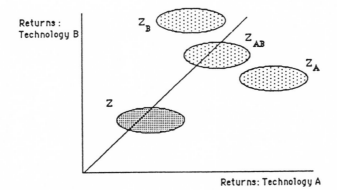

Fig. 2. Distribution of payoffs to adoption of *A* and *B* under a continuum of adopter types

figure 2 the process corresponding to p' converges to x', with probability one; the process corresponding to p'' converges to 0 or to 1, with probability one. Where $p = \underline{p}$, a constant function, the process converges to $\underline{p}$; therefore, the standard strong law (with unit increments added under fixed probabilities) is a special case. Where the allocation function varies with "time" n, this dependent-increment strong-law theorem still goes through, providing that the sequence $\{p_n\}$ converges to a limiting function p faster than $1/n$ converges to zero. The process then converges to one of the stable limit points of p. The theorem can be extended to noncontinuous functions p and to non-unit increments to the allocations (Arthur, Ermoliev, and Kaniovski 1987b).

Allocation processes have a useful property. Fluctuations dominate motions at the outset; hence, they make limit points reachable from any initial conditions. But they die away, leaving the process directed by the equivalent deterministic system and hence convergent to identifiable attractors.

For a given problem, to identify steady-states, we do not need to compute p directly, only its fixed points. A number of studies now use this technique.

Example: When Does Self-Reinforcement Imply Monopoly?

In many models we want to identify "competitive exclusion" or monopoly conditions under which one product, or one technology must eventually gain enough advantage to take 100 percent of the market. In the context of our theorem, we would need to show the existence of stable fixed points only at the vertices of the unit simplex.

As an example, consider a more general version of the "adoption market" model above, in which there is now a continuum of agent types rather than just two. Assume agents—potential adopters—choose between K technologies. Suppose that if n_j previous adopters have chosen technology j previously, the next agent's payoff to adopting j is $\Pi_j(n_j) = a_j + g(n_j)$, where a_j represents the agent's "natural preference" for technology j and the monotonically increasing function g represents the technological improvement that comes with previous adoptions.

Each adopter has a vector of natural preferences $a = (a_1, a_2, \ldots, a_K)$ for the k alternatives, and we can think of the continuum of agents as a distribution of points a (with bounded support Z) on the positive orthant. We assume an adopter is drawn at random from this probability distribution each time a choice is made. (See fig. 2.) The distribution itself shifts either to the right or upward as returns to A or B increase with an adoption of either A or B respectively. Monopoly—in this case lock-in of a single technology—corresponds to positive probability of the distribution of payoffs being driven over the 45° line as the number of adoptions becomes large.

The path-dependent strong law allows us to derive two useful theorems (Arthur 1986). Where the improvement function g increases without upper bound as n_j increases, then the process has stable limit points only at simplex vertices, with probability one. The distribution *must* be driven over the 45° line (as with Z_A and Z_B in fig. 2) and monopoly by one technology must eventually occur. Where returns to adoption increase but are bounded (as when improvement effects become exhausted) monopoly is no longer inevitable. Here certain sequences of adopter types could bid improvements for two or more alternatives upward more or less in concert. These could then reach their increasing returns bounds together, with the adopter payoff distribution still straddled across the 45° line (as with Z_{AB} in fig. 2), and thus with the market shared from then on. The market remains shared from then on. In this case, some "event histories" dynamically lead to a shared market; other event histories lead to monopoly. Competitive exclusion no longer occurs with probability one.

Example: Location by Spin-Off

Consider a particular mechanism in industry location (Arthur 1987b). Assume an industry builds up firm by firm, and firms may locate in one of K possible regions, starting with some set of initial firms, one in each region, say. Assume that new firms are added by "spinning off" from parent firms one at a time; that each new firm stays in its parent region; and that any existing firm is as likely to spin off a new firm as any other. (David Cohen 1984, shows that such spin-offs have been the dominant "birth mechanism" in the U.S. electronics industry.) In this case firms are added incrementally to regions with probabilities exactly equal to the proportions of firms in each region at that time. This random process is therefore a Polya process—a well-known process (see Joel Cohen 1976) that is a special case in our class of allocation processes, one with $p(x) = x$. Any point in the simplex of regions' shares of the industry is now a fixed point; regions' shares can therefore converge to *any* point. There is a continuum of "equilibrium points." From Polya theory we can say more. The random limit vector to which the process must converge has a uniform distribution on the unit simplex. (We could think of a representative outcome—regions' shares of the industry—as the result of placing $N - 1$ points on the unit interval at random, and partitioning the interval at these points to obtain N "shares.") In this model "chance" dominates completely. "Historical accident" in the shape of the early random sequence of spin-offs becomes the sole determining factor of the limiting regional pattern of industry.

Path-Dependence: Recontracting Processes

Allocation processes, as a class of models, might be appropriate for studying how an allocative pattern forms—providing choices made are irreversible. A different, useful class of model would allow recontracting within the market once it has formed. These would assume an already formed "market" or total allocation of fixed size T, divided among K categories. (For example, T hectares of land divided among K landowners; T firms divided among K regions; T voters divided among K candidates.) Transitions of units between categories are possible, with probabilities that depend in general on the market shares, or numbers in each category. Thus, self-reinforcement (or self-inhibition) are once again possible.

We have the advantage that models of this fixed-size, Markov-transition kind are standard in genetics (Ewens 1979), epidemiology, and in parts of physics (Haken 1978). Consider a special, but useful case, where $K = 2$, and transitions can be made only one unit at a time. (Here I follow Weidlich and Haag 1983). To keep matters concrete suppose a total "market" or "population" of $T = 2N$ voters with state variable m, where $N + m$ voters prefer candidate A, and $N - m$ voters prefer candidate B. Let $p_{AB}(m)$ denote the probability that a voter changes preference from A to B, and $p_{BA}(m)$ the probability that a voter changes preference from B to A, in unit time. Then the probability $P(m,t)$ of finding the system at state m at time t (strictly speaking a measure on an ensemble of such systems) evolves as:

$$P(m,t + 1) = P(m,t)[1 - p_{AB}(m) - p_{BA}(m)]$$

$$+ P(m + 1,t)p_{BA}(m + 1) + P(m - 1,t)p_{AB}(m - 1) \qquad (6)$$

which yields the Master Equation

$$\frac{dP(m,t)}{dt} = [P(m + 1,t)p_{BA}(m + 1) - P(m,t)p_{BA}(m)]$$

$$+ [P(m - 1,t)p_{AB}(m - 1) - P(m,t)p_{AB}(m)]. \tag{7}$$

Normalizing to variable x in the continuous interval $(-1,1)$, by setting

$$x = m/N; \quad \epsilon = 1/N; \quad P(x,t) = NP(m,t);$$

$$R(x) = [p_{AB}(m) - p_{BA}(m)]/N; \quad \text{and} \quad Q(x) = [p_{AB}(m) + p_{BA}(m)]/N;$$

we can rewrite Eq. (7) in the form of a one-dimensional Fokker-Planck diffusion equation

$$\frac{\partial P(x,t)}{\partial t} = -\frac{\partial}{\partial x} R(x)P(x,t) + \frac{\epsilon}{2}\frac{\partial^2}{\partial x^2} Q(x)P(x,t). \tag{8}$$

We can substitute particular drift and diffusion functions, R and Q corresponding to particular transition mechanisms and study the evolution of P over time, and its stationary, limiting distribution. In many cases it is possible to solve explicitly for the stationary distribution $P(x)$.

The important difference from allocation process models is that in this type of process transitions in market share remain of constant order of magnitude (rather than fall off at rate $1/n$). "Recontracting processes" therefore show convergence in distribution rather than strong convergence to a point. Unless they have absorbing states, permanent lock-in to one market position is not possible. Instead they exhibit "punctuated equilibria" in the shape of sojourns in the neighborhood of local maxima and transitions between them.

Example: Market Shares with a Conformity Effect

Suppose a luxury car market (of size $2N$) is divided between American and German cars, denoted A and B. Suppose consumers change their preference occasionally, according to

$$p_{AB}(m) = \nu \exp(\delta + \kappa m)(N - m) \quad \text{and}$$

$$p_{BA}(m) = \nu \exp - (\delta + \kappa m)(N + m)$$

where ν denotes frequency of "switches;" δ allows for a preference bias; and κ corresponds to a fashion or conformity effect (Weidlich and Haag 1983). In

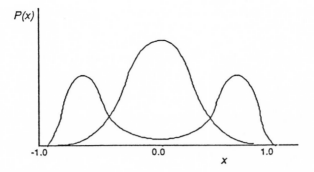

Fig. 3. Stationary distributions of *P*(*x*) for κ = 0.5 and κ = 1.3

the absence of conformity, a larger population of one car type increases the chance of "switches" to the other. Hence there is a centralizing tendency. But this is offset by the conformity effect, which reinforces a concentration of one type. When κ is small, centralization dominates and the stationary distribution is unimodal (fig. 3). But as κ increases the distribution bifurcates and becomes bimodal, with maxima corresponding to the relative prevalence of one type of car over the other. In this case the market lingers at prevalence of one type of car with intermittent transitions to prevalence of the other.

Some Other Questions

Strategic Action

So far, most of the theory and examples I have given do not deal explicitly with the possibility of strategic action—the possibility that economic agents adjust their actions to take into account the possible responses of other agents. Strategic action does not negate the methods or frameworks discussed above. But it can add an overlay of difficulty to the derivation of allocation functions, transition probabilities, and the like.

There are now a number of studies that examine market structure in the presence of strategic action and self-reinforcement. Flaherty (1980) looks at the case where firms can strategically invest to reduce their costs. Multiple (open-loop, noncooperative) equilibria result. Under reasonable conditions, only those equilibria that are asymmetric—where single firms become dominant in market share—are stable. Fudenberg and Tirole (1983) use learning effects as the source of reinforcement and investigate closed-loop, perfect equilibria. Again they find multiple equilibria. (The analysis here, strangely, concentrates on the symmetric equilibrium—the only one likely to be unstable.)

These studies are (deterministically) dynamic in the sense that they derive trajectories that fulfill the usual Nash condition. To examine how one trajectory from the multiplicity of candidates is "selected" however, we need to push the analysis one stage further back and ask how a trajectory itself comes to be chosen or "fallen into." Spence (1981) goes part way toward this, by showing in *ad-hoc* fashion that the order in which firms enter the market makes a difference.

Hanson (1985) allows randomness to solve the "selection" problem, in the case of self-reinforcing duopoly dynamics. In a version of the stochastic adopter-sequence model above, he assumes that the two technologies that improve with adoption are *proprietary* (like VHS and Betamax)— "sponsored" by firms that can manipulate their price. Firms price low early on, possibly taking losses in exchange for market share. If both firms are evenly enough matched to stay in the market, sooner or later the cumulation of "chance events" may allow one firm sufficient adoption advantage to gradually tip the market in its favor. It can then raise its price and take monopoly profits, while keeping the other firm on the contestable margin of the market. Hanson details conditions under which monopoly by a single firm occurs with probability one. It is clear, however, that conditions can also be constructed where markets end up shared. For example, when firms discount heavily so that they are mainly interested in present sales, neither firm may have sufficient incentive to price low early on. Neither eventually wins the "natural customers" of the other with positive probability and the result is a shared market.

Expectations

In the Katz and Shapiro model mentioned earlier, expectations are rational and fulfilled, but static—fixed at the outset. We might assume more generally that agents modify their expectations as market shares change. Suppose agents form beliefs or expectations in the shape of probabilities on the future states of the market process—probabilities that are conditioned on market share or absolute numbers of competing alternatives. We now have a *rational-expectations equilibrium* if the *actual* adoption process that results from agents acting on these beliefs turns out to have conditional probabilities that are identical to the *believed* process. Under increasing returns, if one product gets ahead by "chance," its increased probability of doing well in the market will further enhance expectations of its success. In general, expectations may interact with self-reinforcing mechanisms to further destabilize an already unstable situation. Little work has been done here yet, but it appears that the presence of dynamic, rational expectations leads more easily to monopoly outcomes (Arthur 1985).

Policy

Where there are multiple equilibria and a central authority favors a particular one, it can of course attempt to "tilt" the market toward this outcome. Timing is crucial here: in David's phrase (1986) there are only "narrow windows" in which policy is effective.

In many cases, however, especially where learning is the source of self-reinforcement, it is not clear in advance which equilibrium outcome has most potential promise. A central authority then faces the problem of choosing which improving products, or processes, or technologies to subsidize. This yields a version of the multi-arm bandit problem. Cowan (1988) shows that, where central authorities subsidize increasing-return technologies on the basis of their current estimates of future potential, locking into inferior technologies is less likely than in the uncontrolled adoption case. But it is still possible. An early run of bad luck with a potentially superior technology may cause the central authority, perfectly rationally, to abandon it. Even with central control, escape from inferior outcomes is not guaranteed.

It may sometimes be desirable to keep a multiple-equilibrium market "balanced" to avoid monopoly problems or to retain "requisite variety" as a hedge against future shifts in the economic environment. The question of using well-timed subsidies to prevent the "tipping" and lock-out has not yet been looked at. But its structure—that of artificially stabilizing a naturally unstable dynamical process—is a standard one in stochastic feedback control theory.

Spatial Mechanisms

Economic agents may be influenced by neighboring agents' choices. Puffert (1988) examines historical competitions between railroad gauges where rail companies found it advantageous to adopt a gauge that neighboring railroads were using. Spatial mechanisms have parallels with Ising models and renormalization theory in physics (Holly 1974) and with voter models in probability theory (Liggett 1979; Föllmer 1979). In economics very little work has yet been done on spatial self-reinforcing mechanisms.

REFERENCES

Allen, P., and M. Sanglier. 1981. "Urban Evolution, Self-Organization, and Decision Making." *Environment and Planning A*, 13:167–83.
Arrow, K. 1962. "The Economic Implications of Learning by Doing." *Rev. Econ. Stud.* 29:155–73.

Arrow, K., and F. Hahn. 1971. *General Competitive Analysis.* New York: Holden-Day.

Arthur, W. B. 1983. "Competing Technologies and Lock-In by Historical Events: The Dynamics of Allocation under Increasing Returns." I.I.A.S.A. Paper WP-83-90, Laxenburg, Austria. Revised as C.E.P.R. Paper 43, Stanford University, 1985.

———. 1984. "Competing Technologies and Economic Prediction." *Options.* Laxenburg, Austria: I.I.A.S.A.

———. 1986. "Industry Location and the Importance of History." Center for Economic Policy Research, Paper 84. Stanford University.

———. 1987a. "Competing Technologies: An Overview." *Technical Change and Economic Theory,* eds. G. Dosi, C. Freeman, R. Nelson, G. Silverberg, and L. Soete. London: Pinter.

———. 1987b. "Urban Systems and Historical Path-Dependence." *Urban Systems and Infrastructure,* eds. R. Herman and J. Ausubel. NAS/NAE.

Arthur, W. B., Y. M. Ermoliev, and Y. M. Kaniovski. 1983. "On Generalized Urn Schemes of the Polya Kind." *Kibernetika* 19:49–56. English trans. *Cybernetics* 19:61–71.

———. 1986. "Strong Laws for a Class of Path-Dependent Urn Processes." Proc. International Conf. on Stochastic Optimization, Kiev 1984. Lect. Notes in Control and Info. Sciences 81, eds. V. Arkin, A. Shiryayev, and R. Wets. New York: Springer.

———. 1987a. "Path-Dependent Processes and the Emergence of Macro-Structure." *European J. Operational Research* 30:294–303.

———. 1987b. "Non-Linear Urn Processes: Asymptotic Behavior and Applications." *Kibernetika.*

Brown, D., and G. Heal. 1979. "Equity, Efficiency and Increasing Returns." *Rev. Econ. Stud.* 46:571–85.

Chenery, H. 1959. "The Interdependence of Investment Decisions." *Allocation of Economic Resources,* ed. M. Abramovitz. Stanford: Stanford University Press, 82–120.

Cohen, D. L. 1984. "Locational Patterns in the Electronics Industry: A Survey." Mimeo, Stanford University.

Cohen, J. 1976. "Irreproducible Results and the Breeding of Pigs." *Bioscience* 26: 391–94.

Cowan, R. 1987. "Backing the Wrong Horse: Sequential Technology Choice under Increasing Returns." Ph.D. Diss. Stanford University.

David, P. 1975. *Technical Choice Innovation and Economic Growth.* London: Cambridge University Press.

———. 1985. "Clio and the Economics of QWERTY." *Amer. Econ. Rev. Proc.* 75:332–37.

———. 1986. "Some New Standards for the Economics of Standardization in the Information Age." Paper 79, Center for Economic Policy Research, Stanford University.

Dierker, E. 1972. "Two Remarks on the Number of Equilibria of an Economy." *Econometrica* 40:951–53.

Engländer, O. 1926. "Kritisches und Positives zu einer allgemeinen reinen Lehre vom Standort." *Zeitschrift für Volkswirtschaft und Sozialpolitik.* Neue Folge 5.

Ewens, W. J. 1979. *Mathematical Population Genetics.* New York: Springer.

Faini, R. 1984. "Increasing Returns, Non-Traded Inputs and Regional Development." *Econ. J.* 94:308–23.

Farrell, J., and G. Saloner. 1985. "Standardization, Compatibility, and Innovation." *Rand J. Econ.* 16:70–83.

———. 1986. "Installed Base and Compatibility." *Amer. Econ. Rev.* 76:940–55.

Flaherty, M. T. 1980. "Industry Structure and Cost-Reducing Investment." *Econometrica* 48:1187–1209.

Föllmer, H. 1979. "Local Interactions with a Global Signal: A Voter Model." *Lecture Notes in Biomath 38.* New York: Springer.

Fudenberg, D., and J. Tirole. 1983. "Learning by Doing and Market Performance." *Bell J. Econ.* 14:522–30.

Graham, F. D. 1923. "Some Aspects of Protection Further Considered." *Quart. J. Econ.* 37:199–227.

Haken, H. 1978. *Synergetics.* New York: Springer Verlag.

Hanson, W. A. 1985. "Bandwagons and Orphans: Dynamic Pricing of Competing Systems Subject to Decreasing Costs." Ph.D. Diss. Stanford University.

Heal, G. 1986. "Macrodynamics and Returns to Scale." *Econ. J.* 96:191–98.

Helpman, E., and P. Krugman. 1985. *Market Structure and Foreign Trade.* Cambridge: MIT Press.

Hill, B., D. Lane, and W. Sudderth. 1980. "Strong Convergence for a Class of Urn Schemes." *Annals Prob.* 8:214–26.

Hirshman, A. 1958. *The Strategy of Economic Development.* New Haven: Yale University Press.

Holly, R. 1974. "Recent Results on the Stochastic Ising Model." *Rocky Mtn. J. Math.* 4:479–96.

Kaldor, N. 1970. "The Case for Regional Policies." *Scottish J. Pol. Econ.* 17:337–48.

Katz, M., and C. Shapiro. 1985. "Network Externalities, Competition, and Compatibility." *Amer. Econ. Rev.* 75:424–40.

———. 1986. "Technology Adoption in the Presence of Network Externalities." *J. Pol. Econ.* 94:822–41.

Kauffman, S. 1987. "Towards a General Theory of Adaptive Walks on Rugged Landscapes." *J. Theor. Biol.* 128:11–45.

Kehoe, T. J. 1985. "Multiplicity of Equilibria and Comparative Statics." *Quart. J. Econ.* 100:119–47.

Liggett, T. 1979. "Interacting Markov Processes." *Lect. Notes in Biomath 38.* New York: Springer.

Marshall, A. 1891. *Principles of Economics.* 8th ed. London: Macmillan.

Maruyama, M. 1963. "The Second Cybernetics: Deviation-Amplifying Mutual Causal Processes." *Amer. Scien.* 57:164–79.

Matthews, R. C. O. 1949. "Reciprocal Demand and Increasing Returns." *Rev. Econ. Stud.*: 149–158.

Myrdal, G. 1957. *Economic Theory and Underdeveloped Regions.* London: Duckworth.

Nicolis, G., and I. Prigogine. 1976. *Self-Organization in Nonequilibrium Systems: From Dissipative Structures to Order through Fluctuations.* New York: John Wiley and Sons.

Ohlin, B. 1933. *Interregional and International Trade*. Cambridge: Harvard University Press.

Palander, T. 1935. *Beiträge zur Standortstheorie*. Stockholm: Almqvist and Wicksell.

Puffert, D. 1988. "Network Externalities and Technological Preference in the Selection of Railway Gauges." Ph.D. Diss. Stanford University.

Ritschl, H. 1927. "Reine und historische Dynamik des Standortes der Erzeugungszweige." *Schmollers Jahrbuch* 51:813–70.

Rosenberg, N. 1982. *Inside the Black Box: Technology and Economics*. Cambridge: Cambridge University Press.

Rosenstein-Roden, P. N. 1943. "Problems of Industrialization of Eastern and South-Eastern Europe." *Econ. J.* 55:202–11.

Roughgarden, J. 1979. *Theory of Population Genetics and Evolutionary Ecology*. New York: Macmillan.

Scarf, H. 1981. "Indivisibilities: Part I." *Econometrica* 49:1–32.

Schelling, T. 1978. *Micromotives and Macrobehavior*. New York: Norton.

Solow, R. 1956. "A Contribution to the Theory of Economic Growth." *Quart. J. Econ.* 70:65–94.

Spence, M. 1981. "The Learning Curve and Competition." *Bell. J. Econ.* 12:49–70.

Varian, H. 1975. "A Third Remark on the Number of Equilibria in an Exchange Economy." *Econometrica* 43:985–86.

————. 1981. "Dynamical Systems with Applications to Economics." Vol. 1, *Handbook of Mathematical Economics,* eds. K. Arrow and M. Intriligator. New York: North Holland.

Weber, A. 1909. *Theory of the Location of Industries*. Chicago: University of Chicago Press.

Weidlich, W., and G. Haag. 1983. *Concepts and Models of a Quantitative Sociology*. New York: Springer.

Weitzman, M. 1982. "Increasing Returns and the Foundations of Unemployment Theory." *Econ. J.* 92:787–804.

Young, A. 1928. "Increasing Returns and Economic Progress." *Econ. J.* 38:527–42.

CHAPTER 8

Path Dependence, Self-Reinforcement, and Human Learning

On first thoughts it may appear that the subjects of learning in the economy and of increasing returns have little in common with each other. But in fact there is a strong connection between the two. I show in this paper that a very common context of learning can be viewed as competition among beliefs or actions, with inherent reinforcement of those that pay off well. But as such, the learning process may then lock-in to actions that are not necessarily optimal nor predictable, by the influence of small events.

This paper developed from studies of the dynamics of learning in John Holland's classifier system, where the problem is to design a "classifier competition" algorithm that learns to choose high-payoff actions in a repeated multichoice (or multiarm bandit) setting. The resulting algorithm turns out to replicate actual human learning behavior to a high degree. It can therefore be used to replace the idealized, perfectly rational agents in appropriate neoclassical models with calibrated, "artificially intelligent agents" that represent *actual* human behavior.

The paper appeared in 1990 as Santa Fe Institute Paper 90-026. It was published by the *Journal of Evolutionary Economics,* under the title "On Designing Economic Agents that Behave like Human Agents," 3 (1993):1–22. I have rewritten the first two sections and the conclusion to be more consonant with the themes of this book. A shorter version, "Designing Economic Agents that Act like Human Agents: A Behavioral Approach to Bounded Rationality," appeared in *American Economic Review* (Papers and Proceedings) May 1991.

There is a strong connection between increasing-returns mechanisms and learning problems. Much of learning in fact can be viewed as dynamic competition among different hypotheses or beliefs or actions, with some reinforced and others weakened as fresh evidence and data are obtained. Such competition with reinforcement happens within the brain at the Hebbian neural-synapse level in a literal way—biochemically—when primitive learn-

I thank in particular both John Holland and Richard Herrnstein whose ideas on adaptive behavior and learning did much to stimulate this paper. I also thank Kenneth Arrow, Vincent Crawford, Frank Hahn, David Lane, David Rumelhart, Andrzej Ruszczynski, and Tom Sargent for their insights and discussion, without implicating them in the views expressed here.

ing takes place. And it happens at a higher level in decision problems when agents choose repeatedly among alternative actions whose consequences are to some degree random. In this case agents emphasize or reinforce the choices that appear most promising as they receive information on their consequences from the environment.

My purpose in this paper is to explore the connection between increasing returns and learning in this context of agents choosing repeatedly among discrete actions with initially unknown, random consequences. To do this I will examine the consequences of a family of learning algorithms that appears to fit human learning behavior in this context.

There is a second purpose to constructing and understanding algorithms that fit human learning in the repeated decision context. Modern machine-learning methods from computer science are introducing into economics the possibility of replacing the theoretical, perfectly-rational agents within standard neoclassical models with sophisticated learning algorithms— "artificially-intelligent agents"—that can gather information, improve their actions as they receive feedback from their environment, make sudden discoveries, and "learn to learn" at a meta-level. Such algorithms are used typically when we want to represent humans as "boundedly rational."[1] But while they capture qualitatively the inductive nature of human learning, there is no guarantee they represent actual human learning. If we want to capture bounds to human rationality realistically then, we need to use learning algorithms calibrated against actual human behavior. Ideally in fact we would want to calibrate to reproduce not just the speed of real human learning, but also its style, and its departures from perfect rationality. Neoclassical models containing such calibrated "artificial agents" would then display behavior grounded upon actual behavior and would be useful to contrast with models built upon idealized human behavior.

This exercise of constructing and calibrating algorithms to fit actual human learning behavior, which we may use in designing "artificial agents," allows us to ask several questions. If we succeed in representing human learning by a calibrated algorithm in the iterated choice context, and such learning exhibits elements of self-reinforcement, can we learn our way into multiple (and possibly inferior) decision equilibria? Is learning path-dependent? How fast do humans learn? And in what ways does human learning depart from idealized, "rational" learning?[2]

---

1. For example, see Marimon, McGrattan, and Sargent (1989); Arifovic (1990); and Miller (1989).

2. The interesting recent work of Fudenberg and Kreps (1988) and Milgrom and Roberts (1989) also asks this question. This approach checks putative human learning behavior against particular, well-chosen sets to axioms, to test whether asymptotic behavior will result in standard outcomes. Other learning studies, for example Bray (1982), Marcet and Sargent (1989), view learning as the recursive estimation of parameters within well-defined neoclassical models.

The first section of the paper discusses the iterated multi-choice problem. The second part develops the family of learning algorithms we shall use, interprets them and shows that whether they converge to choosing the "optimal" action in the limit depends on their parameter values. The third part calibrates the algorithm parameters against available human data and shows that the algorithm can replicate human behavior to a high degree. The resulting parameters, it turns out, lie outside the range that guarantees long-run optimality. The last section discusses the possibility of lock-in to inferior actions and shows that the likelihood this happens depends on the degree to which the best action is easy to discriminate from the others. It also explores the possibilities of using this algorithm to represent learning agents in normal-form games and in more general neoclassical models in economics.

The Problem

The problem I will consider here is the well-known iterated-choice problem. The decision maker must choose one of N actions at each time, where the actions result in random payoffs or profits drawn from a stationary distribution that is unknown in advance. For example, the decision maker—a firm, government agency, or consumer, for example—might be faced with a choice among N alternative pricing schemes, or policy options, or research projects, or design features, or personnel policies, each with consequences that are poorly understood at the outset and that vary from "trial" to "trial." The agent chooses one of these at each time, observes its consequence or payoff, and over time updates his choice as a result.

What makes this iterated-choice problem interesting is the tension between *exploitation* of knowledge gained and *exploration* of poorly understood actions. At the beginning many actions will be explored or tried out in an attempt to gain information on their consequences. But in the desire to gain payoff, the agent will begin to emphasize or exploit the "better" ones as they come to the fore. This reinforcement of "good" actions is both natural and economically realistic in this iterated-choice context; and any reasonable algorithm will be forced to take account of it. The question is whether it leads to a convergence of choices to the action with maximal expected payoff over time.

It is easy to imagine cases in which learning may converge upon nonoptimal choices. For example one possible action—drilling for oil in a particular tract—when chosen may result in consistent payoffs clustered around $10M. An alternative—drilling in another tract—may pay zero the first ten times it is undertaken. But there may be 5 percent chance it pays $500M. There is no supposition that the agent—or any learning algorithm—knows this in advance; and it may take considerable exploration to find this out.

Whether learning incorporates enough exploration to eventually uncover and home in on the optimal action will be of interest to us in what follows.

Before I develop a behavioral algorithm that might capture how boundedly-rational humans handle the tradeoff between exploitation and exploration in this problem, let us glance briefly at the perfect-rationality version of the problem. This supposes that an agent must choose repeatedly among N actions that deliver payoffs chosen randomly from a given set of stationary distributions, $F_1, \ldots, F_N$. The agent wishes to maximize a given criterion, typically expected discounted payoff over an infinite horizon. He possesses known, subjective prior distributions on the payoff distributions and updates these in a Bayesian way according to the payoffs experienced for the actions chosen. Defined this way, the problem becomes a multiarm-bandit problem, normally solved by a dynamic programming argument.[3]

The technical details of the solution need not concern us here. What is interesting is the character of the optimal strategy. Under zero discounting it pays to explore forever, so that the agent is assured, in the limit, of converging upon the optimal action. But under positive discounting, it is optimal after some time to narrow choices down to exploit higher payoff actions; and eventually to concentrate on one and choose it alone forever. Sometimes this may be the action with the highest expected payoff. But sometimes it will be an inferior action. This happens when early disappointing payoffs on the superior action make it *appear* unpromising and not worth exploring further; so that exploration of it ceases and learning concentrates upon and "locks in" to a lower-payoff alternative.

Thus in the pure rational-learning case, reinforcement of high-payoff actions occurs naturally, as noted above. But under positive discounting, it may cause lock-in to one of several possible actions: there are multiple equilibria. And the action "selected" in the long-run depends on the random consequences of earlier choices: there is path dependence. This of course is well known in the bandit literature. But it implies that multiple equilibria, path dependence, possibly inefficient outcomes (relative to the perfect-information one), nonpredictability, and lock-in—the standard increasing returns properties—cannot be escaped under rational learning in the presence of positive discounting.

The bandit formulation is of course a normative ideal that does not stand up well against actual human behavior. There is evidence that humans deviate systematically from Bayesian updating (Camerer 1987). And the formulation assumes that agents know the parametrized form of the distribution that gener-

---

3. For an overview of bandit problems, see D. A. Berry and B. Fristedt, *Bandit Problems,* New York: Chapman and Hall, 1985. See also M. Rothschild, "A Two-Armed Bandit Theory of Market Pricing," *J. Economic Theory* 9:185–202, 1974.

ates the payoffs, which is not the case we are considering. Thus we might ask whether the possibilities of path dependency and lock-in carry over to *actual, boundedly-rational human learning*. To answer this, let us explore a class of algorithms that represents actual human behavior and examine *its* consequences.

A Family of Learning Algorithms

How do humans proceed in actual choice behavior? We may think of "learning" in this iterated-choice context as updating the probabilities of choosing actions, as information on their consequences is received. An algorithm that does this is called a *stochastic learning* or *probability learning algorithm* in the psychology literature (Bush and Mosteller 1955; Bush and Estes 1959; Neimark and Estes 1967). One possibility would be to draw upon one of these available algorithms in the psychological literature. These however are unsuitable for several reasons. They concentrate for the most part on two-choice problems where the consequences of the actions are the qualitative values "correct" or "incorrect." Payoffs that are monetary, and random, are difficult to cope with for these algorithms. And often they were designed to converge asymptotically to probability matching. Thus if one action pays one unit randomly 70 percent of the time and the other one unit randomly 30 percent of the time, they converge to triggering the two actions in the ratio 70:30. While there is some support for such behavior in some laboratory experiments, it is unlikely that in the real economy, with actual profits at stake, decision makers would not go for an economic "edge" where it is obvious and easily learned. We do not want to enforce asymptotic optimality in the algorithm, but we do not want to rule it out at the beginning either.

The Algorithm

An algorithm that chooses among alternative actions is called a *learning automaton* in the machine-learning literature (Tsypkin 1973; Narendra and Thathachar 1989). I will use this term here. Consider then a learning automaton that represents a single agent who can undertake one action of N possible actions at each time and who updates his probabilities of taking each action on the basis of the payoffs or outcomes he experiences. Action i brings reward $\Phi(i)$ which is unknown to the agent in advance, is positive, and in general is distributed randomly. The vector of rewards Φ has a stationary distribution.

The automaton—our artificial agent—"learns" via the following simple algorithm. It associates a vector of *strengths*, S_t, with the actions 1 through N, at each time t. C_t is the current sum of these strengths (the component sum of S_t), and the initial strength vector S_0 is strictly positive. The vector p_t represents the agent's probabilities of taking actions 1 through N at time t.

At each time t, the agent:

1. Calculates the probability vector as the relative strengths associated with each action. That is it sets $p_t = S_t/C_t$
2. Chooses one action from the set according to the probabilities p_t and triggers that action
3. Observes the payoff received and updates strengths by adding the chosen action's j's payoff to action j's strength. That is, where action j is chosen, it sets the strengths to $S_t + \beta_t$ where $\beta_t = \Phi(j)e_j$; (e_j is the jth unit vector)
4. Renormalizes the strengths to sum to a pre-chosen constant. That is it sets $C_t = C$.

This algorithm has a simple behavioral interpretation. We may think of the above strength vector as summarizing the current confidence the agent or automaton has learned to associate with actions 1 through N. The confidence associated with an action increases according to the (random) payoff it brings in when taken. This accords well with psychological studies of human choice.[4] The automaton chooses its action with probabilities proportional to its current confidence in the N actions and learning takes place as these probabilities of actions are updated. The summed confidence in all actions is constrained to be constant. S_0, the initial confidence in the actions, represents prior beliefs, possibly carried over from past experience. The speed of learning in this algorithm will turn out to be proportional to $1/C$. Hence C defines a one-parameter family that can be used to fit the algorithm to human behavior.

Notice the algorithm does not ask that the problem be well-defined, or the payoffs stationary, or even that the reasoning be conscious. Most important, it ensures that actions that pay-off better build up "strength" or confidence faster, so that over time superior actions are more likely to be chosen and inferior actions are more likely to be dropped.

The algorithm also has a machine-learning interpretation. A Holland-type *classifier* is a condition/action couple (e.g., "if object appears in left vision field/turn toward object"), where the action is allowed to be activated only if the condition is fulfilled.[5] In a *classifier system*, classifiers are concatenated into an interdependent network, with actions taken serving as conditions

---

4. These behavioral observations have been the basis of the psychological theory of iterated choice at least since Tolman in 1932 and Hull in 1943. In both Tolman and Hull choice or response frequency reflects a latent property of *response strength*. The algorithm bears similarities to the main models of stochastic learning in the psychological literature (Sternberg 1963), being perhaps closest to Luce's (1959) "beta response-strength model," where strengths are updated by multiplicative factors rather than additive factors as here.

5. For classifier systems see Holland *et al.* (1987), Holland (1986), and Goldberg (1989).

for triggering choice among further, dependent actions. If several classifiers have the same condition and that condition is fulfilled, they "compete" to be the one activated. Our algorithm can be viewed then as a set of N classifiers each competing to trigger its own action, where classifier j is the simple couple "if it is time to act / take action j." As is standard in classifier systems, strengths are associated with the classifiers; one classifier is triggered on the basis of current strengths; and the strength of the chosen classifier is updated by the associated reward.

Notice that the algorithm allows reinforcement of promising actions in a natural way. Actions that pay-off well are further strengthened or reinforced and are frequently taken, as in the classic Hebb's rule (Hebb 1949). It is also stochastic in that actions are triggered randomly on the basis of current probabilities, and rewards are drawn randomly from a distribution. Heuristically, reinforcement allows for the exploitation of "useful" actions—ones that pay well tend to be strengthened early on and therefore to be heavily emphasized. And the stochastic property—triggering actions randomly on the basis of their strength—allows for exploration: if a little used action brings in a "jackpot" it may be strengthened sufficiently to become a frequent action.

It will sometimes be useful to work with a more general version of the algorithm. This replaces the renormalization *constant* in step four with a renormalization *sequence*, $C_t = Ct^\nu$. The parameters C and ν, fixed in advance, now define a two-parameter family of algorithms that can be used to calibrate the automaton. C varies the speed as before, and ν now provides a deceleration of "annealing" term in the learning.

Dynamics of the Learning Behavior

To see more clearly how the algorithm works, I now turn to its dynamics. Begin with steps 3 and 4 of the algorithm. From these the strength vector is updated as

$$S_{t+1} = \frac{C_{t+1}}{C_t + B_t} (S_t + \beta_t) \tag{1}$$

where the scalar random variable B_t is the component sum of the vector β_t. We may rewrite this as

$$\frac{S_{t+1}}{C_{t+1}} = \frac{S_t}{C_t + B_t} + \frac{\beta_t}{C_t + B_t}$$

$$= \frac{(C_t + B_t)S_t}{(C_t + B_t)C_t} - \frac{B_t S_t}{(C_t + B_t)C_t} + \frac{\beta_t}{C_t + B_t}. \tag{2}$$

Recall that actions are chosen according to current relative strength, that is $S_t/C_t = p_t$. Denoting the random variable $(C_t + B_t)^{-1}$ by α_t, we may therefore rewrite (2) simply as

$$p_{t+1} = p_t + \alpha_t (\beta_t - B_t p_t). \tag{3}$$

Now define the function $f(p)$ as $E[\beta(p) - Bp \mid p]$, the conditional expectation of the change in the action strengths given the action probabilities p, where the expectation is taken both over the distribution of each action's reward and with respect to the randomly chosen actions. Write the expected reward $E[\Phi(j)]$ as $\Phi(j)$. Now, given action j, the expectation of $\beta - Bp$ is the vector $\phi(j)$ $(e(j) - p)$. Action j is triggered with probability $p(j)$. The function is therefore given by

$$f(p) = \Sigma_j \, \phi(j) \, [e(j) - p] p(j). \tag{4}$$

Note that f is continuous. Now define the random vector $\xi_t(p_t)$ as

$$\xi_t(p_t) = \beta_t - B_t p_t - f(p_t). \tag{5}$$

(By the definition of f, the conditional expectation $E[\xi_t \mid p_t]$ is zero.) We can then finally rewrite the algorithm's dynamics (4) as

$$p_{t+1} = p_t + \alpha_t f(p_t) + \alpha_t \, \xi_t(p_t). \tag{6}$$

Alternatively, from (4) the j-th component of the expected motion vector $f(p)$ is $p(j)\{\phi(j) - \Sigma_i \phi(i)p(i)\}$, so that the jth component of p_t updates as

$$p(j)_{t+1} = p(j)_t + \alpha_t \, p(j)_t \left[\phi(j) - \sum_{i=1}^{N} \phi(i)p(i)_t \right] + \alpha_t \, \xi(j)_t \, .$$

Noting that p_t remains in the interior of the simplex, and writing $\xi(j)/p(j)$ as $\zeta(j)$, we have

$$\frac{p(j)_{t+1} - p(j)_t}{p_t(j)} = \alpha_t \left[\phi(j) - \sum_{i=1}^{N} \phi(i)p(i)_t + \zeta(j)_t \right]. \tag{6'}$$

We now have two representations for the dynamics—the transient learning behavior of the automaton. Equation (6) tells us that the action probabilities are updated at each time by an "expected motion" vector $f(p_t)$, together with an unbiased "perturbation" term ξ_t. And version (6′) tells us that the growth rate of the probability of choosing action j is driven by the difference between *its* expected payoff and the weighted-average expected payoff for *all* actions at the current probabilities p, plus unbiased noise. The step size of the algorithm, α_t, is given in both cases by $(Ct^\nu + B_t)^{-1}$; it is random and is of the order $O(t^{-\nu})$. The overall rate of learning therefore increases both with larger step size and—as is realistic—with larger differences in expected payoff among the actions.

The dynamics in (6) take the form of a *stochastic approximation,* with state vector p, driving function f, and random step-size vector α_t (see Nevelson and Hasminskii 1973). And the alternative version (6′) takes the form of a *replicator system* with noise. Viewed either way, the limiting behavior of the process will depend on the equivalent deterministic system (e.g., (6) without the ξ_t term) and the rate ν at which the step size falls off.

Asymptotic Optimality and Exploration

One question we will want to ask of human learning is whether it is likely to achieve asymptotic optimality by converging over time to activating only the choice with highest expected payoff. Put another way, we want to ask whether humans explore alternative choices sufficiently to be sure to concentrate eventually on the best option. We can settle this by deriving theoretically the range of parameters under which the automaton does sufficient exploration to achieve asymptotic optimality, and later comparing the human, calibrated parameters to see if they fall into this range.

It is certainly not clear *a priori* whether the algorithm I have described learns over time to put all its "confidence" in the optimal action k and activate it only in the limit, or alternatively locks in to actions that are second- or third-best. It shows two apparently contradictory tendencies. On the one hand, its *expected* motion of learning is always in the direction of maximal-payoff action k: the kth component $p_t(k)$ in (6′) shows expected change $\alpha_t p_t(k)[\phi(k) - \Sigma_i\phi(i)p_t(i)]$ at time t and this is always positive. (See fig. 1.) On the other, it is subject to positive feedback—self-reinforcement—in that high-payoff action j, triggered early, may gain in strength and therefore be triggered ever more frequently until it dominates. The maximal-payoff action k may then be insufficiently explored and become shut out.

It turns out that which of these tendencies dominates depends on the rate of decrease of the step size—that is, on the parameter ν. If the step-size remains of constant order ($\nu = 0$), then inferior action j, if emphasized early, may indeed build up sufficient strength to shut k out. In this case, action j's strength—and therefore its probability of activation—may be reinforced rapidly enough that with some positive probability after a finite time alternatives

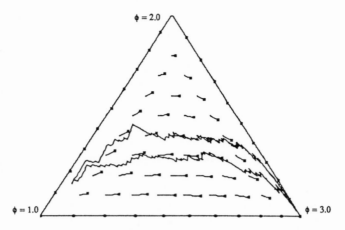

Fig. 1. Expected motions and two learning trajectories for a three-action problem

like k may cease to be triggered at all. In a sense here the algorithm is learning too fast. Learning may thus fall into the "gravitational orbit" of a non-optimal but reasonable action without escaping. If on the other hand ν is sufficiently large ($\nu = 1$) this does not happen. Here the normalizing sequence $C_t = C \cdot t$ increases linearly, and the step size falls at the corresponding rate $1/t$.[6] This keeps action k "in the game" by delaying rapid lock-in to a non-optimal action and thus retains exploration for an arbitrarily long time. Even if j dominates early, sooner or later k will be triggered, further explored, and eventually take over.

Thus, whether long-run optimality is guaranteed depends on whether the value of ν is large enough. I state this more precisely in the following two theorems. Assume (A1): the random payoffs Φ are bounded above and below by positive constants and (A2) expected payoffs are unequal.

Theorem 1. Suppose A1, and that $0 < \nu < 1$. Then the vector sequence p_t converges to nonmaximal-payoff vertex j of the simplex of probabilities S^N, with positive probability.

Theorem 2. Suppose A1 and A2, and that $\nu = 1$. Then the vector sequence p_t converges to optimal-payoff vertex k of the simplex of probabilities S^N, with probability one.

---

6. This "cooling" of motion or step size is common in stochastic optimization to ensure optimality.

These results rely on probabilistic limit arguments that I relegate to an appendix.

These theorems give qualitative results, but they do not say anything about the practical probabilities of locking in to the wrong action. Here the other parameter, C, becomes important. Obviously, non-optimality is more likely if the difference in expected payoffs between k and its next-best alternatives is small and differences are hard to discern. It is less likely the larger the constant C. Larger C means smaller step size; and with small enough steps attraction to a non-optimal action may occur slowly enough to allow "discovery" and exploitation of the optimal action. Also, practically speaking, ν need not be as large as 1 for optimality to occur with probability close to 1. If action k is more than 10 percent better than other actions, above $\nu = 0.5$ or so the probability of locking in to inferior actions becomes insignificant.

Example. Figure 1 shows an example of this learning automaton in practice. Three actions 1, 2, and 3 provide expected rewards of 1.0, 2.0, and 3.0, respectively. The figure maps the vector field of expected motions and shows two sample learning trajectories. Both trajectories have been started at a fairly extreme point (at bottom left) corresponding to high initial confidence in the poorest action 1, and where the activation probability of the best action 3 is low. For a short while the high-probability actions 1 and 2 compete, but then the automaton begins to "discover" and reinforce action 3, and with its higher average reward its frequency of activation rapidly rises. Eventually the main competition is between actions 2 and 3 with convergence to almost 100 percent activation of 3 after about 200 steps. In practice, the algorithm would presumably start with equal probabilities, and convergence would then be considerably faster.

Calibration against Human Subjects

Our next step is to calibrate the parameters C and ν against data on human learning. We are interested in three things here: the degree to which the calibrated algorithm represents human behavior; whether the calibrated value of ν lies within the range that guarantees asymptotically optimal choices; and the general characteristics of learning—such as speed and ability to discriminate —that the calibrated values imply.

To calibrate the algorithm I use the results of a series of two-choice bandit experiments conducted by Laval Robillard at Harvard in 1952–1953 using students as subjects (see Bush and Mosteller 1955).[7] Robillard set up

---

7. Data on humans choosing repeatedly among competing alternatives are scarce. Bush and Mosteller (1955) discuss the available human (and animal) multi-choice experiments. These experiments have gone out of fashion among psychologists, and no recent, more definitive results appear to be available.

seven experiments, each with its own payoff structure, and allocated groups of ten subjects to each. Each subject, in his or her particular experiment, could choose action A or B in one hundred trials. In designating the experiments, 50 : 0 denotes that action A delivers one unit payoff randomly with probability .5, action B one unit payoff with probability zero; 80 : 40 denotes payoffs with probabilities .8 and .4 respectively; and so on. Table 1 summarizes the results. It shows the proportion of A-choices in each sequential block of ten trials, averaged over the group of ten subjects for that experiment.

A comment or two on this data set. The antiquity of these data should not bother us too much—we can presume that human behavior has not changed in the last four decades. But there are several shortcomings. Ideally I would prefer to calibrate on experiments that show wider variation in the expected value of rewards, longer trial lengths to allow for reasonable convergence of choice probabilities (if it is present), and more than just two alternatives. Further, I would want real, not token, monetary reward to be at stake.[8] In spite of these limitations, the experiments appear to have been conducted and documented with care, and I will use them as an expedient, until I possess proper experimental economic data. The resulting calibration should be interpreted as a good indication of human behavior in situations of choice, rather than a definitive statement.

Our artificial agents produce stochastic sequences of choices or frequencies of choosing action A, and so do the Robillard subjects. Goodness of fit (under any appropriate criterion) for fixed parameters is therefore a random variable. The object in calibration is then to choose parameters that maximize *expected* goodness of fit. I proceed therefore by allowing "groups of artificial agents" (computer runs of the algorithm) to reproduce the equivalent of Robillard's data for fixed values of C and ν. I then choose the parameters C and ν to fit the seven experiments taken together, by minimizing the expected sum of errors squared between the automaton-generated frequencies and the corresponding human frequencies for each particular experiment, totaled over the seven experiments.

This operation of choosing C and ν to fit the artificial agents' learning to the human learning data is a relatively simple numerical stochastic optimization problem. It results in $C = 31.1$ and $\nu = 0.00$. Note immediately that ν lies in a region where strong reinforcement of possibly inferior actions means that optimality is far from guaranteed.

Figures 2 and 3 plot artificial agents' learning against human subjects',

---

8. Robillard offered actual monetary reward (1 c and 5 c per correct response) for the second and third experiments only. These showed no observable difference in learning over the first experiment. In the calibration I have thus simply assigned payoff utility 1 to a "correct" action, and 0 to an "incorrect" action.

TABLE 1. "Two-Armed Bandit" Data on Human Learning Obtained by Robillard

Experiment: Trial Block	50 : 0	50 : 0	50 : 0	30 : 0	80 : 0	80 : 40	60 : 30
0–9	0.52	0.51	0.49	0.56	0.59	0.50	0.49
10–19	0.63	0.54	0.58	0.57	0.77	0.59	0.58
20–29	0.69	0.67	0.67	0.55	0.88	0.71	0.62
30–39	0.63	0.59	0.59	0.63	0.88	0.64	0.51
40–49	0.64	0.66	0.63	0.60	0.86	0.63	0.51
50–59	0.75	0.66	0.64	0.66	0.91	0.63	0.61
60–69	0.76	0.77	0.71	0.65	0.92	0.53	0.57
70–79	0.85	0.70	0.73	0.65	0.89	0.71	0.57
80–89	0.87	0.83	0.72	0.65	0.88	0.73	0.65
90–99	0.90	0.83	0.81	0.66	0.89	0.70	0.55

using these calibrated values. More specifically, for a representative seven-experiment set of artificial agent choices, it plots the average frequencies of activation of action A by seven groups of ten automata against the corresponding frequencies from Robillard's seven groups of ten human subjects. ("Representative" here means that the automata seven-experiment choices show goodness of fit to the human data approximately equal to the *expected* goodness of fit for the C and ν values used.) The results, judged by eye, are encouraging. The automata learning plots show roughly the same trend and variation as the human plots in each of the experiments. The parameter values are calibrated over all seven experiments together, and not for each one separately; yet the algorithm does not "average" among the experiments. Instead it varies, the change in choice frequency speeding up when reward differences are easy to discern (as in the 80 : 0 case), slowing down when discernment is difficult (the 60 : 30 case), closely tracking the behavior of the human subjects.

Are there systematic differences that distinguish the human learning from the calibrated automata learning curves? Consider the hypothesis that choice-frequencies identical to those of Robillard's subjects could be generated by our calibrated automata. To test this we can generate for each experiment 100 automata trajectories, measure the error-squared distance between pairs taken at random and compute the distribution, mean, and variance of these pair-distances. We can similarly, for each experiment, compute the mean distance between the human (Robillard) trajectory and 100 corresponding, randomly generated automata ones. We would reject the hypothesis if the human trajectories lie on average far from the automata ones—on the tail of the automata pair-distance distribution. Table 2 shows the t-statistic for the Robillard-automata pair-distances as compared to the inter-automata pair-distance distri-

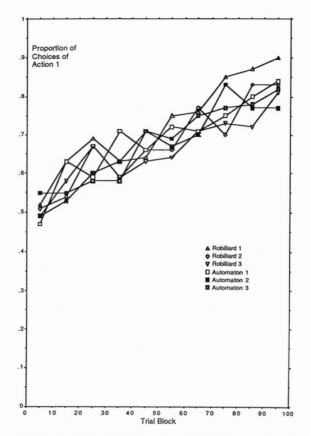

Fig. 2. Calibrated learning automata versus Robillard's human subjects. Choice frequencies in the three 50 : 0 experiments

bution. It shows that six of the seven Robillard trajectories fall well within the distribution of automata trajectories and that the overall calibration is a good fit. Experiment 5 however is an outlier. Here humans learn faster than the calibrated algorithm. The reason is that its 80 : 0 payoff scheme has a close to deterministic outcome and for deterministic payoffs humans appear to speed up learning once they become convinced that actions produce the same payoff each time they are undertaken.[9] Such meta-learning might be built in by making C endogeneous but at the cost of complicating the algorithm.

---

9. This is confirmed in the psychological experiments with deterministic outcomes of Goodnow (p. 295, Bush and Mosteller 1955). For Goodnow's nondeterministic payoff experiments our Robillard-calibrated artificial agents show very similar fits, out of sample, to those in figures 2 and 3.

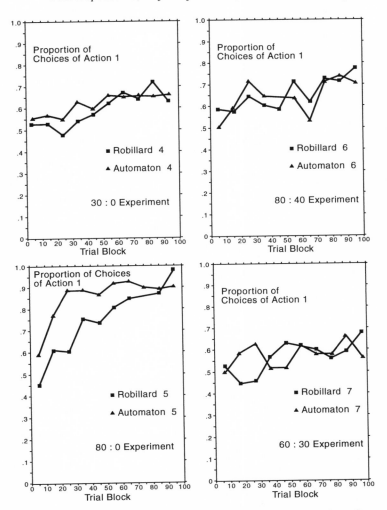

Fig. 3. Automata versus Robillard subjects in the other four experiments.

I would expect too that learning may also speed up somewhat—the parameter C might fall—as the payoffs at stake increased from a few dollars to several millions of dollars and casual decision-making behavior gave way to more calculated behavior. C would likely not fall too far—ignorance that must be narrowed remains ignorance, at any scale—but certainly it would be worth estimating at the high range of payoff to see how it might vary.

More convincing than statistical tests of fit would be tests of whether the algorithm can replicate human behavior in quite different choice problems

TABLE 2. *t*-Distance of Robillard Learning Trajectories from Randomly-Generated Automata Learning Trajectories

Experiment	#1. 50:0	#2. 50:0	#3. 50:0	#4. 30:0	#5. 80:0	#6. 80:40	#7. 60:30
t-statistic	0.58	−0.21	−0.07	−0.76	6.75	0.86	1.14

than those for which it was calibrated. A different problem, with a different style of outcome (but still within our multi-choice context) is provided by recent experiments of Herrnstein, Prelec, Loewenstein, and Vaughan (1990). In these the payoff distributions are no longer fixed, but depend instead on the frequency of actions taken. These are of interest to us because they show a well-documented characteristic behavior called *melioration* (Herrnstein 1979; Herrnstein and Vaughan 1980) and converge to an interior, non-optimal set of frequencies of choice.

In the Herrnstein *et al.* experiments there are two choices and their payoffs are frequency dependent. The payoff to choice A is $\Phi_A = 3^{(1.9 - 3x)}$ and to B is $\Phi_B = 3^{[0.8 - 4.6(1-x)]}$, where x is the frequency of A-choices in the last twenty trials, as shown in figure 5. These payoff functions are deterministic, but unknown in advance to the subject in the experiment. Above a frequency of 75 percent A-choices, option B pays better; below 75 percent option A pays better.

Human subjects, Herrnstein *et al.* find, tend to choose the action with the higher payoff at their current frequency—they "meliorate." Here this implies convergence to choosing A 75 percent of the time. Optimizing behavior on the other hand would maximize frequency-weighted payoff—it would set x, the frequency of A-choices, to maximize $(x\Phi_A + (1 - x)\Phi_B)$. This implies choosing A about 33 percent of the time.

Figure 4 shows the frequency of A-choices in the last 50 of 400 trials, for eight Herrnstein subjects (plotted as triangles at the foot of the graph) and for eight of our calibrated agents (plotted as squares). The human subjects tend to meliorate, with a possible bias in the direction of optimality. The calibrated agents replicate this behavior. They also meliorate, but with no bias toward asymptotic optimality. That our algorithm picks up this characteristic of human behavior is not altogether surprising. Both human and artificial agents are carrying out local search in the frequency-dependent case, on the efficacy of choices at the current frequency of choice. Thus they deviate in the same direction, coming much closer to melioration than optimality.

Findings like this give us confidence that we *can* indeed replicate human behavior for a particular decision context with a simple parametrized learning algorithm.

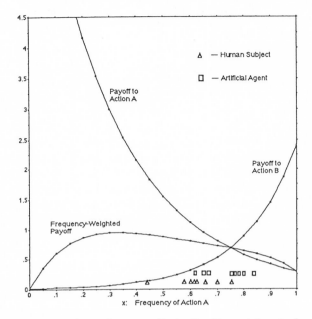

Fig. 4. Frequency-dependent payoffs in the Herrnstein *et al.* experiments

Asymptotic Optimality, Path-Dependence, and Other Questions

Having established that we can replicate or mimic human learning in the basic repeated multi-choice problem by a reinforcement-learning algorithm that fits reasonably well, let us return to some of the questions asked at the start. Where payoffs are independent of frequency, what can we say about the possibilities of path dependence and of long-run optimality? We know from the zero calibrated value for ν that learning may "lock in" with finite probability to an inferior action. Thus to the degree the calibrated algorithm represents human learning, path dependence may indeed be present and optimality is not guaranteed on all occasions where learning takes place. But what does this mean in practice? We can use computer experiments with the algorithm to test how often we might expect human decisions to lock in to less-than-optimal actions.

Consider one such experiment, a decision problem in which there are six choices, with action 1 the maximal choice. Expected payoffs fall off geometrically from action 1 to 6, and payoffs are distributed uniformly, from 0.5 to

1.5 times expected value for each of the actions. For rewarding the actions, average expected payoff over the six actions is scaled to unity. Obviously when expected payoffs are close, with all payoffs varying randomly, the optimal action becomes hard to discriminate. This difficulty of discrimination can be varied in our experiment by a parameter λ, the (common) ratio of expected payoffs between action 1 and action 2, action 2 and action 3, and so on, from a range of 0.7 (easy) to .98 (very difficult).

Table 3 shows the percentage of times action 1 dominated in 100 experiments at the end of 600 trials, using the calibrated algorithm. Human choice—if captured by the calibration—indeed "discovers" and exploits the optimal action unless it becomes difficult to discriminate. When the best action ceases to be more than 10 percent better than the next best, chance variations in payoff cause performance to lock in to a less-than-optimal outcome in a significant percentage of experiments. (Even then, when it is on average only about 2 percent better than its next best competitor ($\lambda = .98$), action 1 dominates more than twice as often as any other.) Of course when all actions are the same ($\lambda = 1$), action 1 emerges about as often as the others. Whether the optimal action dominates in the long run then, depends on how difficult the choice problem is.

It might be objected that the algorithm I have calibrated is to some degree ad-hoc—that the finding that human learning may lock in by chance to inferior choices, is merely an artifact of the algorithm. Would it be robust across other algorithmic specifications? I believe so. As we saw earlier, where current cumulation of rewards matters, it is both reasonable economically and psychologically that actions with higher payoffs be increasingly emphasized—be reinforced. Any reasonable representation of human learning must take this into account. Whether reinforcement leads to path dependence or not, depends upon whether exploration of lower payoff actions continues at a rate sufficient to eventually uncover the action with largest expected value. If exploitation outweighs exploration, learning may converge too rapidly on promising-looking actions. What is crucial then to the emergence of the optimal action is a slowing down in speed of convergence, so that learning has time to explore less-promising alternatives. The data—not the algorithm—show that in human learning such slowing down does not occur. I would therefore expect the result that human learning is path-dependent, nonpredict-

TABLE 3. Frequency of Convergence to the Optimal Action at Varying Difficulty (λ) of Discrimination

λ	.70	.72	.74	.76	.78	.80	.82	.84	.86	.88	.90	.92	.94	.96	.98	1.0
freq%	100	100	99	99	98	96	94	94	86	85	77	70	60	43	38	15

able, and not necessarily optimal to be validated under other well-fitting specifications.

Do similar findings carry over to the question of whether human agents converge to a Nash equilibrium in an iterated game? I believe so. Think now of our calibrated agents representing human agents learning or adapting within a normal-form, stage game (Arthur 1989). The agents can observe their own actions and random payoffs, but are not particularly well informed of other players' actions and payoff functions. Each agent then faces an iterated multi-choice problem as before and so our learning context carries over to this wider problem. (An example might be oligopolistic firms choosing among pricing policies in a decentralized market on the basis of observed end-of-quarter profit.) Of course, in this case where the payoff environment is no longer stationary, each agent's payoff distribution slowly changes as other agents change their choice probabilities.[10]

For some games of this type learning behavior may not converge at all. The fact that learning agents change their choice-probabilities or strategy-profiles as other agents change *their* strategy-profiles may cause probability vectors to cycle. This is a familiar result in the adaptive theory of games. In games where learning *does* converge, to the degree that the calibration captures actual human behavior, we can assert that Nash is likely but not guaranteed. More precisely, as before, the likelihood of convergence to Nash depends on the difficulty of discrimination among the action payoffs. The reason of course is that, once again, where discernment of the optimal (best-reply) action is difficult, agents may come to concentrate their play on "good" actions that are working well, and not explore less known but potentially superior alternatives. Individual behavior may then not be best-reply; and combined behavior may therefore not be Nash.[11]

How might we use calibrated agents to represent actual human adaptive behavior in other standard neoclassical models? As one example, consider a Lucas (1978) stock market. Here there are a constant number of units of a single stock, an alternative financial instrument that pays rate β, and a random dividend. Agents buy or sell the stock in discrete periods. Lucas shows that under rational expectations, there is a price-equilibrium at fundamental value. We might ask whether this equilibrium is likely to be reached by *actual* human buying and selling behavior. Arthur, Holland, Palmer, and Tayler (1990) explore this question using calibrated agents in an adaptive version of this market. Each agent is represented by a collection of classifiers, of the form "If

---

10. We would have to check that the calibration above carries over to this case. I suspect it would: the rate of learning would be little affected providing players' payoff distributions changed slowly.

11. Although in examples with closely clustered payoffs, Nash is not guaranteed, in the simpler games that I have tested with calibrated agents, Nash behavior always emerges.

the current price falls in the range *x* to *x* + *z* / *buy* one unit of stock" or "If the current price falls in the range of *x* to *x* + *z* / *sell* one unit of stock." A specialist sets the price each period with the object of clearing the market. Starting from random behavior—50 percent chance of choosing "buy" or "sell"—we find that the calibrated agents learn to buy and sell stock appropriately as the price is below and above fundamental value. Within about one hundred and fifty buying-selling periods the price indeed converges to small fluctuations around fundamental value. However, we also find that small speculative bubbles sometimes occur, and also localized price "supports" and "ceilings"—a hint that under boundedly-rational learning technical analysis may emerge.

Conclusions

This paper has explored the possibility of calibrating learning models against experimental data with a view to representing actual, boundedly-rational human learning in the iterated choice context.

The calibrated learning algorithm developed here can be used to replace idealized, perfectly rational agents of standard neoclassical models with learning agents whose choice behavior replicates *actual* boundedly-rational human behavior. The data used for calibration come from the psychology literature and are not perfectly suited for economic purposes; so the calibration here should be regarded as preliminary. But they suggest that we can indeed design "artificially intelligent" agents or learning automata that replicate human behavior so that their rate of learning varies with the difficulty of discerning expected payoff in the way the human rate varies; and so that, where payoffs depend on the frequency of choice, they "meliorate" as humans consistently do.

To the degree it replicates human behavior, the calibrated algorithm shows that humans tend to over-exploit "good" actions that pay off well early thereby inheriting the classic properties of strong self-reinforcement: path dependence, nonpredictability, and possible lock-in to an inferior choice. In many circumstances where the superior action stands out clearly, these (possibly unwelcome) properties do not apply. They are prone to occur where payoffs to choices are closely clustered, random, and therefore difficult to discriminate among. This sort of finding is unfamiliar in economics, where our habit of thinking is that if there were a better alternative, it would be chosen. But it is familiar in psychology (for a recent instance see Bailey and Mazur 1990), where it has long been accepted that there are thresholds, beyond which better alternatives become difficult to discriminate. If this finding holds up under better data sets (as I suspect it will) it implies that the question of whether human behavior adapts its way to an optimal steady-state, or a Nash outcome admits of no simple yes or no answer. The answer depends on the problem: If alternatives are distinct and clearly different, we can expect optimal outcomes. But where discrimination is difficult, nonoptimal outcomes —not too distant from optimality—are possible.

Practically speaking, this possible lack of optimality would not matter a great deal—it would merely detract somewhat from efficiency—if decision problems throughout the economy were independent. But often they are not. Earlier actions may determine the options or alternative decisions available later. And knowledge gained in earlier problems may be carried into later, similar ones in the form of expectations or prior beliefs—a phenomenon called *transfer* in psychology. There is thus an "ecology" of decision problems in the economy, with earlier patterns of decisions affecting subsequent decisions. This interlinkage would tend to carry sub-optimality through from one decision setting to another. The overall economy would then follow a path that is partly decided by chance, is history-dependent, and is less than optimal.

How long it takes to uncover "reasonable" or optimal choices depends upon the degree to which payoffs are tightly clustered. But as a rule of thumb for actions with random payoffs that are unknown in advance, we should not expect behavior to have settled down much before 40 to 100 or more trials. In turn this implies that there is a *characteristic learning time* or "relaxation time" for human decisions in the economy that depends on the frequency of observed feedback on actions taken and on the payoff structure of the problem itself. There is also, of course, a time frame or horizon over which the economic environment of a decision problem stays relatively constant. For some parts of the economy, this learning time or learning horizon may be shorter than the problem horizon, and we can expect these parts to be at equilibrium—albeit a slowly changing one. For other parts, learning may take place more slowly than the rate at which the problem shifts. These parts would be always transient—always tracking changes in their decision environment. They by contrast would not be at equilibrium. And they would not be at optimality either, if decisions had not yet "discovered" the optimal action. One part of the economy in learning-motion may form the environment for another part. Thus transience may beget transience, and lack of equilibrium may percolate across the economy.

APPENDIX

Consider the two-parameter learning algorithm with dynamics described by (4), (5), and (6). Recall that starting strengths S_0 are positive. Assume: (A1) the random payoffs Φ are uniformly bounded above and below; and (A2) actions have unequal expected payoffs.

I now show that if $0 \leq \nu < 1$, the process may possibly converge to a non-optimal action.

Theorem 1. *Assume* A1 *and that* $0 \leq \nu < 1$. *Then the vector sequence* p_t *may converge to triggering action* j *only (to vertex* j *of the simplex of probabilities* S^N) *with positive probability.*

Proof. Given A1, there is positive probability that the sequence reaches the interior of an arbitrary ϵ_1-neighborhood of inferior vertex e_j, in finite time. It is then sufficient to show that once the process is in this neighborhood there is positive probability that *only* action j will be triggered from that time on. I show this by straight computation.

Let $A_M(j)$ be the event that p lies within the ϵ_1-neighborhood of e_j and that j only is triggered from time M onward.

$$P\{A_M(j)\} = \prod_M^\infty p_s(j)$$

Now let $p_s(j) = 1 - a_s(j)$. Since $a_s(j) > 0$, for the infinite product $\prod (1 - a_s(j)]$ to converge it is sufficient that the series Σa_s converge. In this case, the event $A_M(j)$ will have positive probability, and p_t will converge to sub-optimal vertex e_j with positive probability.

We therefore investigate the convergence of the series Σa_s. Let action j receive random reward Φ. From (3)

$$p_{s+1}(j) = p_s(j) + (Cs^\nu + \Phi)^{-1} \Phi [1 - p_s(j)]$$

so that

$$a_{s+1}(j) = a_s(j) [1 - \Phi (Cs^\nu + \Phi)^{-1}].$$

Thus the ratio of succeeding terms in the a-series is

$$\frac{a_{s+1}(j)}{a_s(j)} = [1 - \Phi(Cs^\nu + \Phi)^{-1}].$$

Note immediately that if $\nu = 0$, the fact that Φ is bounded below ensures that the a-series decreases at least as fast as a geometric series and therefore converges. Thus, where $\nu = 0$, the sequence p_t may converge to sub-optimal action j with positive probability.

Now let $0 < \nu < 1$. Denote the lower bound on Φ by r. Then, where time $s > C/r$, the ratio

$$1 - \frac{\Phi}{(Cs^\nu + \Phi)} < 1 - \frac{r}{Cs^\nu} < 1 - \frac{1}{s^\nu} = 1 - s^{-\nu}.$$

The convergent series $\Sigma \, s^{-(1+\epsilon)}$ has ratio $(1 - s^{-1})^{1+\epsilon}$. By comparison, since $\nu < 1$, the a-sequence is then also convergent. Therefore, where $0 < \nu < 1$, the stochastic sequence p_t may converge to sub-optimal action j with positive probability. The theorem follows. ∎

I now consider $\nu = 1$. This implies that the step size falls at the rate $1/t$. The process in (6) is therefore a standard stochastic approximation process on the unit simplex, with expected motion toward one point, vertex k. The only complication is that there are zeros at all vertices of the simplex, and no expected motion toward k on the sub-simplices where $p(k) = 0$. I proceed via two lemmas, the first one showing that step size rate $1/t$ is slow enough to rule out convergence to a non-optimal vertex.

Lemma 1. Suppose A1 and $\nu = 1$. Then the algorithm converges to a non-optimal action j (vertex j of the simplex, j $\neq$ k) with probability zero.

Proof. Consider the stochastic process (6) with driving function f as in (4) and perturbations ξ_t as in (5), starting at point p_0. At nonmaximal vertex j, where $p = e_j$, $f(e_j) = 0$. The matrix of derivatives at e_j has an eigenvector $e_k - e_j$ with associated eigenvalue $\phi_k - \phi_j$ which is positive. Therefore the point e_j is linearly unstable. Because the payoffs are bounded above and below, the order of the step-size $\alpha_t = (Ct^\nu + B)^{-1}$ is t^{-1}. The perturbations $\xi_t(p) = \beta_t - B_t p_t - f(p_t)$ are bounded above uniformly on the simplex, and below outside a neighborhood of the vertices. We may now invoke the argument of Pemantle (1988; Theorem 1). This amounts to using probabilistic inequalities together with the above conditions to show that (i) whatever the starting point p_0, at some finite time τ, p_τ will lie outside an ϵ-neighborhood of e_j with probability greater than $\frac{1}{2}$; and (ii) the probability that the process enters an $\epsilon/2$ neighborhood subsequently is less than c. A simple tail argument then shows that (i) and (ii) together rule out convergence to e_j. Therefore, Prob $\{p_t \to e_j\} = 0$. ∎

The next lemma shows that a process of the type we are dealing with cannot stay forever in a region with non-zero expected motion, provided a suitable Lyapunov function exists.

Lemma 2. Let G be an open set and suppose there exists a nonnegative function V(p) defined on the domain t $\geq$ 0, p $\in$ G, such that E[V(p$_{t+1}$) − V(p$_t$) | p$_t$] $\leq$ − α_t const, where α_t is a sequence such that

$$\alpha_t > 0, \quad \sum_{t=0}^{\infty} \alpha_t = \infty.$$

Then the process p$_t$ exits G in a finite time with probability one.

Proof. This is Theorem 2.5.1 of Nevelson and Hasminskii (1976). The argument amounts to showing that if the process stayed in the domain, the cumulated increments of $V(p_t)$ would drive V negative with probability one, which contradicts the positivity of V.   ∎

Theorem 2. Assume A1, A2 and $\nu = 1$. Then the vector sequence p_t converges to the maximal expected-payoff vertex of the simplex with probability one.

Proof. Relabel the vertices in order of expected payoff, so that vertex 1 is maximal, vertex 2 is second best, and so on. Define nonnegative functions V_1, $V_2, \ldots, V_N$ (that map S^N into R) as $V_1 = 1 - p(1)$, $V_2 = 1 - p(2), \ldots, V_N = 1 - p(N)$. Also define $W_2, \ldots, W_N$ as $W_j = V_1 + V_2 + \ldots + V_j$. We first show that $V_1(p_t)$ is a supermartingale. From (6') we have

$$E[V_1(t+1) - V_1(t) \mid p_t] = -E[p_{t+1}(1) - p_t(1) \mid p_t]$$
$$= -\alpha_t p_t(1) \, [\phi(1) - \Sigma_i \phi(i) p_t(i)] \, . \tag{7}$$

Since $\phi(1) > \phi(i)$ for all $i \neq 1$, $E[V_1(t+1) - V_1(t) \mid p_t] \leq 0$. Thus the sequence $\{V_1(p_t)\}$ is a supermartingale on S^N bounded below by zero and is therefore convergent. $W_j(p_t)$ is also a supermartingale. To show this think of actions 1 to j as the composite action j'. This has combined probability $p'_t(j) = p_t(1) + \ldots + p_t(j)$ and, if chosen, expected payoff $\phi'_j = [p_t(1) \, \phi(1) + \ldots + p_t(j)\phi(j)]/p'_t$. Thus j's expected payoff $\phi'(j)$ is a convex combination of the payoffs $\phi(1)$ to $\phi(j)$, which by A2 is strictly greater than the payoffs $\phi(j+1)$ through $\phi(N)$. We then have

$$E[W_j(t + 1) - W_j(t) \mid p_t] = -E[(p'_{t+1}(j) - p'_t(j)) \mid p_t]$$

$$= -\alpha_t p'_t(j)[\phi'(j) - \Sigma_i \phi(i) p_t(i)]$$

$$= -\alpha_t p'_t(j) \left[\phi'(j) - \left\{ p'_t(j)\phi'(j) \right. \right.$$

$$\left. \left. + \sum_{i=j+1}^{N} \phi(i)p_t(i) \right\} \right] \leq 0. \tag{8}$$

W_j is therefore a supermartingale bounded below by $j - 1$ and is convergent with probability one. From the convergence of $V_1(t)$ and $W_2(t)$ follows the convergence of $V_2(t)$; from this and the convergence of $W_3(t)$ follows the convergence of $V_3(t)$. Proceeding this way, all V_j converge. It follows that the sequence $\{p_t\}$ converges to a limit random vector γ with probability one. Now, Lemma 1 shows that, with probability one, γ cannot be a non-optimal vertex point e_j, $j \neq 1$. Suppose then γ is a nonvertex point h. Let the set U_h be an open ϵ-neighborhood of this point. Then there exists a finite time t', for which $p_t \in U_h$ from t' onward. Let j be the index of the first nonzero component of h. Then within U_h, the expected payoff of the composite action j' strictly exceeds that of the other actions by a constant c; and by (8), $E[W_j(t+1) - W_j(t) \mid p_t] < - \alpha_t$ const for $t > t'$. The step size α_t is positive, and by A1, with $\nu = 1$, the summation $\Sigma_t \alpha_t > \Sigma_t (Ct + B)^{-1} = \infty$. But then U_h, W, and α_t fulfill the requirements of Lemma 2, and the process p_t for $t > t'$, must exit U_h in finite time with probability one. This contradicts $\gamma = h$. It follows with probability one that the sequence $\{p_t\}$ can converge only to the maximal vertex e_1. The theorem is proved. ∎

REFERENCES

Arthur, W. B. 1989. "Nash-Discovering Automata for Finite Action Games." Mimeo. Santa Fe Institute.

Arthur, W. B., Ermoliev, Y. M., and Y. M. Kaniovski. 1987a. "Nonlinear Urn Processes: Asymptotic Behavior and Applications." WP-87-85, IIASA, Laxenburg, Austria.

―――. 1987b. "Urn Schemes and Adaptive Processes of Growth," *Kibernetika*, 23:49–58.

Arthur, W. B., Holland, J. H., and R. Palmer. "Adaptive Behavior in the Stock Market." Paper in progress. Santa Fe Institute.

Bailey, J. T., and J. E. Mazur. 1990. "Choice Behavior in Transition: Development of Preference for the Higher Probability of Reinforcement." *Journal of Experimental Analysis and Behavior.*

Bower, G. H., and E. R. Hilgard. 1981. *Theories of Learning.* 5th Ed. Prentice-Hall: New Jersey.

Bray, M. M. 1982. "Learning, Estimation, and the Stability of Rational Expectations." *Journal of Econ. Theory* 26:318–39.

Bush, R. R., and F. Mosteller. 1955. *Stochastic Models for Learning.* Wiley. New York.

Estes, W. K. 1950. "Toward a Statistical Theory of Learning." *Psychological Review.* 57:94–107.

Fudenberg, D., and D. M. Kreps. 1988. "Learning, Experimentation, and Equilibrium in Games." Mimeo. MIT.

Gardner, R. A. 1957. "Probability-Learning with Two and Three Choices." *American Journal of Psychology.* 70:174–85.

Goldberg, D. 1989. *Genetic Algorithms in Search, Optimization, and Machine Learning.* Reading, Mass.: Addison-Wesley.

Goodnow, J. J. 1955. "Determinants of Choice-Distribution in Two-Choice Situations." *American Journal of Psychology.* 68:106–16.

Hebb, D. O. 1949. *The Organization of Behavior.* Wiley, New York.

Herrnstein, R. 1979. "Derivatives of Matching." *Psychological Review.* 86:486–95.

Herrnstein, R., and W. Vaughan. 1980. "Melioration and Behavioral Allocation," in *The Allocation of Individual Behavior,* J. E. Straddon (ed.). 143–76. New York: Academic Press.

Herrnstein, R., D. Prelec, Loewenstein, and W. Vaughan (1990). Paper in progress.

Holland, J. H. 1986. "Escaping Brittleness: The Possibilities of General Purpose Machine Learning Algorithms Applied to Parallel Rule-based Systems." In R. Michalski, J. Carbonell, and T. Mitchell (eds.) *Machine Learning: An Artificial Intelligence Approach,* Vol 2. Kaufman, Los Altos, Calif.

Holland, J. H., K. J. Holyoak, R. E. Nisbet, and P. R. Thagard. 1987. *Induction: Process of Inference, Learning, and Discovery*. MIT Press.

Hull, C. L. 1943. *Principles of Behavior*. New York: Appleton-Century Crofts.

Luce, R. D. 1959. *Individual Choice Behavior: A Theoretical Analysis*. New York: Wiley.

Lucas, R. E. 1978. "Asset Prices in an Exchange Economy." *Econometrica*, 46:1429–45.

Marcet, A., and T. Sargent. 1989. "Convergence of Least Squares Learning Mechanisms in Self-Referential Linear Stochastic Models." *Journ. Econ. Theory* 48: 337–68.

Marimon, R., E. McGrattan, and T. Sargent. 1989. "Money as a Medium of Exchange in an Economy with Artificially Intelligent Agents." Santa Fe Institute, Paper 89-004.

Milgrom, P., and J. Roberts. 1989. "Adaptive and Sophisticated Learning in Repeated Normal Form Games." Mimeo, Stanford University.

Narendra K., and M. A. L. Thathachar. 1989. *Learning Automata: An Introduction*. Prentice-Hall, Englewood Cliffs, New Jersey.

Nevelson, M. B., and R. Z. Hasminskii. *Stochastic Approximation and Recursive Estimation*. Vol. 47. American Math. Soc. Providence.

Pemantle, R. 1988. "Nonconvergence to Unstable Points in Urn Models and Stochastic Approximations." Mimeo. Statistics Department, University of California, Berkeley.

Restle, F., and J. G. Greeno. 1970. *Introduction to Mathematical Psychology*. Addison-Wesley.

Rothschild, M. 1974. "A Two-Armed Bandit Theory of Market Pricing." *Journal of Economic Theory* 9:185–202.

Sternberg, S. 1963. "Stochastic Learning Theory," in *Handbook of Mathematical Psychology*. R. D. Luce, R. R. Bush, E. Galanter, Eds. New York: Wiley.

Tsetlin, M. L. 1973. *Automaton Theory and Modeling of Biological Systems*. Academic Press. New York.

Tsypkin, Y. Z. 1973. *Foundations of the Theory of Learning Systems*. Academic Press. New York.

Turing, A. M. 1956. "Can a Machine Think?" in *The World of Mathematics*, J. R. Newman, Ed. New York: Simon and Schuster, 4:2009–2123.

CHAPTER 9

Strategic Pricing in Markets with Increasing Returns

W. Brian Arthur and Andrzej Ruszczynski

Several of the papers in this book show that where products or technologies experience increasing returns to market share, markets can become unstable, so that in the long run one product or technology can come to dominate and drive out the others. But these assume the absence of strategic manipulation. Thus the question arises: If firms that lose market share (and hence the increasing returns advantage that accrues to market share) can offset this by strategically lowering their prices, are increasing-returns markets still unstable? Does the possibility of strategic pricing mitigate positive feedback effects and stabilize such markets?

In this paper, Andrzej Ruszczynski and I examine the problem by setting up a stochastic duopoly game between two competing firms that can strategically price products that experience positive feedback to market share. We show that whether pricing mitigates the natural instability of the market or enhances it depends on the rate of time preference of the firms. If firms have high discount rates, firms that achieve a large market share tend to quickly lose it by pricing high to exploit it for near-term profit, and so the market stabilizes. If, on the other hand, firms have low discount rates, they price in an effort to lock in and hold onto a dominant position, so that pricing further destabilizes the market.

The paper appeared under the title "Dynamic Equilibria in Markets with a Conformity Effect" in *Archives of Control Sciences,* 37 (1992):7–31. For this version I have rewritten the title, the introduction, and some of the expository parts of the article. Andrzej Ruszczynski is with the Institute of Automatic Control, Warsaw University of Technology, Poland.

1. Introduction

In many markets, competing products are subject to increasing returns in the sense that their natural usefulness or perceived attractiveness or potential profitability increase with their share of the market. For example, in high-technology markets for competing computer software applications, or computer operating systems, or telecommunication systems, network externalities lend advantage to products that gain a lead in user-base. In markets for luxury cars or designer clothing, fashion or conformity effects bestow brand advantage with increases in market share. In the airline industry, the ability to operate efficient hub-and-spoke systems depends greatly on passenger-mile volume and hence market share of the market. In all these markets, we might ask whether such positive-feedback or increasing-returns mechanisms tend to destabilize the market and lead to the eventual domination of one or a small number of monopolizing firms.

Most of the studies of competition under increasing returns to date assume the absence of strategic manipulation. (For a survey see Arthur, chap. 7 in this book.) And so we know little about the effects of pricing or other forms of strategic action in markets with self-reinforcement. The possibility of pricing may give firms that lose market share and its positive-feedback advantage a means to respond by lowering their prices, which would mitigate the effects of positive feedback and possibly stabilize the market. Or, it may give producers a means to further exploit a positive-feedback advantage, which would suggest that the market may be more prone to monopoly and destabilization. *A priori* it is not obvious that in the presence of strategic pricing, positive feedback will still imply instability of the market.

The few studies that explore market structure in the presence of strategic action and self-reinforcement do show indications in the direction of instability and multiple equilibria. Flaherty [8] explores the case where firms strategically invest to reduce their costs. Multiple, open-loop, noncooperative equilibria result. Fudenberg and Tirole [10] use learning effects as a source of reinforcement and investigate closed-loop perfect equilibria. Again they find multiple equilibria. Spence [14] shows in *ad hoc* fashion that the order in which firms enter a market matters, with different orders of entry giving different market-share trajectories. But none of these studies demonstrates precise conditions under which multiple equilibria rather than a single equilibrium might occur. Further, the equilibria derived in these studies are deterministic trajectories. There is no indication of how one trajectory from the multiplicity of candidate trajectories might come to be selected.

In this paper, we explore strategic pricing under increasing returns to market share, and carefully analyze conditions under which the market is stable or unstable. And we deal with the "selection problem" by setting up a stochastic model, in which naturally occurring random events in part determine the trajectory followed.[1]

---

1. In his dissertation, Hanson [11] also solved the selection problem in this way, using a stochastic model of a growing market. He discusses but does not fully derive conditions under which monopoly by a single firm occurs.

In the model we develop, a fixed-size market is divided between two competing firms that each produce one product. Consumers may "switch" stochastically between the two products from time to time, with probabilities that depend on the proportion of consumers using each product. Where the probability of switching to a product increases with its market share, we say the product shows positive feedback (or self-reinforcement or a conformity effect); where it decreases, we say it shows negative feedback (or self-inhibition or a nonconformity effect). We allow for both possibilities when we set up the model in section 2.

The producers in this stochastic duopoly market price dynamically as a function of their current market shares (sec. 3) using Nash-Markov strategies; and an equilibrium probability distribution of market shares results (sec. 4–6). Under certain conditions this equilibrium distribution is unimodal, indicating that most of the time the market is shared in a stable way. Under other conditions it is bimodal, indicating that the market is unstable—or more precisely, bistable—so that it experiences lengthy sojourns at shares that are asymmetric, and transits from time to time between these asymmetric states.

Overall, we find that producers' discount rates are crucial in determining whether the market structure is stable or unstable. High discount rates damp the effect of self-reinforcement and lead to a balanced market, while low discount rates enhance it and destabilize the market (sec. 6 and 7). Under high discount rates, firms that achieve a large market share quickly lose it again by pricing high to exploit their position for near-term profit. And so, in this case the market stabilizes. Under low discount rates, firms price aggressively as they struggle to lock in a future dominant position; and when the market is close to balanced shares, each drops its price heavily in the hope of reaping future monopoly rents. The result is a strong effort by each firm to "tilt" the market in its favor, and to hold it in an asymmetric position if successful. And so, in this case strategic pricing destabilizes the market.

To demonstrate the phenomena, in section 7 we present computational results for a particular example of conformity effects, illustrating how strategic pricing policies and the resulting distribution of market shares are altered as the discount rate varies.

2. A Stochastic Model of the Market

The model we shall analyze has a finite number N of consumers and two producers, A and B. Each consumer uses either product A or B; and the number using A will be called the *state* of the market at time t and denoted $s(t)$.

The state evolves in time, due to new purchases, which are random. We assume that each consumer considers purchasing a new product once in a reference time unit, on average, and intervals between his purchase times are independent and exponentially distributed. Purchase times of different customers are also assumed to be independent, so all purchase times $t_0, t_1, \ldots, t_k, \ldots$ form a Poisson sequence with arrival rate N.

We also assume randomness of customers' decisions with distributions dependent on the state of the market and on the kind of product possessed previously by the customer. We denote by $P_i\{A|B\}$ the probability that at state i a customer who had B will choose A; in a similar way we define $P_i\{B|A\}$. Thus, at purchase times state transitions occur with probabilities

$$q_i^+ = Pr\{s(t_{k+1}) = i + 1 | s(t_k) = i\} = \left(1 - \frac{i}{N}\right) P_i\{A|B\},$$

$$q_i^- = Pr\{s(t_{k+1}) = i - 1 | s(t_k) = i\} = \frac{i}{N} P_i\{B|A\}, \tag{1}$$

$$q_i^0 = Pr\{s(t_{k+1}) = i | s(t_k) = i\} = 1 - q_i^+ - q_i^-.$$

Under these assumptions $s(t)$ is a continuous-time *Markov chain* with a finite state space (see, e.g., Feller [7]). Models of similar forms are commonly used in physics (Risken [13]), genetics (Ewens [6]) and technology (Bertsekas [5]).

The probabilities

$$p_i(t) = Pr\{s(t) = i\}$$

obey the *master equation*

$$\frac{1}{N} \frac{dp_i(t)}{dt} = q_{i-1}^+ p_{i-1}(t) + q_{i+1}^- p_{i+1}(t) - (q_i^+ - q_i^-)p_i(t) \tag{2}$$

and powerful methods exist for analyzing its solutions [7]. In particular, if $P_i\{A|B\} > 0$ for all $i < N$ and $P_i\{B|A\} > 0$ for all $i > 0$, then the limits

$$p_i(\infty) = \lim_{t \to \infty} p_i(t) \tag{3}$$

exist and are independent of the initial state distribution.

Additional insight into the problem can be gained by approximating the distribution $p_i(t)$, $i = 0, 1, \ldots, N$, by a continuous density function $p(x, t)$ in *market share* $x = \frac{i}{N}$, so that $p\left(\frac{i}{N}, t\right) = Np_i(t)$.

Suppose that $q_i^+ = q^+ \left(\frac{i}{N}\right)$ and $q_i^- = q^- \left(\frac{i}{N}\right)$ are twice continuously differentiable functions $q^+(x)$, $q^-(x)$. Then, expanding the right-hand side of (2) at x up to second order terms we arrive to the following *forward Kolmogorov (Fokker-Planck) equation* (see [13]):

$$\frac{\partial p(x,t)}{\partial t} = -\frac{\partial}{\partial x}[H(x)p(x,t)] + \frac{1}{2N}\frac{\partial^2}{\partial x^2}[Q(x)p(x,t)], \qquad (4)$$

with the *drift coefficient*

$$H(x) = q^+(x) - q^-(x)$$

and the *fluctuation coefficient*

$$Q(x) = q^+(x) + q^-(x).$$

Defining the *probability flux* $I = Hp - (Qp)'_x/2N$ we can rewrite (4) as $p'_t = -I'_x$; we also see that the flux must vanish at the ends of the interval $[0,1]$ so that the total probability mass remains unchanged. The *stationary solution* $p(x, \infty)$ is obtained by setting the left hand side of (4) to zero; it can be used to approximate (3).

In the present work we are interested in phenomena arising when customers' preferences depend on the state of the market, i.e.

$$P_i\{A|B\} = f\left(\frac{i}{N}\right),$$

$$P_i\{B|A\} = g\left(\frac{i}{N}\right),$$

with functions $f(x)$ and $g(x)$ reflecting the effect of market share x on purchase probabilities. The examples below illustrate three cases holding pricing issues aside for the moment.

No market-share effect. Suppose that $f(x) = g(x) = c$ for all x. In our original finite state space formulation we obtain the *Ehrenfest model* (see [7]), while in (4) we have $H(x) = -2c\left(x - \frac{1}{2}\right)$, $Q(x) = c$. This corresponds to the *Ornstein-Uhlenbeck process* whose stationary distributions are Gaussian with mean $\bar{x} = \frac{1}{2}$ and variance $\frac{c}{2N}$ [7]. A strong centering effect occurs: the market share has the tendency to fluctuate in a neighborhood of $\bar{x}$.

Linear market-share effect. Suppose now that $f(x) = c\left(x + \frac{1}{N}\right)$ and

$g(x) = c\left(1 - x + \dfrac{1}{N}\right)$ with some constant c. Then in the discrete model

we obtain from (2) a uniform stationary distribution: $p_i(\infty) = \dfrac{1}{N+1}$, $i = 0, 1, \ldots, N$. In the continuous model we get a small centering drift $H(x) = \left(\dfrac{1}{2} - x\right)/2N$, but fluctuations much stronger in the center than near boundaries: $Q(x) = 2x(1 - x) + \dfrac{1}{N}$, which yields flat stationary distributions.

Similar models have been studied in genetics [6].

Superlinear market-share effect. We use this term to denote the situation when both $f(x)$ and its derivative $f'(x)$ are increasing functions of x, while $g(x)$ and $g'(x)$ decrease in x. A particularly simple and interesting case of $f(x) = \nu \exp(\kappa x)$ and $g(x) = \nu \exp(\kappa(1 - x))$ was analysed by Weidlich and Haag [15]. When the constant κ (representing fashion or conformity effects) is small, the centering tendency prevails and the stationary distribution is unimodal. But as κ increases then the distribution bifurcates and becomes bimodal, with maxima corresponding to the relative prevalence of one product over the other. This is illustrated in figure 1.

3. A Stochastic Duopoly Game

Suppose now that producers A and B can influence customers' decisions by setting prices π_i and σ_i on their products, so that

$$P_i\{A|\cdot\} = f\left(\frac{i}{N}, \pi_i, \sigma_i\right),$$

$$P_i\{B|\cdot\} = g\left(\frac{i}{N}, \pi_i, \sigma_i\right),$$

(for simplicity we do not distinguish between $P_i\{A|A\}$ and $P_i\{A|B\}$, etc.; this would only complicate notation).

Function π which assigns prices π_i to market states i will be called the *policy* of A. Similarly, the policy of B is $\sigma = (\sigma_0, \sigma_1, \ldots, \sigma_N)$. Although one could consider here a more general model with prices dependent on state and time, we shall restrict our considerations to *stationary* policies: whenever the state is i, A uses π_i and B uses σ_i.

Let us define the objective of producer A. If a purchase of A's product is made at time t_k and current state is $s(t_k)$, then the producer gains $a_k = \pi_{s(t_k)}$; otherwise $a_k = 0$. Future gains are discounted at rate $\rho > 0$. The objective of A is to maximize his *expected discounted reward*

$$V_i = E\left\{ \sum_{k=0}^{\infty} e^{-\rho t_k} a_k | s(t_0) = i \right\}, \tag{5}$$

where E denotes the expected value. It obviously depends on the initial state i. Similarly, B wishes to maximize

$$W_i = E\left\{ \sum_{k=0}^{\infty} e^{-\rho t_k} b_k | s(t_0) = i \right\} \tag{6}$$

with b_k equal to $\sigma_{s(t_k)}$ or zero, depending on whether B's product is purchased at t_k.

It is convenient to replace our problem by an equivalent form with a discrete clock corresponding to purchase times. Setting $t_0 = 0$ after elementary calculation we get

$$E\{e^{-\rho t_k}\} = \alpha^k \tag{7}$$

with

$$\alpha = \frac{N}{N + \rho}. \tag{8}$$

For every k, purchase time t_k and producers' gains a_k and b_k are independent. Therefore we can substitute (7) into (5) and (6) obtaining a problem in which transitions occur at times $k = 0, 1, 2, \ldots$ and the discount per stage is α.

Let us now describe a *Nash equilibrium* in stationary policies, as a pair of policies $\pi^* = (\pi_0^*, \pi_1^*, \ldots, \pi_N^*)$ and $\sigma^* = (\sigma_0^*, \sigma_1^*, \ldots, \sigma_N^*)$ such that π^* is best for producer A if B uses σ^*, and σ^* is best for B if A uses π^* (see, e.g., Başar and Olsder [3] for a classification of equilibria in dynamic games).

Owing to the symmetry of the problem, we may focus our attention on A's prices, assuming that B follows his policy σ^*.

Let us assume that A's optimal policy π^* exists and that $V^* = (V_0^*, V_1^*, \ldots, V_N^*)$ is the corresponding *value vector* of best expected rewards (5). Then they satisfy the *Dynamic Programming Equation* (Bellman [4]):

$$V_i^* = \max_{\pi_i} \{ \phi_i(\pi_i, \sigma_i^*) + \alpha[q_i^+(\pi_i, \sigma_i^*)V_{i+1}^*$$

$$+ q_i^0(\pi_i, \sigma_i^*)V_i^* + q_i^-(\pi_i, \sigma_i^*)V_{i-1}^*]\}, \tag{9}$$

where for $i = 0,1, \ldots, N$, ϕ_i is the expected instantaneous reward

$$\phi_i(\pi_i, \sigma_i^*) = \pi_i f\left(\frac{i}{N}, \pi_i, \sigma_i^*\right) \tag{10}$$

and q_i^+, q_i^- and q_i^0 are transition probabilities (1):

$$q_i^+(\pi_i, \sigma_i^*) = \left(1 - \frac{i}{N}\right) f\left(\frac{i}{N}, \pi_i, \sigma_i^*\right),$$

$$q_i^-(\pi_i, \sigma_i^*) = \frac{i}{N} g\left(\frac{i}{N}, \pi_i \sigma_i^*\right), \tag{11}$$

$$q_i^0(\pi_i, \sigma_i^*) = 1 - q_i^+(\pi_i, \sigma_i^*) - q_i^-(\pi_i, \sigma_i^*).$$

Moreover, the optimal price π_i^* is the maximizer in (9).

Equations for B's policy σ^* and the corresponding value vector W_i^*, $i = 0,1, \ldots, N$, are analogous:

$$W_i^* = \max_{\sigma_i}\{\psi_i(\pi_i^*, \sigma_i) + \alpha[q_i^+(\pi_i^*, \sigma_i)W_{i+1}^* + q_i^0(\pi_i^*, \sigma_i)W_i^*$$

$$+ q_i^-(\pi_i^*, \sigma_i)W_{i-1}^*]\}, \tag{12}$$

with B's expected instantaneous payoff given by

$$\psi_i(\pi_i^*, \sigma_i) = \sigma_i g\left(\frac{i}{N}, \pi_i^*, \sigma_i\right). \tag{13}$$

Equations (9), (12) are necessary and sufficient conditions for a Nash equilibrium (π^*, σ^*). Existence of equilibria can be proved by specializing the standard argument based on fixed point theorems (see, e.g., Aubin [2]): the boundedness of feasibility intervals and continuity of all functions are sufficient. We shall not pursue this issue here; we shall assume that equilibria exist and shall focus our attention on their properties (the reader interested in the theory of Markovian game models is referred to Hoffman and Karp [12] and Zachrisson [16]).

We start from the following observation which motivates the use of a dynamic model when conformity occurs. Let us assume that maximal instantaneous rewards increase with market share, i.e.

$$\max_{\pi_{i+1}} \phi_{i+1}(\pi_{i+1}, \sigma_{i+1}^*) \geq \max_{\pi_i} \phi_i(\pi_i, \sigma_i^*), \qquad i = 0, 1, \ldots, N - 1.$$

Then we can prove that starting from higher market shares cannot be worse than from lower:

$$V^*_{i+1} \geq V^*_i, \qquad i = 0, 1, \ldots, N - 1. \tag{14}$$

Proof of this intuitively obvious property can be found in Appendix A.

Once (14) has been established, we can sharpen it substantially. Let $\hat{\pi}_i$ denote the *myopic price* corresponding to static optimization

$$\phi_i(\hat{\pi}_i, \sigma^*_i) = \max_{\pi_i} \phi_i(\pi_i, \sigma^*_i). \tag{15}$$

Then (see Appendix A for details)

$$V^*_{i+1} - V^*_i \geq \frac{\phi_{i+1}(\hat{\pi}_{i+1}, \sigma^*_{i+1}) - \phi_i(\hat{\pi}_i, \sigma^*_i)}{1 + \alpha}. \tag{16}$$

Estimates (14) and (16) can be used to establish a simple property of the optimal prices π^*_i. Let us rewrite the dynamic programming equation (9) as follows:

$$(1 - \alpha)V^*_i = \max_{\pi_i}\{\phi_i(\pi_i, \sigma^*_i) + \alpha q^+_i(\pi_i, \sigma^*_i)(V^*_{i+1} - V^*_i)$$

$$+ \alpha q^-_i(\pi_i, \sigma^*_i)(V^*_i - V^*_{i-1})\}. \tag{17}$$

It is reasonable to assume that the probability of purchasing A decreases when the price π_i grows, while the probability of purchasing B does not decrease. This implies that the last two terms in (17) form a nonincreasing function of π_i. When $V^*_{i+1} > V^*_i$, it is strictly decreasing. Now it is obvious that the optimal price π^*_i that maximizes (17) need not be larger than the myopic price defined by (15),

$$\pi^*_i \leq \hat{\pi}_i, \qquad i = 0, 1, \ldots, N. \tag{18}$$

In fact, when ϕ_i is smooth in π_i and the myopic price is in the interior of the feasibility interval, inequality (18) is sharp. It pays to decrease the instantaneous reward because changes in the market share can bring more. It is this fundamental trade-off between present and future incomes that motivates our research. We are going to analyze the influence of conformity on the extent to which it is profitable to decrease price below its myopic value.

4. A Continuous Approximation

As with the classical approach recalled in section 2, additional insight into the problem can be gained by constructing a continuous model in the market share $x \in [0, 1]$. We approximate the optimal reward vector V_i^*, $i = 0, 1, \ldots, N$ by a *normalized reward function* $v^*(x)$ so that

$$v^* \left(\frac{i}{N} \right) = \frac{1}{N} V_i^*, \qquad i = 0, 1, \ldots, N.$$

In a similar way we define the normalized reward function $w^*(x)$ for the second player. We also introduce continuous approximations $\pi(x)$ and $\sigma(x)$, $0 \le x \le 1$, of the policies of the players.

To derive an equation for $v^*(x)$ let us introduce, on the basis of (10) and (11), the functions:

$$\phi(x, \pi, \sigma) = \pi f(x, \pi, \sigma),$$
$$q^+(x, \pi, \sigma) = (1 - x) f(x, \pi, \sigma),$$
$$q^-(x, \pi, \sigma) = x g(x, \pi, \sigma),$$
$$q^0(x, \pi, \sigma) = 1 - q^+(x, \pi, \sigma) - q^-(x, \pi, \sigma).$$

Recalling the definition of α in (8) and rearranging terms, similarly to (17), we can rewrite the dynamic programming equation as follows

$$\frac{\rho N}{N + \rho} v^*(x) = \max_{\pi} \Big\{ \phi[x, \pi, \sigma^*(x)]$$

$$+ \frac{N^2}{N + \rho} q^+[x, \pi, \sigma^*(x)] \left[v^* \left(x + \frac{1}{N} \right) - v^*(x) \right] \quad (19)$$

$$+ \frac{N^2}{N + \rho} q^-[x, \pi, \sigma^*(x)] \left[v^* \left(x - \frac{1}{N} \right) - v^*(x) \right] \Big\}.$$

Near 0 (and 1) the equation is slightly different, with $v^* \left(x - \frac{1}{N} \right) \Big[$ or $v^* \left(x + \frac{1}{N} \right) \Big]$ replaced by $v^*(0)$ [and $v^*(1)$]. Assuming that $v^*(x)$ is twice continuously differentiable we can expand it up to second order terms and obtain from (19) the differential equation

$$\rho v^*(x) = \max_{\pi} \Big\{ \left(1 + \frac{\rho}{N} \right) \phi[x, \pi, \sigma^*(x)] + H[x, \pi, \sigma^*(x)] \frac{dv^*(x)}{dx}$$

$$+ \frac{1}{2N} \, Q[x, \pi, \sigma^*(x)] \, \frac{d^2 v^*(x)}{dx^2} \Bigg\} , \tag{20}$$

where, exactly as in (4), drift and fluctuation and coefficients are defined by

$$H(x, \pi, \sigma) = q^+(x, \pi, \sigma) - q^-(x, \pi, \sigma),$$
$$Q(x, \pi, \sigma) = q^+(x, \pi, \sigma) + q^-(x, \pi, \sigma).$$

This differential dynamic programming equation can be interpreted as a description of the flow of value in our system: the left hand side is the outflow due to discounting, while on the right we have inflows due to instantaneous rewards, systematic drift and fluctuations. It is similar to the backward-type equations developed by Fleming and Rishel in [9] for optimal control of diffusion processes.

It is clear that an equation identical with (20) can be written for the second player, with only $v^*(x)$ and $\phi[x, \pi, \sigma^*(x)]$ replaced by $w^*(x)$ and $\psi[x, \pi^*(x), \sigma] = \sigma g[x, \pi^*(x), \sigma]$, respectively (cf. [12], [13]).

5. The Critical Discount Rate

Following the approach of the previous section, let us derive an equation for the derivative

$$y(x) = \frac{dv^*(x)}{dx}.$$

We assume that strategies of both players are fixed at their equilibrium values and we denote by $\phi(x)$, $q^+(x)$, $q^-(x)$ and $q^0(x)$ the resulting instantaneous reward and transition probabilities. We also suppose that all functions involved are continuously differentiable.

Differentiating both sides of (19) and rearranging terms we obtain for $\frac{1}{N} < x < 1 - \frac{1}{N}$ the integral equation

$$y(x) = \frac{1}{N} \frac{d\phi(x)}{dx} + \frac{N}{N + \rho} \left\{ [\mathscr{E}_N y](x) + \frac{dq^+(x)}{dx} \int_x^{x + (1/N)} y(s) ds \right.$$

$$\left. - \frac{dq^-(x)}{dx} \int_{x - (1/N)}^{x} y(s) ds \right\} , \tag{21}$$

where $\mathcal{E}_N$ is the local expectation operator

$$[\mathcal{E}_N y](x) = q^-(x, \pi, \sigma) y \left(x - \frac{1}{N} \right)$$

$$+ q^0(x, \pi, \sigma) y(x) + q^+(x, \pi, \sigma) \nu \left(x + \frac{1}{N} \right). \tag{22}$$

(For $x < \dfrac{1}{N}$ the equation is slightly different: $[\mathcal{E}_N y](x)$ is replaced by $q^0(x)y(x)$ $+ q^+(x)y \left(x + \dfrac{1}{N} \right)$ and the last integral is over $[0,x]$. Similar corrections should be made for x close to 1.)

Detailed analysis of the integral equation (21) in its full form is difficult, so we shall restrict our considerations to an approximation obtained as follows. Using the estimates

$$\int_x^{x+(1/N)} y(s)\,ds \approx \int_{x-(1/N)}^x y(s)\,ds \approx \frac{1}{N} y(x)$$

we can (for large N) replace (21) by a much simpler equation

$$y(x) = \frac{1}{N} \frac{d\phi(x)}{dx} + \frac{N}{N + \rho} [\mathcal{E}_N y](x) + \frac{1}{N + \rho} \frac{dH(x)}{dx} y(x). \tag{23}$$

Assume that

$$\rho > \max_{0 \leq x \leq 1} \left| \frac{dH(x)}{dx} \right|. \tag{24}$$

Then (23) has a solution $y(x)$ and a uniform bound for its norm can be obtained (see Appendix B):

$$\max_{0 \leq x \leq 1} |y(x)| \leq \frac{N + \rho}{N} \left(\rho - \max_{0 \leq x \leq 1} \left| \frac{dH(x)}{dx} \right| \right)^{-1} \max_{0 \leq x \leq 1} \left| \frac{d\phi(x)}{dx} \right|. \tag{25}$$

The right hand side of (25) does not grow with N.

If condition (24) is violated, no such estimates can be derived. In fact, our assumption that we can approximate (19) by (20) with small errors is no longer valid: the derivative $dv^*(x)/dx$ need not exist.

Condition (24), although derived by approximations and non-rigorous arguments, appears to be crucial for our problem. Recalling the definition of the drift $H(x)$ as the expected rate of gains in the market share, we see that $dH(x)/dx$ is the expected acceleration rate (*self-reinforcement*). On the other hand, the discount coefficient ρ is the damping rate. So, in (24) we require that *the discount rate is larger than the self-reinforcement rate*. It is an understandable condition: otherwise there would be no price for ignition of the self-reinforcing process.

6. Strategic Pricing Rule

It is difficult to solve our continuous model (20) exactly, but we can still use it to gain more understanding of our game. We shall continue, therefore, the approximations that we derived in sections 4 and 5.

Let us assume that the functions ϕ, q^+, q^- and the optimal policies π^* and σ^* are continuously differentiable in all their arguments. We also assume that condition (24) is satisfied.

Using for large N the approximation

$$\mathscr{E}_N \frac{dv^*}{dx} \approx \frac{dv^*}{dx}$$

(with $\mathscr{E}_N$ defined by (22)) we obtain from (23) an approximation of the derivative of the value function

$$\frac{dv^*}{dx} \approx \left(\rho - \frac{dH}{dx} \right)^{-1} \frac{d\phi}{dx}. \tag{26}$$

Next, assuming that the maximum in (20) is attained in the interior of the feasibility interval and neglecting terms with $\frac{1}{N}$ we get

$$\frac{\partial}{\partial \pi} \left\{ \phi[x, \pi^*(x), \sigma^*(x)] + H[x, \pi^*(x), \sigma^*(x)] \frac{dv^*(x)}{dx} \right\} \approx 0. \tag{27}$$

Substitution of (26) into (27) and expansion of complete derivatives dH/dx and $d\phi/dx$, after simple but lengthy transformations leads to the equation

$$\left(\frac{1}{\pi^*} \frac{f}{f'_\pi} + 1 \right) (\rho - H'_x - H'_\sigma \sigma^{*'})$$

$$+ (f'_x + f'_\sigma \sigma^{*'}) \left[1 - x \left(1 + \frac{g'_\pi}{f'_\pi} \right) \right] = 0. \tag{28}$$

Let $\hat{\pi}(x)$ be the myopic price at x (i.e. the price that maximizes the expected instantaneous reward ϕ). Then $\hat{\pi}(x)$ satisfies the equation

$$\frac{d\phi}{d\pi} = \hat{\pi}f'_\pi + f = 0.$$

If we interpret f as a normalized demand function, we see that the myopic price is just the monopoly price. The first order approximation of the myopic price can be calculated at $\pi^*(x)$ by

$$\hat{\pi}(x) \approx - \frac{f[x, \pi^*(x), \sigma^*(x)]}{f'_\pi[x, \pi^*(x), \sigma^*(x)]}.$$

We also introduce the *substitution rate*

$$\mu_A(x) = - \frac{g'_\pi[x, \pi^*(x), \sigma^*(x)]}{f'_\pi[x, \pi^*(x), \sigma^*(x)]};$$

μ_A is the proportion of the number of customers gained by B to the number of customers lost by A, when A increases his prices.

With such notation equation (28) can be simplified as follows

$$\frac{\hat{\pi}(x)}{\pi^*(x)} - 1 = \frac{(f'_x + f'_\sigma \sigma^{*\prime})[1 - x(1 - \mu_A)]}{\rho - H'_x - H'_\sigma \sigma^{*\prime}_x}. \tag{29}$$

We shall call the above equation the *strategic pricing rule*.

A number of conclusions can be drawn from (29). First, if the market share x has no influence on customers' preferences (if there is no conformity), we have $df/dx = 0$ and (29) yields $\pi^*(x) = \hat{\pi}(x)$.

Secondly, if positive market-share effects are present ($df/dx > 0$) then the optimal price is smaller than the myopic price. The optimal discount quotient $\hat{\pi}/\pi^*$ increases faster than the conformity rate f'_x, because the denominator of (29) decreases.

Thirdly, we use higher prices when the substitution rate μ_A is small (close to 0). The difference between these two cases increases when the market share x grows. In particular, if $\mu_A = 0$ our price $\pi^*(x)$ tends to the myopic price when $x \to 1$, i.e., when A has an almost monopolistic position. So, with μ_A small, the optimal price at first decreases in x and, after reaching its minimum, goes up to the monopoly price. For μ_A close to 1 the end value is smaller, because even in an almost monopolistic position customers can still switch to B. All these effects can be substantially amplified by decreasing the discount rate ρ. Especially, in the presence of strong market-share effects, at balanced market shares the numerator of (29) and the drift derivative H'_x are close to their largest values, so by small ρ the discount quotient can be very large.

Equation for the second player's strategy is similar

$$\frac{\hat{\sigma}(x)}{\sigma^*(x)} - 1 = - \frac{(g'_x + g'_\pi \pi^{*\prime}_x)[1 - (1 - x)(1 - \mu_B)]}{\rho - H'_x - H'_\pi \pi^{*\prime}_x} \tag{30}$$

with

$$\mu_B(x) = - \frac{f'_\sigma[x, \pi^*(x), \sigma^*(x)]}{g'_\sigma[x, \pi^*(x), \sigma^*(x)]}.$$

Again, when $\mu_A \approx 0$ and $\mu_B \approx 0$ we conclude that for small market shares $(x \to 0)$

$$\frac{\pi^*}{\hat{\pi}} < \frac{\sigma^*}{\hat{\sigma}} \to 1$$

while for $x \to 1$ one has

$$\frac{\sigma^*}{\hat{\sigma}} < \frac{\pi^*}{\hat{\pi}} \to 1.$$

Thus, near the boundaries the winner uses monopoly prices while the loser lowers his prices. Therefore, equilibrium prices introduce an additional centering effect in comparison with constant pricing. However, the relation of the prices in the middle of the interval [0, 1] depends on the strength of positive market-share effects.

If conformity is strong enough, we can expect that the graphs of $\pi^*(x)/\hat{\pi}(x)$ and $\sigma^*(x)/\hat{\sigma}(x)$ cross three times in [0, 1]. Consequently, there will be an interval in the center with an additional polarizing trend: to the right for x slightly greater than the middle cross-point and to the left for x smaller than the cross-point. Thus we shall observe a form of *synergy* in our model: reinforcement of positive feedback to market share by equilibrium strategic pricing.

7. An Example

To illustrate the theory we present results of the numerical analysis of a simple example with increasing returns to market share that may derive from network externalities, fashion effects, or other positive feedback mechanisms. For simplicity, we call these conformity effects.

We assume that the preferences of customers are driven by a *superlinear conformity* effect similar to that of the example of market-share effects. A customer prefers product A with probability

$$P_A = \frac{e^{\kappa x}}{e^{\kappa x} + e^{\kappa(1-x)}}$$

and product B with probability

$$P_B = \frac{e^{\kappa(1-x)}}{e^{\kappa x} + e^{\kappa(1-x)}}$$

He purchases his desired product with probability $\exp(-\pi/\hat{\pi})$ or $\exp(-\sigma/\hat{\sigma})$, respectively. (And if he does not purchase, he stays with his current product.) Setting for simplicity $\hat{\pi} = 1$ and $\hat{\sigma} = 1$, in the notation (5) we have:

$$f(x, \pi, \sigma) = e^{-\pi} \frac{e^{\kappa x}}{e^{\kappa x} + e^{\kappa(1-x)}},$$

$$g(x, \pi, \sigma) = e^{-\sigma} \frac{e^{\kappa(1-x)}}{e^{\kappa x} + e^{\kappa(1-x)}}.$$

Since $f'_\sigma = 0$ and $g'_\pi = 0$, we have $\mu_A = \mu_B = 0$ in equations (30).

We realize these "demand functions" are somewhat ad hoc: but we choose them for ease of numerical computation.

We may now solve the game numerically, with the number of customers (customer groups) $N = 100$ and with the conformity constant $\kappa = 2.2$, which corresponds to the bifurcation in figure 1. Prices of both players are restricted to nonnegative values.

In figures 2, 3, and 4 we show equilibrium prices of both players for three characteristic values of the discount rate: $\rho = 0.5$, $\rho = 0.4$ and $\rho = 0.1$ and in figure 5 we present the evolution of A's policy for $\rho \in [0.1, 1.0]$. A striking change in the form of the solution can be observed. For large ρ the equilibrium policy behaves in a regular way, with small discounting when the share is small and with large prices when the market is dominated. However, near the critical value $\rho_{crit} \approx 0.4$ a struggle for market shares begins to take place. Both players use zero prices with the aim to dominate the market; the player who wins (has a bigger share) uses lower prices (for x close to 0.5) than the loser so as to hold on to his advantage. If he succeeds in dominating the market, he then raises his price to take advantage of his monopoly position. The value function (fig. 6) increases very fast for small ρ; the steep slope

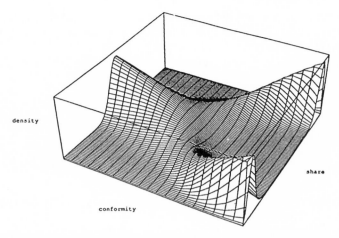

Fig. 1. Stationary distribution of market shares with the conformity constant ranging from 1 (left) to 3 (right)

encourages substantial price decrements. In every case the lowest prices are not used at very small shares, but rather near the center, at pivotal states.

This struggle for market shares has a strong polarizing effect on the distribution of market shares (see fig. 7). It is worth noting that for medium discount rates $(0.5 < \rho < 1.0)$ the distribution is centered in comparison with the case when both players use myopic prices (cf. fig. 1). Near the critical

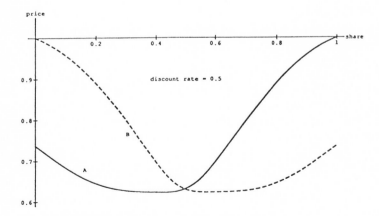

Fig. 2. Equilibrium prices at high discount rate.

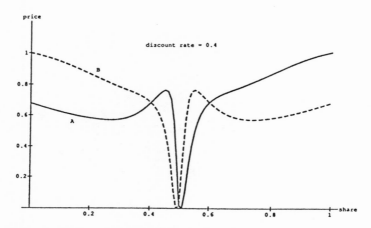

Fig. 3. Equilibrium prices at critical discount rate.

value of the discount rate, however, bifurcation occurs and for smaller ρ the distribution is strongly polarized.

In figures 8, 9, and 10 we show simulation results for the three characteristic discount rates. We see that as ρ decreases, the trajectory has an increasing tendency to stay for long periods in regions with relative preva-

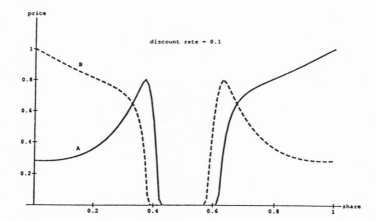

Fig. 4. Equilibrium prices at low discount rate.

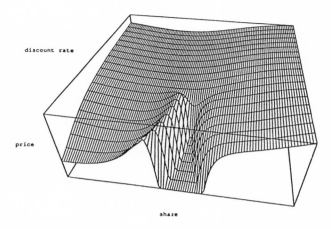

Fig. 5. Evolution of *A*'s policy when the discount rate drops from 1.0 (back) to 0.1 (front).

lence of one product. It should be stressed that we use a rather small N in our experiments, which corresponds to a rather dynamic (flexible) market. When N grows, then the diffusion term $Q(x)/2N$ in (4) decreases and the probability of passing from one maximum to another becomes smaller.

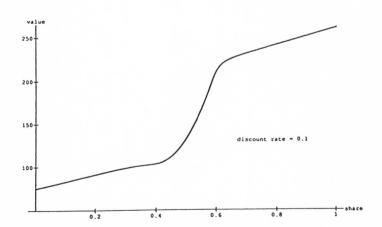

Fig. 6. The value function of *A* at low discount rate.

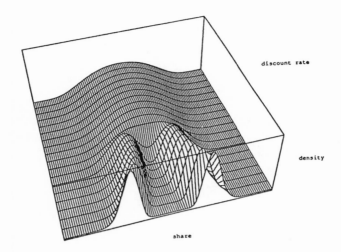

Fig. 7. Evolution of the stationary distribution when the discount rate falls from 1.0 (back) to 0.1 (front).

We have also carried out experiments that allow significant nonzero substitution rates. Here two new phenomena appear. First, near $x = 0.5$ the loser uses prices that are *higher* than the myopic value. This stems from a local decrease of the value function when approaching 0.5. Starting near 0.5

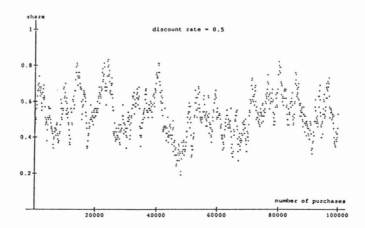

Fig. 8. Trajectory of market states at equilibrium at high discount rate.

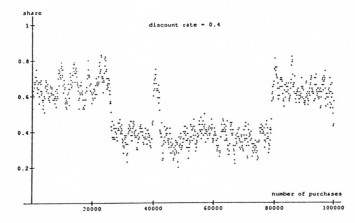

Fig. 9. Trajectory of market states at equilibrium at critical discount rate.

(but below it) is disadvantages because the opponent will be forced to use zero prices and the chances of success will be negligible anyway. Thus the loser may as well price high. This phenomenon sharply polarizes the market-share distribution. Second, both players use almost identical prices far from the critical region results from nonzero substitution rates.

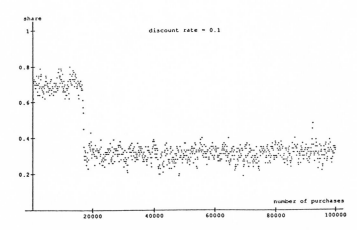

Fig. 10. Trajectory of market states at equilibrium at low discount rate.

Conclusions

The simple dynamic and stochastic model of market competition analyzed in this paper reveals striking properties.

First, positive-feedback or self-reinforcement to market share may result in bistable stationary distributions with higher probabilities assigned to assymetric market shares. The stronger the positive-feedback, the lower the probability of passing from the region of relative prevalence of one product to that of the other.

Second, when producers can influence purchase probabilities by prices, in the presence of positive feedback, optimal pricing is highly state-dependent. The producers struggle for market shares by lowering prices, especially near pivot states with balanced shares.

Third, there is a fundamental relation between positive-feedback effects and the discount rate. If the discount rate is high, producers are less concerned with capturing market share for future use; this damps the influence of self-reinforcing phenomena and stabilizes the market. The resulting market state distribution is centered. On the other hand, if the discount rate is low, producers use pricing to hold onto monopoly positions associated with high market share and its positive-feedback advantages. This locks in these positions temporarily, and so equilibrium pricing strategies amplify self-reinforcing phenomena and the market is more strongly polarized than at constant pricing.

APPENDIX A

Lemma 1. If

$$\max_{\pi_{i+1}} \phi_{i+1}(\pi_{i+1}, \sigma^*_{i+1}) \geq \max_{\pi_i} \phi_i(\pi_i, \sigma^*_i),$$

$$i = 0, 1, \ldots, N - 1. \tag{A.1}$$

Then

$$V^*_{i+1} \geq V^*_i, \qquad i = 0, 1, \ldots, N - 1. \tag{A.2}$$

Proof. Suppose that $V^*_{i+1} \geq V^*_i$, $i = j, j + 1, \ldots, N$ (for $j = N$ we define $V^*_{N+1} = V^*_N$).

Let

$$\gamma_j = \max_{\pi_i} \{\phi_j(\pi_j) + \alpha p_j^+(\pi_j)(V_{j+1}^* - V_j^*)\}$$

(we skip σ_j^* for brevity), and let $\tilde{\pi}_j$ be the maximizer of this expression. The dynamic programming equation (9) yields an upper bound

$$V_j^* = \max_{\pi_j} \{\phi_j(\pi_j) + \alpha p_j^+(\pi_j)(V_{j+1}^* - V_j^*) + \alpha p_j^-(\pi_j)V_{j-1}^*$$

$$+ \alpha[1 - p_j^-(\pi_j)]V_j^*\} \le \gamma_j + \alpha \max_{\pi_j} \{p_j^-(\pi_j)V_{j-1}^*$$

$$+ [1 - p_j^-(\pi_j)]V_j^*\}. \tag{A.3}$$

Let us now estimate V_{j-1}^*. Almost every trajectory starting from $j - 1$ reaches j at some random stage n ($n < \infty$ with probability 1). For $k < n$ we have by (A.1) and the definition of γ_j

$$\phi_k(\pi_k^*) \le \max_{\pi_k} \phi_k(\pi_k) \le \max_{\pi_j} \phi_j(\pi_j) \le \gamma_j,$$

because $V_{j+1}^* \ge V_j^*$. Therefore

$$V_{j-1}^* = E\left\{\sum_{k=0}^{n-1} \alpha^k \phi_k(\pi_k^*) + \alpha^n V_j^*\right\}$$

$$\le E\{\gamma(1 - \alpha^n)/(1 - \alpha) + \alpha^n V_j^*\}. \tag{A.4}$$

Substituting (A.4) into (A.3) we observe that $V_j^* \le \gamma_j/(1 - \alpha)$. Then (A.4) yields the bound $V_{j-1}^* \le \gamma_j/(1 - \alpha)$. Using $\tilde{\pi}_j$ on the left side of (A.3) instead of π_j^* we can estimate V_j^* from below:

$$V_j^* \ge \gamma_j - (1 - \alpha)V_{j-1}^* + V_{j-1}^* - \alpha[1 - p_j^-(\tilde{\pi}_j)]V_{j-1}^*$$
$$+ \alpha[1 - p_j^-(\tilde{\pi}_j)]V_j^*.$$

Substituting the recently obtained bound for V_{j-1}^* and rearranging terms we get $V_j^* \ge V_{j-1}^*$. This ends the induction step and proves (A.2).

Lemma 2. Let the conditions of Lemma 1 hold and let $\hat{\pi}_i$ denote the myopic price:

$$\phi_i(\hat{\pi}_i, \sigma_i^*) = \max_{\pi_i} \phi_i(\pi_i, \sigma_i^*).$$

Then

$$V^*_{i+1} - V^*_i \geq [\phi_{i+1}(\hat{\pi}_{i+1}, \sigma^*_{i+1}) - \phi_i(\hat{\pi}_i, \sigma^*_i)]/(1 + \alpha).$$

Proof. By Lemma 1, replacing in (9) both V^*_{i-1} and V^*_i by V^*_{i+1} can only increase the right hand side, so

$$V^*_i \leq \max_{\pi_i}\{\phi_i(\pi_i, \sigma^*_i) + \alpha V^*_{i+1}\} = \phi_i(\hat{\pi}_i, \sigma^*_i) + \alpha V^*_{i+1}.$$

Consider (9) for $i + 1$ and replace all values on the right by V^*_i. Then, by Lemma 1,

$$V^*_{i+1} \geq \max_{\pi_i}\{\phi_{i+1}(\pi_{i+1}, \sigma^*_{i+1}) + \alpha V^*_i\} = \phi_{i+1}(\hat{\pi}_{i+1}, \sigma^*_{i+1}) + \alpha V^*_i.$$

Combining the last two inequalities we get the required result.

APPENDIX B

Lemma 3. Let $\mathcal{R}:\mathscr{C}[0, 1] \rightarrow \mathscr{C}[0, 1]$ be defined by

$$[\mathcal{R}y](x) = \frac{1}{N}\frac{d\phi(x)}{dx} + \frac{N}{N + \rho}[\mathscr{E}_N y](x)$$

$$+ \frac{1}{N + \rho}\frac{dH(x)}{dx}y(x), \qquad 0 \leq x \leq 1.$$

Assume that

$$\rho > \max_{0 \leq x \leq 1}\left|\frac{dH(x)}{dx}\right|. \tag{B.1}$$

Then $\mathcal{R}$ is a contraction mapping in $\mathscr{C}[0, 1]$, the equation

$$y = \mathcal{R}y \tag{B.2}$$

has a unique solution y and its sup norm $\|y\|$ can be bounded by

$$\|y\| \leq \frac{N + \rho}{N}\left(\rho - \left\|\frac{dH}{dx}\right\|\right)^{-1}\left\|\frac{d\phi}{dx}\right\|. \tag{B.3}$$

Proof. Since $\|E_N\| = 1$, for arbitrary y_1 and y_2 we have

$$\|\mathcal{R}y_2 - \mathcal{R}y_1\| \le \frac{N}{N + \rho} \|E_N(y_2 - y_1)\|$$

$$+ \frac{1}{N + \rho} \left\| \frac{dH}{dx} \right\| \|y_2 - y_1\| \le q\|y_2 - y_1\|,$$

where, by (B.1),

$$q = 1 - \frac{1}{N + \rho} \left(\rho - \left\| \frac{dH}{dx} \right\| \right) < 1.$$

By the contraction mapping principle, (B.2) has a solution in $\mathscr{C}[',\infty]$. Estimating the right hand side of (B.2) we get:

$$\|y\| \le \frac{1}{N} \left\| \frac{d\phi}{dx} \right\| + q\|y\|,$$

which yields the bound (B.3).

REFERENCES

1. W. B. Arthur. 1988. Self-Reinforcing Mechanisms in Economics. In *The Economy as an Evolving Complex System.* P. W. Anderson, K. J. Arrow, and D. Pines (eds.), *SFI Studies in the Sciences of Complexity.* Reading: Addison-Wesley.
2. J. P. Aubin. 1979. *Mathematical Methods of Game and Economic Theory.* Amsterdam: North-Holland.
3. T. Başar and G. J. Olsder. 1982. *Dynamic Noncooperative Game Theory.* London: Academic Press.
4. R. Bellman. 1957. *Dynamic Programming.* Princeton: Princeton University Press.
5. D. P. Bertsekas. 1987. *Dynamic Programming: Deterministic and Stochastic Models.* Englewood Cliffs: Prentice-Hall.
6. W. J. Ewens. 1979. *Mathematical Population Genetics.* New York: Springer-Verlag.
7. W. Feller. 1966. *An Introduction to Probability Theory and Its Applications.* Vol 2. New York: Wiley.
8. M. T. Flaherty. 1980. Industry Structure and Cost-Reducing Investment. *Econometrica,* 48:1187–1209.
9. W. H. Fleming and R. W. Rishel. 1975. *Deterministic and Stochastic Control.* New York: Springer-Verlag.
10. D. Fudenberg and J. Tirole. 1983. Learning by Doing and Market Performance. *Bell J. Economics,* 14:522–30.

11. W. A. Hanson. 1985. Bandwagons and Orphans: Dynamic Pricing of Competing Systems Subject to Decreasing Costs. *Ph.D. Diss.*, Stanford University.
12. A. J. Hoffman and R. M. Karp. 1966. On Nonterminating Stochastic Games. *Management Science,* 12:359–70.
13. H. Risken. 1989. *The Fokker-Planck Equation. Methods of Solution and Applications.* Berlin: Springer-Verlag.
14. M. Spence. 1981. The Learning Curve and Competition. *Bell J. Economics,* 12:49–70.
15. W. Weidlich and G. Haag. 1983. *Concepts and Models of Quantitative Sociology.* Berlin: Springer-Verlag.
16. L. E. Zachrisson. 1964. Markov Games. In *Advances in Game Theory,* M. Dresher, L. S. Shapley, and A. W. Tucker (eds.), *Ann. Mathematical Studies,* 52. Princeton: Princeton University Press.

CHAPTER 10

Strong Laws for a Class of Path-Dependent Stochastic Processes

W. Brian Arthur, Yuri M. Ermoliev, and Yuri M. Kaniovski

In this 1984 paper, Yuri Ermoliev, Yuri Kaniovski, and I explore a class of nonlinear stochastic processes particularly applicable to positive-feedback problems in economics. We call them generalized urn schemes of the Polya kind, and investigate both their dynamics and long-run limiting behavior. Generalized urn schemes were discussed earlier, in chapter 3. This chapter offers a more technical account of these processes.

This paper was one of a series of papers that Ermoliev, Kaniovski, and I published in Russian and English on generalized urn processes throughout the 1980s. Other papers include: "On Generalized Urn Schemes of the Polya Kind, *Kibernetika* 19 (1983):49–56, (English translation in *Cybernetics* 19:61–71); "Urn Schemes and Adaptive Process of Growth, *Kibernetika* 23 (1987):49–58; "Non-Linear Urn Processes: Asymptotic Behavior and Applications," WP-87-85, IIASA, Laxenburg, Austria, 1987; "Limit Theorems for Proportions of Balls in a Generalized Urn Scheme," WP-87-111, IIASA, Laxenburg, Austria, 1987; and "Nonlinear Adaptive Processes of Growth with General Increments: Attainable and Unattainable Components of the Terminal Set," WP-88-86, IIASA, Laxenburg, Austria, 1988. An early and elegant paper on such processes is "Strong Convergence for a Class of Urn Schemes," by Bruce Hill, David Lane, and William Sudderth, *Annals of Probability* 8 (1980):214–26.

This paper appeared in the *Proceedings of the International Conference on Stochastic Optimization, Kiev 1984*, edited by V. Arkin, A. Shiryayev, and R. Wets, published as vol. 81 in the series Lecture Notes in Control and Information Sciences, Springer, New York, 1986. Yuri Ermoliev and Yuri Kaniovski are with the Glushkov Institute of Cybernetics, Kiev, Ukraine.

1. Introduction

In many simple sequential processes (rolls of a die say), outcomes at each time may be labelled by category or type (the die turns up 1, or 2, or 3, etc.), with type i having fixed probability $q(i)$, and $\Sigma_i\, q(i) = 1$. The strong law of large numbers then tells us that over time the proportion of outcomes of each type must converge to the probability for that type.

We consider an important generalization of such processes, wherein the probability $q(i)$ is no longer fixed, but becomes itself a function of the proportions at each moment. This is the case, for example, where new firms in a growing industry each in turn make a locational choice between N possible cities, but where the probability that a given city is chosen next for location depends on the number of firms already located there. Transitions in the proportions of the industry in the various cities now depend upon the path these proportions follow. We seek strong laws for processes of this path-dependent type.

It is convenient to formulate such path-dependent processes as generalized urn schemes of the Polya kind. Consider an urn of infinite capacity that contains balls of N possible colors or types. Let the vector $X_n = (X_n^1, X_n^2, \ldots, X_n^N)$ describe the proportions of balls of type 1 to N respectively, at time n; and let $\{q_n\}_{n=1}^\infty$ be a sequence of Borel functions from the N-dimensional unit simplex S into itself. One ball is added to the urn at each time n; it is of type i with probability $q_n^i(X_n)$. Starting with an *initial vector* of balls $b_1 = (b_1^1, b_1^2, \ldots, b_1^N)$ the process is iterated to yield $X_1, X_2, X_3, \ldots$. We investigate conditions under which X_n converges to a limit random vector X, and the support set of X, under different specifications of the urn functions q_n. In general, we find that where q_n possesses a limit function q and where the process converges, it converges to a limit which belongs to a subset of the fixed points of q.

The literature on this problem is small. In a recent elegant paper, Hill, Lane, and Sudderth [1] analyze the special case where $N = 2$ and the urn functions q_n are stationary. Blum and Brennan [2] present strong laws for a related problem (with $N = 2$) where additions to each category are also restricted to 0 or 1. In this paper we extend our own previous results [3] for the general N-dimensional, time-varying case. We use, for the most part, Lyapunov techniques and stochastic approximation methods. We pay special attention to unstable points (fixed points of q that are not in the support of X); and to convergence to the vertices of the simplex (where a single color dominates). We also present examples of path-dependent processes in economic theory, optimization theory, and chemical kinetics, for which this N-dimensional, nonstationary, path-dependent process is a natural model.

Nonstationary functions arise even in simple urn schemes. Consider Example 1.1. *A Sampled Urn.* (a) An urn contains red and white balls. Sample at random r balls. If m, where $0 \leq m \leq r$, or more are white, replace the sample and add a white. Otherwise add a red. (b) As before, but if m or more are white, replace the sample and add a *red*. Otherwise add a *white*. In (a) the probability that a white is added is

$$q_n^w = \sum_{k=m}^{r} H(k; n, n_w, r)$$

where H is the Hypergeometric distribution parametrized by n, r, and n_w, the number of white balls at time n. In this sampled urn scheme the urn function (path-dependent on n_w) is nonstationary: the Hypergeometric varies with n.

As a simple N-dimensional urn example consider

Example 1.2. An urn contains balls of N colors. Choose one ball. If it is of type j replace it and add a ball of type i with probability $q(i, j)$, where

$$\sum_{i=1}^{N} q(i, j) = 1, \text{ for all } j.$$

For example, when $N = 3$, we might have the rule: Choose one ball, replace it and add a ball which is one of the two possible other colors with equal probability one half.

Notice that the well-known basic Polya scheme [1] (sample one ball and replace it together with a ball of the same color) is a special case both of 1.1 (a) (where r and m are 1) and of 1.2 (where $q(i, i) = 1$ and $N = 2$). For this scheme, the proportion of white balls, n_w/n, converges almost surely to a random limit variable that has a beta distribution with parameters dependent on the initial urn composition. This case however, is singular. When r in 1.1 (a) is greater than 2, our results below show that n_w/n converges to a random variable with support $\{0, 1\}$ only. In 1.1 (b) they show that it converges to a single interior point $\{p\}$. The process of 1.2 also converges, as we will show later.

The general scheme above covers other path-dependent processes.

Example 1.3. *A Position-Dependent Random Walk.* Consider a simple one-dimensional random walk, where $Y_i = \pm 1$, with the position at n given by partial sum $S_n = \sum_{i=1}^{n} Y_i$, but with position-dependent transition probabilities $P(Y_i = +1) = p_n(S_n)$. If we add a white ball to the urn when $Y_i = +1$, a red ball when $Y_i = -1$ (starting from an empty urn), the position of the random walk, S_n, is given by $(2X_n - 1)n$, where X_n is the proportion of white balls in the total n. We can then treat the limiting behavior of the random walk within our present framework.

The general N-dimensional time-varying urn process described above does not always converge. Theorem 3.1 establishes a test for convergence, expressed in terms of the existence of a limit function for $\{q_n\}$ and of an appropriate Lyapunov Function. Theorem 6.1 shows more general conditions, for the particular case where the q_n functions are separable. In general, continuity of the q_n functions is not required for convergence. Where the process does converge and the q_n functions are continuous, the support of the limit vector lies within the set $\left\{ X : q(X) = X, \ q(X) = \lim_{n \to \infty} q_n(X), \ X \epsilon S \right\}$,

that is, within the set of fixed points of the limit function q. (A slight modification is required for noncontinuous urn functions.) However, not all fixed points of q are in the support. Theorems 5.1 and 5.2 show that certain fixed points can be classed as *stable* and *unstable*, with stable fixed points in the support, but unstable ones excluded. We pay particular attention in theorems 4.1 and 6.4 to conditions under which the vertices of the simplex are in the support, that is conditions under which the process tends to single-color dominance. In a final section applications in economic theory, optimization theory, and chemical kinetics are outlined.

2. Preliminaries

The general process starts at time 1 with a vector $b_1 = (b_1^1, b_1^2, \ldots, b_1^N)$ of balls in the urn, with total $\gamma = \Sigma_i b_1^i$. Balls are added indefinitely, according to the urn probability functions q_n. At time n, define the random variable

$$\beta_n^i(x) = \begin{cases} 1 & \text{with probability } q_n^i(x) \\ 0 & \text{with probability } 1 - q_n^i(x), \end{cases} \qquad i = 1, \ldots, N.$$

Then additions of i-type balls to the urn follow the dynamics

$$b_{n+1}^i = b_n^i + \beta_n^i(X_n) \qquad i = 1, \ldots, N.$$

Thus the evolution of the proportion of i-types, $X_n^i = b_n^i/(\gamma + n - 1)$, is described by

$$X_{n+1}^i = X_n^i - \frac{1}{\gamma + n} [X_n^i - \beta_n^i(X_n)] \qquad n = 1, 2, \ldots \qquad (1)$$

with

$$X_1^i = b_1^i/\gamma.$$

We can rewrite (1) in the form

$$X_{n+1}^i = X_n^i - \frac{1}{\gamma + n} [X_n^i - q_n^i(X_n)] + \frac{1}{\gamma + n} \eta_n^i(X_n) \qquad (2)$$

$$X_1^i = b_1^i/\gamma,$$

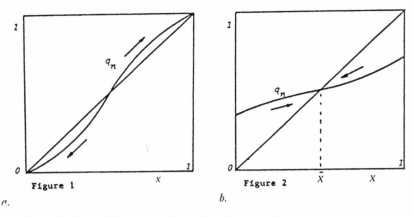

Fig. 1a–b. Probability q_n as a function of proportion x in two different one-dimensional cases.

where

$$\eta_n^i(X_n) = \beta_n^i(X_n) - q_n^i(X_n).$$

Noting that the conditional expectation of η_n^i with respect to X_n is zero, we can derive the expected motion of X_{n+1} as

$$E\{X_{n+1}^i | X_n\} = X_n^i - \frac{1}{\gamma + n} [X_n^i - q_n^i(X_n)]. \tag{3}$$

Thus we see that motion tends to be directed by the term $q_n(X_n) - X_n$. In figure 1, for example, this tendency is toward 0 or 1. In figure 2 it is toward $\bar{X}$.

3. A Convergence Test

We begin with a convergence theorem that is a stochastic analog of the Lyapunov asymptotic stability theorem for deterministic systems. It serves as a very general test for convergence in the N-dimensional case. We denote the N-dimensional unit simplex by S, and use $\| \cdot \|$ to denote the Euclidean norm.

Theorem 3.1. Given continuous urn functions $\{q_n\}$, suppose there exists a Borel function $q: S \to S$, constants $\{a_n\}$, and a (Lyapunov) function $v: S \to R$ such that:

(a) $\displaystyle \sup_{x \in S} \|q_n(x) - q(x)\| \le a_n, \ \sum_{n=1}^{\infty} a_n/n < \infty$

(b) The set
$$B = \{x : q(x) = x, \ x \in S\}$$
contains a finite number of connected components

(c) (i) v is twice differentiable

   (ii) $v(x) \ge 0, \qquad x \in S$

   (iii) $\langle q(x) - x, \ v_x(x) \rangle < 0, \qquad x \in S \backslash U(B)$

   where $U(B)$ is an open neighborhood of B.

Then $\{x_n\}$ converges to a point of B or to the border of a connected component.

Proof. The theorem follows from stochastic approximation results of Nevelson and Hasminskii [4], ch. 2. Applied to our problem, we can summarize the argument as follow. Note first that $v(X_n)$ eventually becomes a non-negative supermartingale on S. On the set $S \backslash U(B)$, v has expected increment always less than some $-\delta$; hence the process must exit this set in finite time. It thus enters $U(B)$ infinitely often. Next, the cumulated perturbations

$$\sum_{n=0}^{t} \frac{1}{(n + \gamma)} \ \eta_n$$

form a martingale and converge; thus after sufficient time the process cannot cumulate sufficient perturbation to counter expected motion and exit an ϵ-neighborhood surrounding $U(B)$. Now the B-components are separated by finite distances. Hence the process converges to a single component of B or its border. Finally, since expected motions within B are zero, and cumulated perturbations converge, the process cannot visit distinct points inside B infinitely often. Thus $\{X_n\}$ converges to a point of B, or to the border of a connected component.   ∎

For the most general cases, an appropriate Lyapunov function may be difficult to find. For the special case $N = 2$, an appropriate Lyapunov function is simply the norm

$$v(x) = \int_0^x [t - q(t)]dt + a$$

providing q is differentiable. (For this reason a norm can be used in place of Lyapunov functions in the two-color case in [1]. We can also construct a Lyapunov function in the case of $N > 2$, providing the q^i are differentiable and symmetric in the sense that

$$\partial q^i / \partial x^k = \partial q^k / \partial x^i, \quad x \epsilon S.$$

Remark 3.1. In the case of example 1.2 it is easily shown that

$$q_n(x) = Qx$$

where the matrix $Q = [q(i,j)]$. We can take $v(x) = \langle (I - Q)x, x \rangle$ for

$$B = \{x : (I - Q)x = 0\}$$

where I is the identity matrix. The theorem then tells us that the scheme converges to a fixed point $\bar{x} = Q\bar{x}$.

4. Convergence to the Vertices

We next establish conditions under which the urn may converge to single-color dominance, that is, conditions under which X_n may converge to a vertex of the simplex S. Without loss of generality we take the vertex to be

$$(0, 0, \ldots , 1).$$

Theorem 4.1. Given the process characterized by initial urn vector b_1 and $\{q_n\}$. Let $\bar{b}_n^i = b_1^i$, for $i = 1, \ldots , N - 1$; $\bar{b}_n^N = b_1^N + n - 1$.

If (a)
$$\sum_{i=1}^{N-1} q_n^i \left(\frac{n}{\gamma + n - 1} \right) \geq 1, \, n \geq 1$$

and (b)
$$\sum_{n=1}^{\infty} \sum_{i=1}^{N-1} q_n^i \left(\frac{\bar{b}_n}{\gamma + n - 1} \right) < \infty$$

then

$$P \left\{ \bigcap_{i=1}^{N-1} \left[\lim_{n \to \infty} X_n^i = 0 \right] \right\} > 0.$$

Proof. Let

$$A_n = \{\omega \mid b_n^i = b_1^i, i = 1, \ldots, N - 1; b_n^N = b_1^N + n - 1\}$$

then

$$P\left\{ \bigcap_{i=1}^{N-1} \left[\lim_{n\to\infty} X_n^i = 0 \right] \right\} \geq P\left\{ \bigcap_{n=1}^{\infty} A_n \right\}$$

$$= \prod_{n=1}^{\infty} \left\{ 1 - \sum_{i=1}^{N-1} q_n^i \left(\frac{\bar{b}_n}{\gamma + n - 1} \right) \right\} > 0,$$

the inequality following from standard results on the convergence of infinite products. The theorem then follows. ∎

Notice that this theorem is independent of the previous one—no special conditions are imposed on the $\{q_n\}$ beyond the condition (a) that the vertex is reachable from the starting point, and the condition (b) that $q^N(X)$ approaches 1 sufficiently fast as X approaches the vertex.

5. Stable and Unstable Fixed Points

We now wish to show that convergence is restricted to only certain subsets of the fixed points of q. We will find useful a lemma of Hill, Lane, and Sudderth [1] extended to the N-dimensional case.

Lemma 5.1. Suppose $\{X_n\}$ and $\{Y_n\}$ are generalized urn processes with the same initial urn compositions and with urn functions $\{f_n\}$ and $\{g_n\}$ respectively. Suppose all urn functions map the interior of S into itself, and suppose f_n and g_n agree a.e. in a neighborhood U of the point θ. Then $\{X_n\}$ converges to θ with positive probability if and only if $\{Y_n\}$ does.

Proof. The argument follows that in [1]. In essence, if $\{X_n\}$ converges to θ, the process must be contained within U from some stage k onward and must therefore have reached some point a within U at that stage. Since the q_n map the interior of the simplex into itself, a must also be reachable by $\{Y_n\}$ at stage k with positive probability, and once in this state a at k the two processes become identical. Hence $\{Y_n\}$ converges to θ with positive probability, and the lemma is proved. ∎

We now consider fixed points θ of q of two special types. Given θ and a neighborhood U of θ, we will say that θ is a *stable point* if there exists a symmetric positive-definite matrix C such that

$$\langle C[x - q(x)], x - \theta \rangle > 0, \text{ for } x \neq \theta \quad x \in U \cap S. \tag{4}$$

Similarly we will call θ an *unstable point* if θ is such that

$$\langle C[x - q(x)], x - \theta \rangle < 0, \quad \text{for} \quad x \neq \theta \quad x \in U \cap S. \tag{5}$$

Notice that we impose no requirement that q is continuous within U. In the $N = 2$ case, stable points are those where q downcrosses the diagonal, unstable ones are where q upcrosses the diagonal. In N-dimensions downcrossing and upcrossing are inappropriate: the Lyapunov criterion (4) tests whether expected motion is locally always toward θ, the Lyapunov criterion (5) tests whether it is locally always away from θ.

We now show that the process converges to stable points with positive probability:

> Theorem 5.1. Let θ be a stable point in the interior of S. Given a process with transition functions $\{q_n\}$ which map the interior of S into itself, and which converge in the sense that
>
> $$\sup_{x \in U \subset S} \| q_n(x) - q(x) \| \leq a_n, \quad \sum_{n=1}^{\infty} a_n/n < \infty$$
>
> then
>
> $$P\{X_n \to \theta\} > 0.$$

Proof. Construct the functions $\{\bar{q}_n\}$ and $\{\bar{q}\}$ which are identical to $\{q_n\}$ and $\{q\}$ respectively within the neighborhood U, and are equal to θ outside it. Let $\{Y_n\}$ be the urn scheme corresponding to $\{\bar{q}_n\}$, with initial state identical to that of the X-scheme. It is clear that $\{\bar{q}_n\}$ converges to $\bar{q}$, in the sense given above, and that θ is the unique solution of $\bar{q}(y) = y$. Now introduce the function

$$v(y) = \langle C(y - \theta), y - \theta \rangle$$

using the fact that θ is a stable point to select C, a positive-definite symmetric matrix. It is easy to check that v is a Lyapunov function, as specified in Thm. 3.1. It follows from Thm. 3.1 (the discontinuity in $\tilde{q}$ does not affect the argument) that $\{Y_n\}$ converges to θ with probability 1. Finally, $\{X_n\}$ and $\{Y_n\}$ as a pair fulfill the conditions of Lemma 5.1. Therefore $\{X_n\}$ converges to θ with positive probability, and the theorem is proved.   ∎

Remark 5.1. If the Lyapunov criterion (4) holds over the interior of S, so that θ is the only stable point, then, by Thm. 3.1 or as shown in [3], $\{X_n\}$ converges to θ with probability 1.

We now wish to establish that, given an additional Hölder condition, convergence to unstable points has probability zero. We adapt a stochastic approximation result of Nevelson and Hasminskii [4] (chap. 5) in the lemma that follows. Consider the process

$$z_{n+1} = z_n - a_n F_n(z_n) + \beta_n \gamma_n(z_n, \omega) \tag{6}$$

where $F_n : R^N \to R^N$, where γ_n is a random vector, where F_n converges uniformly to F, and where $\Sigma_{n=1}^{\infty} a_n^2 < \infty$, $\Sigma_{n=1}^{\infty} \beta_n^2 < \infty$.

Lemma 5.2. Given the process described by (6), such that:

(a) If $B = \{z : F(z) = 0\}$, and $\bar{B}$ is a subset of B such that, for $\bar{z} \in \bar{B}$ and all z in a neighborhood of $\bar{z}$, there exists a symmetric positive-definite matrix C such that $\langle C(z - \bar{z}), F(z) \rangle < 0$;

(b) $\{\gamma_n\}$ has bounded fourth moments, and there exist positive constants a_1 and a_2 such that

$$a_1 \leq Tr\, D(n, \bar{z}) \leq a_2$$

where $D(n, z)$ is the matrix $E\, [\gamma_n^i(z, \omega) \times \gamma_n^j(z, \omega)]$;

(c) $|F(z)|^2 + |Tr[D(n, z) - D(n, \bar{z})]| \leq k\, |z - \bar{z}|^\mu$

for some k and some $\mu \in (0, 1)$.

Then $P\, \{z_n \to \bar{z} \in \bar{B}\} = 0$.

Proof. See [4]. Proof involves constructing a Lyapunov function w, infinite on $\bar{B}$, and such that $w(z_n)$ becomes a non-negative supermartingale. $\{z_n\}$ then cannot converge to any $\bar{z} \in \bar{B}$.

We now apply this lemma to our urn scheme $\{X_n\}$, assuming as before that $\{q_n\}$ converges to some function q.

Theorem 5.2. Suppose θ is a non-vertex unstable point with a neighborhood U such that:

$$\|q(x) - q(\theta)\| \le k \, \| \, x \, - \, \theta \, \|^\mu \text{ for } x \in U, \text{ and for some } k, \text{ and}$$

$\mu \in (0, 1)$. Then $P\{x_n \to \theta\} = 0$.

Proof. Using the previous lemma, and the dynamic equation (2), we identify z_n with X_n, F_n with $[X - q_n(X)]$, γ_n with η_n, and $\bar{z}$ with θ. Then condition (a) of the lemma is fulfilled and we need only check (b) and (c). Now η_n and q_n are bounded and η_n has a fourth moment. It is easy to see that the diffusion matrix $D(n, X) = E[\eta_n^i(X) \times \eta_n^j(X)]$ approaches a limiting matrix $D(X)$ uniformly for $x \in U$. We also have

$$E[\eta_n^i(X)^2] = q_n^i(X) \, [1 - q_n^i(X)]$$

and since $q(\theta) = \theta$, we have $[D(\theta)]_{ii} = \theta_i(1 - \theta_i)$. Finally, since

$$Tr\, D(\theta) = \sum_{i=1}^{N} \theta_i(1 - \theta_i),$$

we have $Tr\, D(\theta)$, given θ nonvertex, bounded above and below. Then all requirements of Lemma 5.2 are fulfilled and the theorem follows. ∎

6. Separable Urn Functions

Until now we have used Lyapunov techniques to prove or rule out convergence to points in the simplex. For a certain restricted class of urn functions we can dispense with Lyapunov techniques and instead use martingale methods, the restrictions allowing us to sharpen our results. We will say that the urn function q is *separable* if

$$q(x) = \left[q^1(x^1), q^2(x^2), \ldots, q^{N-1}(x^{N-1}), q^N(x) = 1 - \sum_{i=1}^{N-1} q^i(x^i) \right]$$

where the indices are of course arbitrarily determined. Note that this restricted class always includes the important case where $N = 2$. We further impose a requirement that the urn function does not cross the diagonal "too often." That is, we suppose that for each open interval $J \in [0, 1]$ and $i = 1, \ldots, N - 1$, there exists a subinterval $J_1 \subset J$ such that $x^i - q^i(x^i) \leq 0$, or $x^i - q^i(x^i) \geq 0$ for $x^i \in J_1$. The theorems in this section assume separable urn functions that fulfill this condition. For reasons of brevity, we state the theorems that follow in terms of a stationary urn function q. All proofs extend rather simply to the nonstationary case, providing $\{q_n\}$ converges to q in the sense given in theorem 3.1 and providing that $\{q_n\}$ fulfills the above subinterval condition (with the same subinterval for all q_n) for n greater than some time n_1.

We begin by establishing convergence to the fixed points of q.

Theorem 6.1. Given a continuous (and separable) urn function q, $\{X_n\}$ converges with probability one to a random variable X which has support in the set of fixed points of q.

Proof. Let B_n be the σ-field generated by $X_1, X_2, \ldots, X_n$. Using the dynamical system (2), consider, for index i:

$$\mu_n^i = \sum_{t=1}^{n} \eta_t^i(X_t)(\gamma + t)^{-1}$$

Since

$$E(\eta_t^i \mid B_t) = 0, \text{ and } |\eta_t^i| \leq 2,$$

the pair μ_n^i, B_n, for $n \geq 1$ define a martingale, with $E \mid \mu_n^i \mid^2 <$ constant. It follows that there exists a $\mu^i < \infty$ such that $\mu_n^i \rightarrow \mu^i$ with probability one. From (2) we thus obtain the convergence:

$$X_{n+1}^i - X_1^i + \sum_{t=1}^{n} [X_t^i - q^i(X_t^i)](\gamma + t)^{-1} \rightarrow \mu^i \tag{7}$$

for all events ω in $\bar{\Omega}_i$, the set where μ_n^i converges. (Note that $P\{\bar{\Omega}_i\} = 1$.)

Now, to establish the convergence of X_n^i on $\bar{\Omega}_i$ suppose the contrary, that is,

$$\varliminf_{n \rightarrow \infty} X_n^i < \varlimsup_{n \rightarrow \infty} X_n^i.$$

Under our specified condition, we may now choose a subinterval J_1 of $(\underline{\lim} X_n^i, \overline{\lim} X_n^i)$ within which (without loss of generality) $x^i - q(x^i) \geq 0$. Choose within this a further subinterval (a^i, b^i). There must exist times

m_k, n_k, $m_k < n_k$, $k = 1, 2, \ldots$, such that

$X_{m_k}^i < a^i$, $X_{n_k}^i > b^i$ and $a^i \leq X_n^i \leq b^i$ for $m_k < n < n_k$.

Summing (2) between m_k and n_k we have

$$\mu_{n_k}^i - \mu_{m_k}^i = X_{n_k}^i - X_{m_k}^i + \sum_{t=m_{k+1}}^{n_{k-1}} [X_t^i - q^i(X_t^i)](\gamma + t)^{-1} \geq a^i - b^i,$$

which, for k large enough, contradicts (7). Convergence for index i with probability one to a point X^i is established.

Now suppose X_n^i fails to converge to a fixed point of q. That is that $X^i - q^i (X^i) = \beta > 0$. From the argument above, the quantity

$$\sum_{t=\tau}^{\infty} [X_t^i - q^i(X_t^i)](\gamma + t)^{-1} \to 0 \tag{8}$$

with probability one, as τ goes to infinity. Since X_n^i converges to X^i, it eventually lies within a neighborhood U of X^i where, by continuity of q^i, $X_t^i - q^i (X_t^i) > \beta/2$. But then the summation in (8) becomes infinite, which contradicts (8). Thus X_n^i converges to a fixed point of q^i.

A similar argument holds for other indices j $(\neq N)$: X_n^j converges to a fixed point of q^j, on the set $\tilde{\Omega}_j$. We have

$$P\left\{ \bigcap_1^{N-1} \tilde{\Omega}_j \right\} = 1.$$

Therefore the residual, X_n^N, is constrained to converge, with probability 1, to a fixed point $q^N = X^N$. The theorem is proved. ∎

Remark 6.1. Note that continuity of q is required only for the fixed-point property, and not for the overall convergence of the process.

As before, we wish to narrow the set of points to which the process may converge. We call the inferior fixed point θ a *downcrossing* point of the function q, if for all indices $i = 1$ through $N - 1$ in some neighborhood U of θ:

$$x^i < q^i(x^i) \qquad \text{where} \qquad x^i < \theta^i$$

$$x^i > q^i(x^i) \qquad \text{where} \qquad x^i > \theta^i.$$

(It is easy to check that it follows that $x^N < q^N$ where $x^N < \theta^N$, and $x^N > q^N$ where $x^N > \theta^N$, so that the term downcrossing is consistent.) Upcrossing can be defined analogously.

Theorem 6.2. If q: *Int S* $\rightarrow$ *Int S*, then the process converges to downcrossing points θ with positive probability.

Proof. Let θ be a downcrossing point. Then the function

$$\sum_{i=1}^{N-1} \langle x^i - q^i(x^i), x^i - \theta^i \rangle + \langle x^N - q^N(x^N), x^N - \theta^N \rangle$$

is positive where $x \neq \theta$ in a neighborhood U of θ. Hence θ qualifies as a stable point and, by theorem 5.1,

$$P\{X_n \rightarrow \theta\} > 0.$$

Remark 6.2. The restriction that q should map the interior of S into the interior of S ensures that the neighborhood of θ is reachable from any starting conditions. This is a stronger condition than normally required in practice.

Corollary 6.1. If θ is the only fixed point of q continuous on S, and if $q^i > 0$ at $x^i = 0$, for all $i = 1$ to $N - 1$, then θ is a downcrossing point and convergence to θ follows with probability 1.

Theorem 6.3. If for any single index i, q^i upcrosses the diagonal at θ, and the upcrossing satisfies the Hölder condition of theorem 5.2, then

$$P\{X_n \rightarrow \theta\} = 0.$$

Proof. Follows from Theorem 5.2.   ∎

Finally, we give a useful condition for convergence to the vertices. We will say that q possess the strong S-property, if it has a single interior fixed point θ, which is a point of upcrossing for each index i, and where each upcrossing satisfies the Hölder condition (see theorem 5.2).

Theorem 6.4. Suppose q is continuous and satisfies the strong S-property. Then the process converges to one of the vertices with probability one.

Proof. Consider index i. The function q^i, it is easy to show, must have fixed points $\{0, \theta^i, 1\}$. By theorem 5.2 convergence to θ^i has probability zero. In combination over all indices, the only other fixed points are vertices. ∎

7. Conclusion

To summarize, we can conclude that where a limiting urn function exists and where a suitable Lyapunov function can be found (we have shown several), the process in N dimensions converges. If the limiting urn function is continuous, only fixed points of this urn function belong to the support of the limiting random variable. Where expected motion is *toward* a reachable fixed point, it is in the support: where it is *away* from a fixed point, it is not in the support. In the special case of separable urn functions, we may talk about "upcrossing" and "downcrossing" in N dimensions, with results that become extensions of the two-dimensional case. And where the strong S-property is fulfilled (see also [3]), the process must converge to a vertex.

Applications

Economic Allocation

Economic agents, drawn from a large pool, each demand a single unit of a durable good that comes in N different types or brands. The agents, in general, are heterogeneous and they choose in random sequence. Where there are increasing or decreasing supply costs; or where agents' preferences are endogenous (their tastes are influenced by the purchases of others); or where agents gain information on the products by learning of other agents' use of them; then the probability that the nth agent to choose purchases brand i depends upon the market-share proportions of the N brands at his time of purchase. Market-share dynamics for this type of allocation problem are thus path-dependent and we may enquire as to the limiting market share outcome as the market expands to an indefinitely large size. For the case where agents choose between competing *technologies,* rather than goods, see [6]. This market-share problem becomes more complex [7] when sellers of goods (or technologies) can strategically price to gain market share; but the overall structure remains the same.

Industrial Location

As outlined in the introduction, firms in a growing industry may each make a locational choice between N cities in random sequence. Choice will be influenced both by internal firm needs and by economies of agglomeration—returns from locating where other firms of the industry have established themselves. We might inquire as to whether cities eventually share the industry, or whether the industry coalesces and agglomerates in a single city (in a vertex solution). For analysis of this locational problem see [8].

Chemical Kinetics

Consider the dual autocatalytic chemical reaction:

$$S + 2W \rightarrow 3W + E$$

$$S + 2R \rightarrow 3R + E$$

A single substrate molecule S is converted into either W or R form (with waste molecules E and F) according to whether it encounters two W-molecules before two R-molecules. Given initial concentrations, we may inquire as to the final proportions of chemical products. Notice that this example is equivalent to example 1.1(a) above; if we think of the process as "sampling" the next three W or R molecules encountered and adding one to W or R according as 2 out of the 3 molecules sampled are W or R. More general N-dimensional kinetics can be similarly modeled.

Stochastic Optimization

In stochastic optimization methods based on the Kiefer-Wolfowitz procedure or its modern variants, an approximation to the solution is iteratively updated as:

$$X_{n+1} = X_n - \rho_n[Y_n(X_n, \omega)] \tag{9}$$

where X_n is an N-dimensional vector in R^N; the step-size ρ_n satisfies

$$\sum_n \rho_n = \infty, \qquad \sum_n \rho_n^2 < \infty;$$

and Y_n is a random vector, serving as an estimate for or approximation to the gradient of the function to be minimized. Often it is computationally expedient to calculate only the sign of Y_n. This gives the Fabian procedure [9]:

$$X_{n+1} = X_n - \rho_n \; sgn \; [Y_n(X_n), \; \omega].$$ (10)

We leave it to the reader to show that (10) can be put in the form of (2). Thus convergence of the Fabian algorithm to a local minimum can now be established.

REFERENCES

1. Hill, Bruce M., David Lane, and William Sudderth. 1980. A Strong Law for Some Generalized Urn Processes. *Ann. Prob.,* 214–16.
2. Blum, J. R., and M. Brennan. 1980. On the Strong Law of Large Numbers for Dependent Random Variables. *Israeli J. Math.* 37, 241–45.
3. Arthur, W. B., Y. M. Ermoliev, and Y. M. Kaniovski. 1983. A Generalized Urn Problem and Its Applications. *Kibernetika* 19:49–57 (in Russian). Translated in *Cybernetics* 19:61–71.
4. Nevelson, M. B., and R. Z. Hasminskii. 1972. *Stochastic Approximation and Recursive Estimation.* American Math. Society Translations of Math. Monographs, Vol. 47. Providence.
5. Ljung, L. 1978. Strong Convergence of a Stochastic Approximation Algorithm. *Annals of Stat.* 6:680–96.
6. Arthur, W. B. 1983. Competing Technologies and Lock-In By Historical Small Events: The Dynamics of Allocation under Increasing Returns. Committee for Economic Policy Research, Paper No. 43. Stanford University.
7. Hanson, W. A. 1985. Bandwagons and Orphans: Dynamic Pricing of Competing Systems Subject to Decreasing Costs. Ph.D. diss. Stanford University.
8. Arthur, W. B. 1984. Industry Location and the Economies of Agglomeration: Why a Silicon Valley? Mimeo, Stanford University.
9. Fabian, V. 1965. Stochastic Approximation of Constrained Minima. In *Transactions of the 4th Prague Conference on Information Theory, Statistical Decision Functions, and Random Processes.* Prague.